European Multi-Level Governance

European Multi-Level Governance

Contrasting Images in National Research

Edited by

Beate Kohler-Koch

Professor Emeritus of Political Science, Mannheim Centre for European Social Research (MZES), University of Mannheim, former Coordinator of the Network of Excellence CONNEX

Fabrice Larat

Director of the Centre d'Expertise et de Recherche Administrative (CERA), Ecole Nationale d'Administration, France, former Manager of the Network of Excellence CONNEX

Edward Elgar
Cheltenham, UK • Northampton, MA, USA

Published by
Edward Elgar Publishing Limited
The Lypiatts
15 Lansdown Road
Cheltenham
Glos GL50 2JA
UK

Edward Elgar Publishing, Inc.
William Pratt House
9 Dewey Court
Northampton
Massachusetts 01060
USA

A catalogue record for this book
is available from the British Library

Library of Congress Control Number: 2009921521

ISBN 978 1 84720 222 2

Mixed Sources
Product group from well-managed
forests and other controlled sources
www.fsc.org Cert no. SA-COC-1565
© 1996 Forest Stewardship Council
FSC

Printed and bound in Great Britain by
the MPG Books Group

Contents

PART III   TRENDS AND PATTERNS IN RESEARCH

List of Tables

List of Figures

List of Contributors

Bulmer, Simon
Simon Bulmer is professor at the University of Sheffield. He co-edited the Journal of Common Market Studies from 1991–98.

Eckert, Sandra
Sandra Eckert is a research assistant at the Robert Schuman Centre for Advanced Studies, European University Institute, Florence.

Edler-Wollstein, Stefanie
Stefanie Edler-Wollstein has studied Political Science at the University of Mannheim and the Johns Hopkins University, Baltimore. She has researched ethnicity and nationalism.

Falkner, Gerda
Gerda Falkner is professor of Political Science at the University of Vienna and Director of the Institute for European Integration Research of the Austrian Academy of Sciences, Vienna.

Groenendijk, Nico
Nico Groenendijk is Jean Monnet Professor of European Economic Governance and Co-Director of the Centre for European Studies at the University of Twente, Netherlands.

Iszkowski, Krzysztof
Krzysztof Iszkowski was researcher in the European Studies Unit of the Institute of Philosophy and Sociology, the Polish Academy of Sciences, Warsaw, Poland and now works as Socio-Economic Analyst in the European Commission, DG Employment, Social Affairs and Equal Opportunities.

Kohler-Koch, Beate
Beate Kohler-Koch is professor emeritus of Political Sciences at the University of Mannheim and Bremen Distinguished Professor at the Bremen International Graduate School of Social Sciences. She was Network Coordinator of the CONNEX Network of Excellence. She is member of the Berlin-Brandenburg Academy of Sciences.

Larat, Fabrice
Fabrice Larat was Network Manager of the Network of Excellence CONNEX and is director of the Centre of Expertise and Research of Public Administration (CERA), École Nationale d'Administration, Strasbourg.

Niżnik, Josef
Josef Niznik is professor and co-founder of the international Graduate School for Social Research at the Institute of Philosophy and Sociology, the Polish Academy of Sciences, Warsaw.

Olsen, Johan P.
Johan P. Olsen is professor emeritus. He was founder and Research Director of ARENA, Oslo. Olsen is also Fellow at the Center for Advanced Studies in the Behavioural Sciences, Stanford University and a member of the Norwegian Academy of Science and Letters.

O'Mahony, Joan
Joan O' Mahony is Alcoa Research Fellow at the Centre for Environmental Policy and Governance, London School of Economics and Political Science.

Ottaway, Jim
Jim Ottaway is Research Officer at the BIOS Centre, London School of Economics and Political Science.

Rittberger, Berthold
Berthold Rittberger is professor of Political Science and Contemporary History at the University of Mannheim. He is the Research Agenda Section Editor of the Journal of European Public Policy.

Rosema, Martin
Martin Rosema is assistant professor of political science at the University of Twente, Netherlands and member of the editorial team of Res Publica.

Schneider, Thomas
Thomas Schneider was IT manager of the CONNEX Network of Excellence, MZES, University of Mannheim.

Sverdrup, Ulf
Ulf Sverdrup is senior researcher at ARENA, University of Oslo. He also worked in the Norwegian Ministry of Foreign Affairs.

Thomassen, Jacques

Jacques Thomassen is professor and chair at the Department of Political Science in the School of Business, Public Administration and Technology, University of Twente.

Vignon, Jérôme

Jérôme Vignon is director "Social Protection and Integration" in the Directorate General for Employment, Social Affairs and Equal Opportunities of the Commission. He was director of the "Forward Studies Unit" and was heading the Task Force in charge of the White Paper on European Governance.

Wessel, Ramses

Ramses Wessel is Professor of the Law of the European Union and other International Organizations at the University of Twente, Netherlands. He is editor-in-chief and founder of the International Organizations Law Review.

Preface: The White Paper on EU Governance: An Innovative Initiative?

Jérôme Vignon

When the new team led by Romano Prodi took, at the end of 1999, the Head of the European Commission, at the closure of one of the most severe confidence crisis ever experienced by this institution, governance or "new governance" ideas were floated around western socio-democratic leaders, such as Bill Clinton, Tony Blair and Antonio Guttierez. The idea was that democratic confidence had been lost, not so much because of ideological failure (public opinion had no illusion that any new world could emerge from a fundamental renewed political paradigm), but because of procedural failure; mainly the quality of the political dialogue with the citizens, in the mass-communication era, should be upgraded so as to become a full policy in itself, and policy implementation through "joint up government", involving all interested stakeholders, should be given more importance than the tabling of new legislation.

Such ideas were certainly in the back of the mind of President Prodi when he decided to set up in mid-2000 the preparation of a White paper on European governance.

The governance team in charge of that preparation could at this time draw from an already rich collection of academic studies and research outcomes which had been flourishing during the last decade under the umbrella of governance, or "governing without government". They were reflecting a shift in the focus of EU political studies, from the normative approach to a more interpretative attempt of understanding the particular nature of the EU democratic process taking place in a transnational context; that is the focus of governance studies was no more about how or whether this process should (or should not) lead to a state-type (that is federal type) EU polity, but rather on the sort of mechanisms which allowed various state and non-state agents to influence the decisions and outcomes of the EU complex set of institutions.

Notwithstanding this approach, the White paper team took a normative view, with the aim of designing procedural changes about how to improve the mutual interaction of the key institutions, starting with the Commission, in order to "bring the EU closer to the citizens", as the previous crisis was mainly interpreted as a legitimacy crisis.

How could a, by nature, extremely complex process become closer to the citizens? The basic hypothesis underpinning most of the work and proposals finally adopted in 2001 and later on systematically implemented, including under the still active process of "Better law making", owes to the different properties of "representative" and "participatory" democracy. It was felt that the EU as a multiple level democratic entity, could never rely exclusively on a purely representative legitimacy, built upon the articulation of regional, national and European elections; it should be complemented with participatory democracy, which would instil experience and knowledge of the various stakeholders concerned with EU policies, from the bottom to the top.

Looking back retrospectively, seven years after the adoption of the EU governance White paper and in view of the follow-up process under the heading of "better law-making", it is still in my view, very difficult to judge whether this approach towards reinforcing the participatory component of the EU was wrong or not.

In a first instance, it is striking that one of the most salient political feature of the modernisation of the EU institutions has been the strengthening of the role of the European Parliament, both in practice (as it was evidenced by the debate on the "service directive" between 2004 and 2006) and from an institutional point of view (as illustrated by the extended powers conferred by the Lisbon Treaty to the European Parliament).

However there is no evidence that the strengthening of the present or future role of representative democracy in the EU policy making has been translated in an increased confidence towards the EU process itself. Of course, we should hope that the turn-over in the 2009 elections of the EP will show some improvement, but this cannot be taken for granted, when we look at the overall usual figures displayed by the Eurobarometer about citizens' confidence.

And finally, the apparently modest impact of participatory governance, driven notably by the "better law making process", might not necessarily be attributed to its lack of relevance, but to its cautious implementation. To a large extent, the involvement of local or regional authorities in the EU law-making process has remained limited; and the effectiveness of the role of the European civil society in channelling the experience and knowledge from the bottom to the top is certainly questionable, as the EU institutions keep a strong grip upon the consultative process and also because the ability of the Brussels-based civil society to really connect with the national civil societies is, to say the least, uneven.

Therefore I believe that the fundamental question of better linking participatory and representative democracy across the EU is still open. This makes the CONNEX research programme led by Beate Kohler-Koch under the auspices of the 6th European Research Framework Programme particularly valuable. It helps us in particular, to take better account of some key conditions under which this articulation will best take place, which were unnoticed or insufficiently identified at the start of the decade, such as:

- the crucial importance of the national filters conveying the European message to the citizens and the feedback from the citizens to the European institutions. From this point of view, institutional innovations embedded in the Lisbon Treaty, like the subsidiarity check by the national Parliaments and the "European citizens' initiative" might trigger a renewed dynamism of national and regional stakeholders in relation to EU issues;

- the relevance of the role of national political parties and discourses, when dealing with the combination of national identities with the political agenda of the EU, notably in those policy domains where there is an obvious EU added-value, like climate change and external policy; and

- the strengthening of the accountability of the participatory mechanisms themselves, which in turn might encourage the stakeholders towards more responsibility and representativity.

We can just hope that the various avenues opened by the "European governance study programme" will continue to be developed, in order to match and check the future development of EU policy making.

Introduction: Research on EU Multi-Level Governance

Beate Kohler-Koch and Fabrice Larat

Integrating research to further our understanding of efficient and democratic governance in a multi-level Europe has been the main objective of CONNEX, a network aimed at building a Europe-wide research community which stands for scientific excellence and can contribute to deepen the existing knowledge of the present state and likely future development of the European polity.[1] One basis of excellence is that the state-of-the-art is common knowledge within a research community. But is there a commonly agreed on state-of-the-art in our area? And how can we be sure that we are standing on the shoulders of the most eminent scholars in the field? Those who rely on the peer review journals published in English are easily misled by the false belief that what they read represents the whole range of the scholarly debate. Thus, the idea to build a research network starts from the opposite assumption, namely that a wealth of knowledge exists beyond the mainstream literature and that it will take a concentrated effort to bring the accumulated knowledge of different disciplines and in the many languages of Europe to the fore. The productive forces of communication and integration of research can only grow when we are aware of the diversity of approaches and the scientific achievements beyond the internationalised core community of European studies. Even though the proliferation of international conferences and research funding by the EU have spurred the trend to internationalisation, social science research is fragmented and a great part of the scientific knowledge produced by research in the different parts of Europe is not easily accessible. Language barriers, disciplinary self-sufficiency, issue boundaries, the diversity of academic cultures and segmented publication markets contribute to this fragmentation.

TAKING STOCK OF A WEALTH OF RESEARCH

Consequently, CONNEX was not content with the usual state-of-the-art report, but has engaged in a more encompassing stock-taking exercise. It started with a review of the EU governance debate in the mostly English speaking academic literature (Kohler-Koch and Rittberger 2006) and with an evaluation of recent and on-going research on specific aspects of EU governance in thematic oriented conferences. Topics were chosen in view of issue relevance and available knowledge, both in terms of the amount and variety of empirical research projects and theoretical writings.[2] Despite valuable insights gained, both approaches can not reflect the diversity of EU governance research across Europe. This was to be achieved by an encompassing survey on recent and on-going academic research projects in all the EU member states[3] and, in addition, Norway, Switzerland, Russia and former Yugoslavia. The resulting database has been made accessible online (GOVDATA), and has been complemented by a bibliographic database (GOVLIT).[4]

It was not just for practical reasons, such as language proficiency and insider knowledge concerning the organisation of research in a country, that we chose to set up a network of national experts to do the stock-taking.[5] Rather, it was a tribute to the insight from the sociology of science which argues convincingly and provides robust empirical evidence that research is context specific. Based on a secondary analysis of a large research programme on "global governance", Renate Mayntz (2005) has well exemplified how perspectives on a given object are shaped by the cognitive features of the dominant paradigm, by the social organisation of the science system, and by external factors such as the geopolitical context. "Internalist" and "externalist" variables have always been brought into play to account for the changes in EU studies (Rosamond 2007). The raise of governance research may well be explained by the changing nature of the EU from a common market to what Giandomenico Majone called a "regulatory state". Since EU governance as a research object has a genuine multi-level and thus transnational dimension, a strong Europeanisation of the intellectual evolution of the field may be expected. However, the reality of EU-governance is not just happening at "Brussels", much rather it gets straight down to the daily practices and procedures in the member states, and because of their quite divergent institutional structures, the experiences at national, regional and local level account for quite diverging perceptions of what EU governance is about. Thus, there is no uniform object of research. Furthermore, research conditions and the intellectual environment that shape the investigations remain mainly national. The intellectual repertoire that animated the conceptual debate on governance was different in the United Kingdom, where governance was developed as a contrasting image to the stylised concept of the Westminster model (Rhodes 1988), as compared to Germany, where federalism and neo-corporatism had induced systematic reflections on political steering (Mayntz and Scharpf 1995), or to France, where an "étatiste" perception and a tradition of centralised administration left little room for reflecting on institutionalised public–private cooperation.[6] The divergence in the imagined and real national constitution and state–

society relations thus constrains the Europeanisation of theoretical approaches and research strategies.

Accordingly, in her evaluation of the political and academic reception of the governance concept, Ioana Popa (2008) has called for a critical reflection on the range and limits of the internationalisation of knowledge production in EU studies. She echoes the argument of Nicolai Genov and Ulrike Becker (2001) that scientific achievements in the social sciences can only be understood by taking account of the dual reference to the respective national and international environment. Despite a marked trend towards the internationalisation of social sciences in general and European studies in particular, the way EU governance is studied cannot be dissociated from the country of origin or from its disciplinary background. France is a well studied case to illustrate (Smith 2000) what has been established in abstract, namely that national science communities have a framing effect and that they are shaped by the role of specific disciplines and the way they have been dominated by leading personalities and schools of thought (Kuhn and Remøe 2005). Correspondingly, the national experts were asked to provide background information on the structural conditions (for example the institutionalisation of research, availability of material resources, incentive structures for research) and on the intellectual contexts (for example academic traditions, relationship between disciplines, level of internationalisation), which are likely to have an impact on national EU governance research. By doing it this way, not just the diversity and richness of EU governance research would be documented but also the reasons for plurality would come to light.

The survey focused on recent (starting with 1994) and at the time on-going research projects on EU governance in Europe and gathered key data on the individual research projects or networks.[7] The intention was to be rather inclusive than exclusive and, therefore, "EU governance research" was defined as encompassing all aspects of governing as far as it was related to the EU and to the incorporation of national or sub-national entities in the multi-level system of EU governance.[8] The selection criteria were meant to identify relevant research projects on the basis of the object of research and not on the basis of a theoretical concept. This decision seems plausible for two reasons; firstly, the governance concept has not matured to a theoretical and precise concept as argued in Chapter 1 and, secondly, the dissemination of the concept has been slow and uneven across countries and disciplines. All in all, information on 1700 academic research projects is now accessible online. In addition, all "National Reports" describing context conditions and analysing the advance of EU governance research in the 25 countries covered by the survey have been published online and are accessible through the GOVDATA website (see list in Annex 1 to this volume).

The present volume builds on this stock-taking effort, both on the survey database and on the national reports written by the national correspondents.

Experts, who mostly had already been involved in gathering the data, were asked to give account of the distinctiveness of EU governance research in the different parts of Europe. Whereas the seven geographically focused chapters bring to light the diversity of research, general patterns and tendencies are examined in the introductory and concluding chapters. Accordingly, the volume is structured in three parts. The first part is dedicated to EU governance as a topic of research. The first contribution by *Beate Kohler-Koch* and *Berthold Rittberger* gives an assessment of the development of the concept known as the 'governance turn' in EU studies and reflects on the characteristic features of EU governance. The second chapter by *Joan O'Mahony* investigates the publication output on EU governance and explores the dissemination of the concept and the diversity of its application.

Part two aims at reflecting the diversity of research traditions. In each chapter, after having recalled the material, structural and intellectual settings influencing national research, the authors take a closer look at the common and distinct features of EU governance research as mirrored in the projects identified by the stock-taking survey. Only two countries are presented separately, namely the United Kingdom (*Simon Bulmer*) and Germany (*Beate Kohler-Koch*), due to the wealth of research they produce on EU governance. Since the national reports revealed similarities between groups of countries, with regards to the material and intellectual conditions for research or to the dedication to governance research, four "regional" clusters were added. Thus, Norway (*Ulf Sverdrup*) and the Netherlands (*Nico Groenendijk, Martin Rosema, Jacques Thomassen, Ramses Wessel*) were put together since both countries are strong in EU governance research and it is worthwhile to compare research infrastructure and strategies that might have spurred related research activities.

Subsequently, *Stefanie Edler-Wollstein* and *Gerda Falkner* analyse the performance and perspective of EU governance research in a group of small states (Austria, Belgium, Denmark, Finland, Sweden and Switzerland) which all benefit from a strong social science tradition. Nevertheless, the intensity of research is not as pronounced as in the countries mentioned above. Also, when compared to each other, research activities and thematic interests vary considerably and contrasting images of EU governance emerge. "Europe's south" includes countries of different size, namely France, Italy, Spain, Portugal and Greece, although they have some cultural and structural features in common that might explain why even the larger countries are not at the core of governance research. *Fabrice Larat* focuses on similarities and differences and underscores the importance of the language barrier which accounts for the weak integration of south Europe in the international academic debate in Chapter Seven. *Josef Niznik* and *Krzysztof Iszkowski* then depict the distinctive situation in the central and eastern European countries who are latecomers to the EU, have no longstanding tradition in the social sciences and suffer from a lack of financial resources in Chapter Eight.

Research at the European University Institute, Florence, presented by *Sandra Eckert,* is a special case since it is a centre for doctoral and post-doc research with a (perceived) European denomination that attracts scholars from all over Europe and beyond and so should be very open to new issues and concepts such as EU governance. In the third and last part *Fabrice Larat* and *Thomas Schneider* provide a general evaluation based on a statistical analysis of the survey data and elaborate Europe-wide trends and patterns. In an epilogue to the book *Johan P. Olsen* looks at how we progress from the stock-taking of recent advances in EU governance research to suggestions on how we could or should redirect our research agenda.

THE VARIOUS FACETS OF THE 'GOVERNANCE TURN' IN EU STUDIES

The 'governance turn' in EU studies is well documented in the survey data. Whereas in the first decades the main research issue was integration – the building of a common market, European law and the common political institutions – the focus is now on the ways and means of governing the EU and on the interdependence of EU and national systems of governance. The 'governance turn' has, however, spread unevenly across countries and disciplines.

Whilst the aggregated survey data give the impression that the changing nature of the EU itself has been a stimulus for reordering EU studies as well as for changes in the theoretical repertoire, a closer look reveals significant disparity among countries and disciplines. Apparently, there are distinct international and interregional differentiations in how the phenomenon of EU-governance is perceived and analysed, with strong variations in approaches, thematic foci and the scope of research. As depicted in Chapter Ten, marked variations can be found between old and new member states. In comparison, research in eastern European member states is more focused on the effects of EU policies at member state level, whereas less attention is paid to the structure and modes of governance.

Thematic preoccupations also change over time. Regional governance was a favourite topic in the 1990s, relating either to the debate on the regionalisation of Europe and the new role of regions in EU governance or to the investigation of new modes of governance such as the implementation of the 'partnership principle' and the ensuing effects on learning, stakeholder participation and improvements in problem-solving capacities. When in the last round of accession the topic once more gained prominence, research was then more geared to pave the way for managing transborder regional cooperation and supporting regional interest representation in EU decision-making. Since economic integration is still the main rationale of the EU and the regulation of market activities are spreading, governance issues are mostly related to the first pillar. Only very recently, with the increased EU competence in the second and third pillar, has research turned to explore the governance of the common foreign, security and defence policy and policing.

It is notable that only a few projects are dedicated to advancing the theoretical understanding of governance. Governance research in times of accession responds to the strong demand for more practical knowledge concerning the legal framework and the functioning of EU institutions, the challenge to domestic administration and the likely impact of the EU on national policies. This tendency was most pronounced in the enlargement to the east and the south, since countries with a weak social science base are generally inclined to engage in applied research. In the academic prosperous north-western belt, the demand for practical knowledge is also strong, but it is often supplied by specialised research institutes and by research executed on commission. At the same time, university research is strong but directed more towards fundamental research. In countries like Germany, the Nordic countries and the Netherlands, the academic prevalence results in putting emphasis on fundamental research, whereas the United Kingdom adheres to its tradition of applied policy research. Nevertheless, empirical research is strong all over Europe and most of it is theoretically well grounded, in particular the research exploring more general issues such as the "governance of complexity", "multi-level administration" or "institutional learning". For the most part, scholars do not aim at developing a new governance theory but draw on established social science theories and adapt those to the EU context. The research profile also differs between disciplines. In general, policy-relevant knowledge is more often expected from and produced by economics and law than by political science or sociology, a tendency that is most pronounced in the south and east of Europe.

Three main issues are at the heart of the more focused governance research: multi-level governance, new modes of governance, and public-private actor relations. Multi-level governance research explores above all the linking of levels of authority, the effect of integration on domestic structures at the national and sub-national levels, and is mainly concerned with the problem-solving capacity of EU governance. New modes of governance are a new growth industry not just in political science, but also in economics and recently also in law. Numerous case studies address the empirical variance of policy coordination as applied in different policy fields and search for evolving patterns and indications for the efficient use of the new instruments. On a more abstract level, the debate concentrates on performance criteria and on the relation to hierarchy and traditional modes of governance. A recurrent field of interest is the public–private actor relationship in EU governance. Research on interest intermediation has a long tradition, but became invigorated by introducing more formal research methodologies to capture exchange relations and by a shift in public attention from lobbying to 'stake-holder participation' and 'civil society' involvement.

The governance debate has always been linked to normative considerations, but issues of democracy and legitimacy take a back seat in research. Despite a growing awareness in the social science community of the "democratic deficit" of the EU and a controversial debate on the positive or detrimental impact of network governance on the EU's democratic quality, the survey shows that less than one fifth of the projects addresses questions of democracy or legitimacy. Part of the research is dedicated to examining the performance of parties and parliaments as agents of democratic representation and public accountability in the European system of multi-level governance, other projects examine the appropriateness of alternative models. The debate on "deliberative democracy" and "associational" or "participatory democracy" had been already firmly established on the European research agenda when the Commission's White Paper on Governance and the debate on the aborted Constitutional Treaty gave it a new impetus.

Last but not least, it is worth mentioning that little attention has been paid to the societal dimension of EU governance. The social basis of European democracy and legitimate governance has long been neglected in European research. The empirical exploration of Europe's civil society and of the emergent transnational public space started with a sudden leap at the end of the 1990s. Since then, academic interest is steady but at a low level, which is not unexpected since the "social space" is, by tradition, the domain of sociology and sociological research in Europe is still fraught by "methodological nationalism" and takes little notice of the transnational dimension of societies.

GOVERNANCE: A UNIVERSAL APPROACH?

The CONNEX stock-taking exercise revealed large discrepancies in EU governance research. The governance concept is well established in political science in the United Kingdom and Germany, where it originated, and has soon been incorporated in the north-western belt with its strong social science tradition. The reception in the southern periphery has been slow and seemingly more reluctant, which is not surprising in view of a different constitutional context and paradigmatic traditions, but also a weaker position of political science within the family of social sciences. Governance is still very much a political science concept; its use is contested in law and in economics where the focus is predominantly on corporate and not on political governance.

The core-periphery discrepancy in research on EU multi-level governance, manifest in the national reports and the survey, points to material shortcomings, such as a weak social infrastructure and limited funds and a social science research tradition that has only recently been built-up. Consequently, in spite of noteworthy individual projects, the research output in many countries of the east and the south neither shapes the national academic and political debate nor does it have a noticeable impact on the international research community. In the case of multi-level governance, the main theoretical and heuristic concepts are imported, though they may not always match the research questions addressing the most pertinent problems in their specific national context. The situation is partially redressed by European funded cooperation in transnational research networks and advanced training in high standard international institutions.

Networking, the mobility of young researchers, and the free flow of ideas, with English as academic *lingua franca,* propel the Europeanisation of the social sciences in general and of EU studies in particular. Concepts travel easily through peer review journals, online publications that are readily available, and through international conferences. Hence, one may wonder if in the future researchers from different parts of Europe will sing from the same hymn sheet. Another pertinent question is who will write the song book. When it comes to the establishing of leading concepts, up to now, American and British scholars are still privileged thanks to a large domestic market, language dominance in the international scientific market, a competent textbook tradition and, in the case of the US, a competitive academic community well versed in conceptual controversies. German research on European governance is also impressive and linked to a vivid conceptual debate. Nevertheless, with a few exceptions, neither the theoretical contributions nor the empirical research findings have entered the US–UK mainstream debate. A telling example is the German "state theory" debate of the 1980s and 1990s, in particular the "Steuerungstheorie" (steering theory), which informed German thinking on the transformation of governance, but had hardly any impact on the debate on governance abroad. Thus, although scholars from Romance and Slavic speaking countries are increasingly publishing in English now, it is not guaranteed that their way of thinking will have the same impact on the conceptual debate as the concepts of Anglo-American origin. In general, looking at the rich and differentiated picture of research represented in the CONNEX database, one can deduce that the wealth of knowledge accumulated across Europe does not really feed back into the conceptual debate. One reason for this is that theoretical concepts on EU governance are just like many other social science concepts developed in abstract and only then tested via empirical research. Not only do the still-existing language and disciplinary barriers get in the way of a systematic and comprehensive evaluation of research findings, the sheer wealth of research and the many different approaches makes it an insurmountable task.

It would be demanding too much from research networks such as CONNEX to deliver a governance theory after only a few years of working together. Rather, the institutionalisation of communication and research cooperation across disciplines and research communities is raising the awareness of the diversity of approaches. Here are two examples. Whereas political science tends to explore the soft modes of governance and looks at the social mechanisms that make it work, the discipline of law elaborates on the multiplicity of regulations and legal rules that constrain actor choices. This, in turn, has induced political scientists to reconsider the conventional wisdom on EU governance and to ask if the downgrading of hierarchy and the "Community method" was indeed not "a death too early foretold" (Dehousse 2008). Research cooperation also brings to light distinct realities that ought to be incorporated into a general concept. The differentiated implementation of new modes of governance and, in particular, the low key involvement of civil society in the new member states of the East draw attention to the general phenomenon that a well functioning public-private partnership does not just need strong civil society associations but also a strong state.

Thus, contrasting images of EU governance reflect different theoretical approaches and also distinct realities which should not be levelled out by premature generalisations. Where do we go from here? "Unity in diversity" is a catchy slogan which, however, conceals the fundamental difference in theoretical objectives. While some scholars have the ambition to make governance a universal concept (Stoker 1998; Schuppert 2008), others, like Olsen in this volume, are more cautious and advocate relating "the analysis of the EU system of governance (...) to some enduring and recurrent themes in the theoretical study of democratic governance and thereby to the long history of ideas about how societies can and should be governed best".

NOTES

1. CONNEX ("Connecting excellence on European governance") is a so-called Network of Excellence funded by the EU under the 6 Framework Programme of Research. 42 partner institutions are members of the consortium. The project started in July 2004 and lasted 4 years. See www. connex-network.org.
2. Since several conferences had already been organised before the official start of CONNEX – for example on the governance of financial markets, on EU governance and external relations, on interest intermediation in EU governance and on the democratic deficits – CONNEX chose to concentrate on "multilevel governance in Europe", an issue that was both well researched and open to controversial theoretical explanations (Conzelmann and Smith 2008).
3. The survey included the at that time prospective members; because of size Luxembourg, Cyprus and Malta were not considered.
4. See GOVDATA database at http://www.connex-network.org/govdata/ and GOVLIT at http://www.connex-network.org/govlit/.

5. For more details see Chapter 10, 'Trends and patterns in governance research' in this volume.
6. We owe these reflections to Yannis Papadopoulos.
7. Each selected project is documented with details on its duration, the name and institutional affiliation of the researcher(s) coordinating the projects as well as references to the resulting publications, if available.
8. The different dimensions related to the EU system of governance have been systematised in a list of keywords used for coding the projects. For technical details about how the survey was conducted and which kind of data is available in the database, see Chapter 10.

REFERENCES

Dehousse, Renaud (2008), 'The "Community Method": Chronicle of a Death too Early Foretold', in Renaud Dehousse and Laurie Boussaguet (eds), *The Transformation of EU Policies – Governance at Work*, CONNEX Report Series Vol. 8, Mannheim, pp. 7–35.

Genov, Nicolai and Ulricke Becker (2001), *Social Sciences in South-eastern Europe*, Bonn: GESIS – IZ Sozialwissenschaften.

Kohler-Koch, Beate and Berthold Rittberger (2006), 'The "Governance Turn" in EU Studies', *Journal of Common Market Studies*, **44**, 27–49.

Kuhn, Michael and Svend Otto Remøe (eds) (2005), 'Implications for the European Socio-economic Research Area', in Michael Kuhn & Svend Otto Remøe (eds), *Building the European Research Area. Socio-economic Research in Practice*, Bern: Peter Lang, pp. 280–301.

Mayntz, Renate (2005), 'Embedded Theorizing. Perspectives on Globalization and Global Governance', *MPIfG Discussion Paper*, 05/14, http://www.mpi-fg-koeln.mpg.de/pu/dp_abstracts/dp05-14.asp.

Mayntz, Renate and Fritz W. Scharpf (eds) (1995), *Gesellschaftliche Selbstregelung und politische Steuerung*, Frankfurt: Campus.

Popa, Ioana (2008), 'La structuration internationale des études européennes: un espace scientifique dissymétrique', in Didier Georgakakis and Marine de Lasalle (eds), *La 'nouvelle gouvernance européenne'. Genèses et usages politiques d'un livre blanc*, Strasbourg: Presse Universitaires de Strasbourg, pp. 92–117.

Rosamond, Ben (2007), 'The political sciences of European integration: Disciplinary history and EU studies', in Knud Erik Jorgensen, Mark Pollack and Ben Rosamond (eds), *Handbook of European Union politics*, London: Sage, pp. 7–30.

Rhodes, Roderick A. W. (1988), *Beyond Westminster and Whitehall*, London: Unwin Hyman.

Schuppert, Gunnar Folke (2008), 'Governance – auf der Suche nach Konturen eines "anerkannt uneindeutigen Begriffs"', in Gunnar Folke Schuppert and Michael Zürn (eds.), *Governance in einer sich wandelnden Welt*, PVS Sonderheft, 41/2008, pp. 13–40.

Smith, Andy (2000), 'French political science and European integration', *Journal of European Public Policy*, **7** (4), 663–669.

Stoker, Gerry (1998), 'Governance as Theory: five Propositions', *International Social Science Journal*, **50** (155), pp. 17–28.

PART I

EU MULTI-LEVEL GOVERNANCE AS A TOPIC
OF RESEARCH

1. A Futile Quest for Coherence: The Many Frames of EU Governance[1]

Beate Kohler-Koch and Berthold Rittberger

INTRODUCTION: THE 'GOVERNANCE TURN' IN EU STUDIES

Research on governance and the European Union constitutes a major focus of research in EU studies. In the recent past, scores of articles and volumes have been dedicated to exploring the origins and characteristics of governance across policy sectors, different levels of jurisdictions, as well as to investigation from the perspective of different disciplinary backgrounds (see, for instance, the contributions in Tömmel 2008; Schuppert 2005; Bache and Flinders 2004). What is implied by the term 'governance turn' in EU studies? For most of the past decades, research on the EU grappled predominantly with the question of how European integration – the process in which EU member states pool sovereignty or delegate decision-making authority from the domestic to the European level – can be explained by employing various theories of European integration which are well-rehearsed by every student of European politics (see Schimmelfennig and Rittberger 2006 for an overview). While this first phase of EU research took the political system of the EU – its institutions and policies – as its *explanandum*, research on EU governance takes the EU polity as given and analyses the structure and processes of the EU political system and its impact on national and European policies and politics (see Jachtenfuchs 2001, 2003; Diez and Wiener 2004).

What are the reasons behind the 'governance turn' in European studies? Our contention is that the 'governance turn' is founded on conceptual, empirical and 'institutional' developments. Conceptually, with the gradual increase in supranational competencies, 'policy-making' in the EU became a new focus of scholarly attention. In European studies, the late 1980s and early 1990s were increasingly marked by importing concepts from the field of policy analysis, such as policy cycles and policy network, to illuminate the process of policy formulation and implementation in the EU (see Tömmel 2008: 15–16). Empirically, this development coincided with, and was stimulated by a significant increase in European-level policy-making competencies in the wake of the Single European Act and the single market programme in the 1980s. Questions of EU 'government' and governance – policy-making and policy co-ordination – began to challenge 'European integration' as the first and foremost focus of scholarly research in EU studies. The specific thematic orientation of research on governance has, however, changed over time. Governance and the regions and also interest intermediation in EU governance were favourite topics in the 1990s, followed by research on new modes of governance and civil society participation, as well as the problem-solving capacities of governance arrangements. 'First-pillar' issues still dominate the agenda of policy-oriented governance research; only recently several research projects have been dedicated to exploring the governance of the common foreign, security and defence policy and policing as well as the 'external dimension' of EU governance (see the survey evaluation by Larat and Schneider in this volume). Institutionally, several large-scale research programmes, increasingly funded by the EU (such as CONNEX and NEWGOV), as well as research institutions (such as the Arena centre and programme in Oslo, the European University Institute in Florence, the Mannheim Centre for European Social Research or the former Max Planck Group for the Research on Collective Goods, Bonn) accompanied and provided special intellectual impetus to the 'governance turn' in European studies.

In this chapter, we explore the 'governance turn' in EU studies by addressing the following themes. First, we argue that there is not one single, let alone coherent EU governance research programme or research agenda; that is governance research is rather informed by different research traditions or 'frames' emanating from different political science sub-disciplines, most notably Comparative Politics and International Relations. Secondly, we posit that governance in the EU bears a set of characteristic features that make it distinct from other systems of governance. Thirdly, we show that the distinctiveness which characterizes EU governance offers an interesting range of normative and empirical-analytical questions about the political stability of domestic and European governance arrangements and their democratic legitimacy.

GOVERNANCE: A COHERENT RESEARCH PROGRAMME?

After over a decade of productive research on EU governance, we have to concede that the 'governance turn' has not reduced the diversity of research questions but has left us with even more open questions than we started out with. Pollitt's dictum, that governance research has 'not reached the state of maturity at which (we as scholars) can ... see through the trees to the wood' (Pollitt 2006: 82) seems to be of undisputed validity. It is doubtful that EU governance research will ever reach a state of maturity so as to claim the undisputed existence of a coherent governance concept, let alone a theory of governance. Even though research is ever more theoretically sophisticated and empirically well-grounded, different authors continue to attach quite different and even contradictory characteristics to 'governance'. The reason for this state of affairs is mainly due to the divergent framing of governance research, which is rooted in different disciplinary traditions. Furthermore, it is also the result of a lack of methodological discipline which has fostered conceptual blurring (see Treib et al. 2007).

Turning to the different 'frames' of EU governance research, we observe that research on governance is difficult to channel into a more coherent research programme, since it originates from different research traditions, most notably those relating to research in Comparative Politics and International Relations. Research on EU governance, hence, carries the imprint of the respective research interests when defining what EU governance is about and when formulating research questions and developing a research design.

Governance in a Comparative Politics perspective: a 'business as usual' approach

EU Governance research mainly resides in political science and there it often originates from studies in Comparative Politics and policy research. Scholars working in this tradition can be said to take a 'business as usual' approach treating features of the system of EU governance as part of a set of features which belong to a specific category of cases that can be compared and analyzed by using established concepts and theories. Scholarship that takes this assumption as its point of departure hence suggests that the EU 'is just like any other political system' and can thus be 'treated' as such by researchers (see Hix 1999). This is a reasonable assumption: empirical research reveals a high variety of governance arrangements among domestic political systems. There are, thus, many good reasons to treat the political systems and features thereof as one case within a category or family of comparable cases. The analytical gain of such a comparative approach is quite obvious in that we can draw from the accumulated empirical knowledge on patterns of national and sub-national governance and we can build on already established theories and enrich our understanding by broadening the range of comparison.

The achievements of governance research in the tradition of Comparative Politics and policy research is impressive. Fields of interest are, among others, different modes of governance and their benefits and drawbacks, variation of different governance modes across policy areas, and the differential impact of Europe on national patterns of governance. The insights gained from research in the Comparative Politics-tradition are also of prescriptive value since they help to illuminate the conditions for efficient decision-making and the effectiveness of alternative governance arrangements. In short, a lot can be learned about the problem solving capacity of different modes of governance in particular political settings.

Lessons learned from International Relations: governance beyond the nation-state

A second crucial input to the EU governance debate originated from the field of International Relations (IR). Governance research from an IR-perspective is mainly concerned with the issue of effective and efficient governance beyond the nation-state. Changes in the international system in the post Cold War era elevated the notion of effective and efficient 'problem-solving' to a guiding principle which was to be pursued through different forms of international (institutionalized) co-operation (Rosenau and Czempiel, 1992; Jachtenfuchs 2003). The issue of effective and efficient problem-solving became even more pertinent as a focus for research resulting from the processes of economic globalization and societal denationalization, denoting that the capacity of national political systems to achieve desired policy outcomes comes under strain as the boundaries of social transactions increasingly transcend the confines of the nation-state (Zürn 1998; Scharpf 1999). Questions pertaining to the performance of political systems are closely associated with questions of the legitimacy of the respective political systems: The problem-solving capacity of the nation-state being strained, states delegate powers to international and supranational institutions. Consequently, the question of the democratic legitimacy of these new venues for problem-solving became a central issue in the debate surrounding governance beyond the nation-state (Kohler-Koch 1998).

One central tenet of the discussion about democratically legitimate governance beyond the nation-state relates to the adequacy of exporting or transferring established concepts for democratically legitimate governance from the domestic to the international or European realm (see, for example, Eriksen and Fossum 2007). The debate brings to the fore concepts such as civil society and participatory democracy as alternatives or complements to representative parliamentary democracy (see, for example, the contributions in Kohler-Koch and Rittberger 2007). Furthermore, scholars are gauging different sets of criteria for participation and system performance which have to be met by all systems of democratically legitimate governance irrespective of whether they are primarily demarcated by territorial, sectoral or functional boundaries. The discussion about governance beyond the nation-state has had lasting consequences for research on EU governance in that it revived the normative debate and triggered an intensive discussion of other forms of democratic legitimacy than those offered by representative parliamentary democracy. In the ensuing section, we will offer an assessment of the dominant features of EU governance, before turning to the implications which can be derived from these characteristics for a new research agenda.

FEATURES OF EU GOVERNANCE

As a concept, EU governance requires considerable 'stretching' to include all areas of EU policy-making activity. Some of the concept's central features, such as its multi-level nature, apply to the whole EU 'pillar' structure; other core features, such as the key role of supranational actors in the 'community method', the dominance of regulatory politics or public-private policy networks are characteristic of only the 'first pillar'. Over the years, policy cooperation has developed in additional areas, including economic and monetary affairs, security and defence, as well as police and judicial cooperation. Here, the policy-making process that brought about integration is characterized by 'intensive trans-governmentalism'. In the case of the single currency it resulted in delegating institutional powers to a function-specific agency, the European Central Bank. In all other areas no centralized and hierarchical institutional process has been introduced. Rather, 'intensive trans-governmentalism' prevails that breeds special forms of policy-coordination involving national and Community officials that allow the member state governments to retain considerable control but still transform the ways in which states traditionally go about doing their business (Wallace 2005: 80, 87–9).

The *community method*, however, is crucial and, in practice, the dominant feature of EU governance. Scharpf (2003) has dubbed this method as the 'joint-decision mode', characterized by a strong role for the European Commission in the formulation and execution of Community legislation, with the European Parliament (EP) gaining power and influence. All legislation is adopted by the Council of Ministers by a qualified majority or unanimous vote. In the preparation, formulation and implementation of policies, the Commission and Parliament consult or even co-opt private groups and organizations for information and expertise. Furthermore, 'comitology committees' of national civil servants and outside experts work out compromise solutions for implementation (Joerges and Vos 1999) to smooth transposition and compliance at the national and sub-national level.

Another prominent feature of EU governance is its multi-level nature. Marks (1993: 392; Marks et al. 1996) developed the concept of *multi-level governance* (MLG), which is a 'system of continuous negotiation among nested governments at several territorial tiers'. MLG posits that decision-making authority is not monopolized by the governments of the member states but is diffused to different levels of decision-making, the sub-national,

national and supranational levels. Aiming at a general theory of MLG, Hooghe and Marks (2001: 4) later emphasized that governance is interconnected, not nested: 'While national arenas remain important arenas for the formation of national government preferences, the multi-level governance model rejects the view that subnational actors are nested exclusively within them. Instead, subnational actors operate in both national and supranational arenas ... National governments ... share, rather than monopolize, control over many activities that take place in their respective territories.' *Multi-level* thus signifies the interdependence of actors operating at different territorial levels – local, regional, national, supranational – while *governance* refers to the growing importance of non-hierarchical forms of policy-making, such as dynamic networks which involve public authorities as well as private actors (Hooghe and Marks 2001).

These two features – the multi-level nature of the EU 'political system' and the growing importance of private actors in the policy process – are also among the defining characteristics for the concept of *network governance* (Eising and Kohler-Koch 1999; Kohler-Koch 1999). Network governance is distinct from other forms of governance, such as corporatism, pluralism and statism. In a system of network governance '[t]he 'state' is vertically and horizontally segmented and its role has changed from authoritative allocation 'from above' to the role of an 'activator'. Governing the EU involves bringing together the relevant state and societal actors and building issue-specific constituencies' (Eising and Kohler-Koch 1999: 5). Furthermore, given the dominance of regulatory policy-making and the marginality of redistributive conflicts in the EU, network governance is characterized by an orientation towards problem-solving instead of individual utility-maximisation (Eising and Kohler-Koch 1999: 6).

While these three features are indicative for the EU as a system of governance, they are by no means 'unique' features. For example, the multi-level nature of the EU, that is, the allocation of decision-making to several levels of authority and to functionally differentiated arenas is characteristic for modern federal polities and thus does not capture what is specific about the EU system of governance. Similarly, network governance is equally characteristic for sectoral policy formulation and implementation in governance systems other than the EU.

We will draw attention to a fourth characteristic which we consider to be particular to the EU system of governance. That is, the EU is a *single-market* but a *two-tier system* of politics. With the elimination of all barriers to the free movement of productive forces *(negative integration),* a single space of economic action was established, where the mechanisms of market allocation enfold freely. An encompassing programme of harmonization, mutual recognition and re-regulation *(positive integration)* has been introduced to control and compensate for unwanted consequences of the mechanisms of market allocation. These political interventions support the transformation of the national economies into a single space of economic interaction, but do not transform it into a single space of politics. The EU is still a multi-level system of government and, in particular, a system of 'governance with governments' (Sbragia 2002). Governments negotiate among each other, with the Commission and the European Parliament on the basis of territorially aggregated interests. They reach valid agreements just because they are *authorized* and *accountable representatives,* that is they have the power to commit their citizens and they have the democratic legitimacy to do so. Without the assurance that they can rely on the legitimate authorization of the other governments, compromise decisions would not be feasible. According to Albert Weale (2008), this is the rationale for member state representation in the EU.

Thus, the two-level system of EU governance is constitutive to the well functioning of the EU system. The multi-level character of EU governance is well acknowledged. Less attention is paid to the particularity of the EU system when compared to other multi-level systems such as the Federal Republic of Germany. Whereas in the German federal system political power is gained or lost by party competition at both levels, in the EU two different 'logics of politics' have to be accommodated. The logic of political party competition prevalent at the member state level does not extend in a similar way to the EU level as it does in the German case.

At the national level, political conflicts are resolved by competition for public support (and votes) whereby politically relevant preferences are drawn into party competition. Majority rule is considered to be the legitimate decision rule in democratic systems of governance, even though majority rule is constrained in many countries by corporatism, party coalitions, and federalism (see Lijphart 1998). Furthermore, political decisions are usually taken 'in the shadow' of potential politicization; political issues are always susceptible to become contested among a broadening circle of political actors and spill over into the wider public debate.

In the EU, the dominant policy-making bodies, the Council and the Commission, are shielded from electoral accountability and for structural reasons composed as all-party coalitions. Decision-making follows the logic of consociation; sensitive political issues are decided by supermajorities or unanimity. Consensus, quite obviously, is considered to be the legitimate way of accommodating rival interests and, above all, the Commission shies away from political conflicts reflecting *Weltanschauungen* or party ideologies. Conflict resolution both in the Commission and in the Council is geared towards finding common ground with stakeholders and accommodating nationally aggregated interests through compromise. The forging of ideology-based majorities is seen as counter-productive to decision-making efficiency.

Arthur Benz calls the EU a system of compounded representation which in itself 'fuses incompatible components of competitive and consociational democracies' (Benz 2003:84). In abstract, both elements are present at EU level since only the European Council and the Council as federal institutions embody the consociational element, whereas the European Parliament is structured along party lines and gives ideological cleavages precedence to national interests (Thomassen et al. 2004). It is expected that with the expanding competence of the European Parliament party competition will become more dominant in EU governance, and some authors have come strongly out in favour of more open political competition in order to promote policy efficiency and to make EU governance democratically more responsive (Hix 2008). We rather take side with authors who are sceptical that national cleavage structures can be transformed into European wide cleavages (Bartolini 2005; Olsen 2007) and also do not consider the EU 'mature' enough for majority rule (Bartolini 2005; Scharpf 2007).

As Lipset and Rokkan (1967) have convincingly argued in their pioneering work, cleavage structures within society have a long history: They originate from past socio-economic and cultural macro conflicts, become institutionalized in political organizations and find their expression in party systems and systems of functional and cultural interest representation. The forms of interest intermediation may differ – some are more pluralist, others more corporatist – but they have in common that they are always deeply entrenched in the competition between parties. Party competition is central because it paves the way to executive power.

At the EU level, party competition in elections to the European Parliament is about votes and influence on policy outcomes, like in any other system of representative government, but not about office and thus not about executive power. Therefore, it is plausible to assume that political parties will rather increase their stakes in national than in EP elections. Consequently, if contestations over EU issues are divisive for the national party and lessen the attractiveness of the party for voters at home, it is most likely that such issues will not be presented to the voter in EP election campaigns. Cees van der Eijk and Mark N. Franklin (2004) showed that most EU parties do not reflect the diversity of opinions among the electorate. Most noticeable is that, except for small parties at the extreme of the political spectrum, EU parties 'offer only limited choice in terms of pro- and anti-European orientations.' (Eijk and Franklin 2004: 33) They refrain from introducing contested issues that might attract votes but have the potential to restructure the national party systems. Hence, party competition at the EU level is heavily constrained by national considerations and, consequently, the European Parliament is mirroring the political party divide in member states. We would argue that this is because of and not despite the fact that '(...) there is not much of a *process* of political representation at the European level' (Mair and Thomassen 2008: 10).

Even though the EU is undergoing a continuous process of institutional reform geared at empowering the European Parliament (Rittberger 2005) and in spite of its openness and responsiveness to a plethora of actors – special interest groups and all kinds of advocacy coalitions – effective accountability and responsiveness to voters' concerns are remarkably limited. Mair argues that 'Europe appears to have been constructed as a safeguard sphere, protected from the demands of voters and their representatives' (Mair 2005: 9). We do not intend to take issue with the argument that political elites engage in conscious and intentional de-politicization, yet by stressing that the politics of conflict resolution in the EU are different from those in domestic polities, this chapter carries a central message: The EU is a two level system of governance where politics operates according to a different 'logic'.

This argument is supported by the empirical findings concerning the attractiveness of the 'new modes of governance' (NMG) at EU level.[2] Even though public policy making, by side stepping parliament and being based on legally non-binding agreements with private actors, is well-established also at national, sub-national and local level, it has gained prominence as a preferred instrument of EU governance. Even though the new modes of governance have not substituted the 'Community method' (Dehousse 2008), they have proliferated significantly in all areas where member states prefer a low key approach to avoid party political conflict. The active involvement of experts and 'stakeholders' promises to achieve efficient problem-solving without stimulating contestation over core policy goals.

EU GOVERNANCE: AVENUES FOR FUTURE RESEARCH

In recent years research has complemented the analysis of the emergence, evolution and execution of the different modes of EU governance by a thorough evaluation. Policy analysis is mainly concerned with a functional evaluation aimed at assessing the efficiency and effectiveness of old and new modes of governance in terms of goal attainment (Citi and Rhodes 2007). Political Theory and Law reflect on the wider normative implications for European democracy (see the contributions in Kohler-Koch and Rittberger 2007; Follesdal 2007) and have done so by addressing different modes of generating democratic legitimacy. Research on electoral democracy (Marsh et al. 2007), deliberative democracy (Kohler-Koch and Finke 2007; Sabel and Zeitlin 2008), functional (Saurugger 2009) and participatory democracy (Ruzza and Sala 2007; Smismans 2006; Steffek et al. 2007) provides differentiated theoretical reasoning and empirical insights into the democratic potential and limits of EU governance.

EU governance, representation and accountability

The pertinent question is how EU governance can be reconciled with democratic representation and accountability. The challenge of EU governance to accountability has attracted the attention of both political scientists and lawyers (see the contributions in the special issue of the European Law Journal edited by Benz, Harlow and Papadopoulos 2007; Curtin and Wille 2008). Papadopoulos (2007) has drawn our attention to the many features of network and multi-level governance which work to the detriment of accountability. He suggests that the lack of visibility of the responsible actors impedes accountability, and the problem of the 'many hands' (Bovens 2007) is aggravated by the inclusion of private actors because only few decision-makers are, at least in principle, politically responsible while in practice even those are difficult to be hold to account due to a long chain of delegation from the level of citizens up. When examining electoral accountability, the good news is that the European Parliament progressively turns into a forum in which Council members and the Commission have an obligation to explain and to justify their conduct; it can pose questions and pass judgement. But its political power to inflict consequences is limited and the link to a public debate is weak and, consequently, democratic accountability is not at its best. In the functional approach, the participation of stakeholders is seen as a potential corrective by bringing in the interests of those who are immediately affected. However, empirical research provides ample evidence that functional representation does not meet the standards of democratic representativeness (Persson 2007; Quittkat 2008), and even when a plurality of views is represented, stakeholders are trapped by the segmented functional policy approach and, as a rule, will not take negative external effects into account. When examining the widely alleged virtues of civil society for EU democracy, the research results are equally sobering. Civil society organizations do not qualify as agents of public accountability and the capacity of civil society at large is constrained by the very factors that make parliamentary accountability so difficult, namely an underdeveloped public sphere and no power to impose consequences (Kohler-Koch 2008 = IPSA).

EU governance and political integration

Whereas research on the democratic legitimacy of EU governance is well under way, the effects on political integration in Europe are less known. Investigations of the new modes of governance have come to the conclusion that their proliferation may be seen as a mixed blessing for the future deepening of EU integration. The greater informality of the coordination procedures and the substitution of legally binding regulations through political agreements are regarded as a weakening of the institutional system of the EU. But with the introduction of softer ways of coordination, new policy fields were defined as areas of common interest and member states were accepting transnational interference. On balance it is difficult to say if soft coordination will 'harden' over time and strengthen EU institutions or if the new modes of governance are a devise to block the 'state-building' of Europe.

When only examining the choice and implementation of governance instruments we will hardly find an answer. It looks more promising to explore how different modes of governance may trigger a dynamic change in the 'compounded' political system of the EU. In the case that the inclusive methods of EU governance shift interest intermediation and the resolution of political conflicts from the national to the EU level, national societies will become more entrenched in a process of European wide, cross-national restructuring of political cleavage lines. This will affect the capacity of national political systems to master political conflicts and accommodate rival aspirations in a democratically legitimate way (see, among others, Bartolini 2005; Scharpf 2007). EU governance – to differing degrees – increases the availability of exit options and opens windows of opportunity for socio-economic and political actors. More and more actors may escape the domestic arrangements of interest intermediation and opt for the European arena because it offers more attractive exchange conditions, as the literature on interest group politics (see the contributions in Kohler-Koch and Eising 2005 and Coen 2007) and social movements convincingly demonstrates (Imig and Tarrow 2001; Tarrow 2005; Della Porta 2007). Since actors can use these opportunities to different degrees, depending on resource endowment, some may leave whereas others are stuck in the national 'community of solidarity'. At any rate, the established equilibrium of interest intermediation that emerged in a long history of contestation and power struggle in the national systems will come under strain. Political dissatisfaction is most likely to spread beyond the directly affected interest group constituencies when in the public perception the powerful gain and the weak lose influence. When standards of appropriateness and fairness are violated, national integration may be at risk. In other words, the much praised opening of EU governance to civil society may turn out to set stumbling stones for political integration at member state level, while it provides – at best – slippery stepping stones for European integration.

EU governance research still needs to explore the effects of EU governance on member state systems beyond the narrow confines of their impact on individual policies. It is plausible to assume that different modes of governance are more or less conducive to system change (Kohler-Koch, 2005). The traditional 'community method' is more likely to preserve the compounded character of the EU system than the new modes of governance which draw private and sub-national public actors directly into the process of EU policy-making. As long as the Council is the main legislative body, politics in terms of competition for party based political power is kept at the national level and EU governance does little to interfere with national political integration. In comparison, an instrument of the new modes of governance such as the 'Open Method of Coordination' (OMC) has the potential to open the national 'containers' of interest aggregation to trans-national and supranational interaction and interference (see, for example, De la Porte and Nanz 2004). Furthermore, the convention method and "participatory democracy", which according to the Lisbon Treaty is synonymous with promoting and involving civil society in EU politics, is expected to contribute to the formation of a European civil society (Trenz 2007) which supports the emergence of a single political space. These different modes of governance – the community method, OMC, civil dialogue – give expression to differing concepts of the preferred location of politics. But only systematic empirical analysis will reveal whether they also contribute to a real shift in the location of politics. It requires a good deal of empirical research to know how deep EU governance cuts into the process of political integration and by doing so affects the structuring of society.

In the preceding sections we have demonstrated that research on EU governance has covered a large area in exploring both normative and empirical-analytical dimensions. Research questions and theoretical approaches still carry the imprint from the discipline where they originated. Comparative Government, Policy Analysis and IR are interested in different aspects of EU governance. In addition, the analytical perspective changes with a different understanding of the nature of the European Union and the underlying forces for political and social change. In view of these different frames of the governance debate, it is not a surprise that the concept of governance looks so ambiguous and under-specified. A concept that stretches over many different research questions provides answers that are difficult to be reconciled. Nevertheless, it looks as if the normative debate on the democratic credentials of EU governance touches some common ground.

NOTES

1. This contribution draws selectively from Kohler-Koch and Rittberger (2006).
2. See the findings of the EU funded Integrated Project NewGov which was dedicated exclusively to the new modes of governance; http://www.cu-newgov.org/database/DELIV/D02D09_Classifying_and_Mapping_OMC.pdf (accessed, 01/08/2008).

REFERENCES

Bache, Ian and Matthew Flinders (2004), 'Themes and Issues in Multi-level Governance', in Ian Bache and Matthew Flinders (eds), *Multi-level Governance*, Oxford: Oxford University Press, pp. 13–15.
Bartolini, Stefano (2005), *Restructuring Europe: Centre Formation, System Building, and Political Structuring Between the Nation State and the European Union*, Oxford: Oxford University Press.
Benz, Arthur (2003), 'Compounded Representation in EU Multi-Level Governance', in Beate Kohler-Koch (ed.), *Linking EU and National Governance*, Oxford: Oxford University Press, pp. 82–111.

Benz, Arthur, Carol Harlow and Yannis Papadopoulos (eds) (2007), Special Issue *European Law Journal*, **13** (4).

Bovens, Mark (2007), 'Analysing and Assessing Public Accountability. A Conceptual Framework', *European Law Journal*, **13** (4), 447–468.

Citi, Manuele and Martin Rhodes (2007), 'New Modes of Governance in the European Union: A Critical Survey and Analysis', in Knud E. Jorgensen, Mark Pollack and Ben J. Rosamond (eds), *Handbook of European Union Politics*, London: Sage Publications Ltd, pp. 463–482.

Coen, David (2007), 'Empirical and theoretical studies in EU lobbying', *Journal of European Public Policy*, **14** (3), 333–345.

Curtin, Deirdre and Anchrit Wille (eds) (2008), *Meanings and Practice of Accountability in the EU Multi-Level Context*, Connex Report Series Vol. 7, Mannheim.

Dehousse, Renaud (2008), 'The Community Method: Chronicle of a death too early foretold', in Renaud Dehousse and Laurie Boussaguet (eds), *The Transformation of EU Policies? EU Governance at Work*, Connex Report Series Vol. 8, Mannheim, 7–35.

de la Porte, Caroline and Patrizia Nanz (2004), 'OMC – A Deliberative-Democratic Mode of Governance? The Cases of Employment and Pensions', *Journal of European Public Policy*, **11** (2), 267–88.

della Porta, Donatella (2007), 'The Europeanization of Protest: A Typology and Empirical Evidence', in Beate Kohler-Koch and Berthold Rittberger (eds), *Debating the Democratic Legitimacy of the European Union*, Lanham: Rowman & Littlefield, 189–208.

Diez, Thomas and Antje Wiener (2004), 'Introducing the Mosaic of Integration Theory', in Antje Wiener and Thomas Diez (eds), *European Integration Theory*, Oxford: Oxford University Press, pp. 1–21.

Eijk, Cees van der and Mark Franklin (2004), 'Potential for contestation on European matters at national elections in Europe', in Gary Marks and Marco Steenbergen (eds), *European Integration and Political Conflict*, Cambridge: Cambridge University Press, pp. 32–50.

Eising, Rainer and Beate Kohler-Koch (1999), 'Governance in the European Union: A Comparative Assessment', in Beate Kohler-Koch and Rainer Eising (eds), *The Transformation of Governance in the European Union*, London: Routledge, pp. 267–286.

Eriksen, Erik O. and John Erik Fossum (2007), 'Europe in Transformation. How to Reconstitute Democracy?' *Recon Online Working Paper* 01.

Follesdal, Andreas (2007), 'Normative Political Theory and the European Union', in Knud E. Jorgensen, Mark Pollack and Ben Rosamond (eds), *Handbook of EU Politics*, London: Sage Publications Ltd, pp. 317–337.

Hix, Simon (1999), *The Political System of the European Union*, Basingstoke: Palgrave Macmillan.

Hix, Simon (2008), *What's Wrong with the European Union and How to Fix it*, Cambridge: Cambridge Polity Press.

Hooghe, Liesbeth and Gary Marks (2001), *Multi-Level Governance and European Integration*, Lanham: Rowman & Littlefield.

Imig, Doug and Sidney Tarrow (2001), *Contentious Europeans: Protest and Politics in a Europeanizing Polity*, Lanham: Rowman and Littlefield.

Jachtenfuchs, Markus (2001), 'The Governance Approach to European Integration', *Journal of Common Market Studies*, **39** (2), 245–64.

Jachtenfuchs, Markus (2003), 'Regieren jenseits der Staatlichkeit', in Gunther Hellmann, Klaus Dieter Wolf and Michael Zürn (eds*), Die neuen Internationalen Beziehungen: Forschungsstand und Perspektiven in Deutschland*, Baden-Baden: Nomos, pp. 495–518.

Joerges, Christian and Ellen Vos (eds) (1999), *EU-Committees: Social Regulation, Law and Politics*, Oxford: Hart Publishing.

Kohler-Koch, Beate (1999), 'The Evolution and Transformation of European Governance', in Beate Kohler-Koch and Rainer Eising (eds), *The Transformation of Governance in the European Union*, London: Routledge, pp. 14–35.

Kohler-Koch, B. (2005), 'European Governance and System Integration', *European Governance Papers (EUROGOV)*, C-05-01.

Kohler-Koch, Beate and Rainer Eising (eds) (2005), *Interessenpolitik in Europa*, Baden-Baden: Nomos.

Kohler-Koch, Beate and Barbara Finke (2007), 'The Institutional Shaping of EU-Society Relations: A Contribution to Democracy via Participation?', *Journal of Civil Society*, **3** (3), 205–221.

Kohler-Koch, Beate and Berthold Rittberger (2006), 'The "Governance Turn" in EU Studies', *Journal of Common Market Studies* **44** (Annual Review), 27-49.

Kohler-Koch, Beate and Berthold Rittberger (2007), 'Charting Crowded Territory: Union Debating the Democratic Legitimacy of the European Union', in Beate Kohler-Koch and Berthold Rittberger (eds), *Debating the Democratic Legitimacy of the European Union*, Lanham: Rowman & Littlefield, pp. 1–29.

Kohler-Koch, Beate (2008), 'Civil society in EU governance – a remedy to the democratic accountability deficit?', *Concepts & Methods*, **4** (1).

Lijphart, Arend (1998), *Electoral systems and party systems. A study of twenty-seven democracies, 1945–1990*, Oxford: Oxford University Press.

Lipset, Martin S. and Stein Rokkan (eds) (1967), *Party Systems and Voter Alignments. Cross-National Perspectives*, New York: Free Press, pp. 1–64.

Mair, Peter (2005), 'Popular Democracy and the European Union Polity', *European Governance Papers (EUROGOV)*, No. C-05-03.

Mair, Peter and Jacques Thomassen (2008), 'Electoral Democracy and Political Representation in the European Union', Paper prepared for the *Connex Workshop on Representation*, European University Institute, 23–24 April 2008.

Marks, Gary (1993), 'Structural Policy and Multilevel Governance in the EC', in Alan Cafruny and Glenda Rosenthal (eds), *The State of the European Community. The Maastricht Debates and Beyond*, Boulder: Lynne Rienner, pp. 391–410.

Marks, Gary, Liesbeth Hooghe and Kermit Blank, (1996), 'European integration from the 1980s: state-centric v. multi-level governance', *Journal of Common Market Studies*, **34** (3), 341–78.

Marsh, Michael, Slava Mikhaylov and Hermann Schmitt (eds) (2007), *European Elections after Eastern Enlargement: Preliminary Results from the European Election Study 2004*, CONNEX Report Series No. 1, Mannheim.

Olsen, Johan P. (2007), *Europe in Search of Political Order. An Institutional Perspective on Unity/Diversity, Citizens/Their Helpers, Democratic Design/Historical Drift and the Co-existence of Orders*, Oxford: Oxford University Press.

Papadopoulos, Yannis (2007), 'Problems of Democratic Accountability in Network and Multilevel Governance', *European Law Journal*, **13** (4), 469–486.

Persson, Thomas (2007), 'Democratizing European Chemicals Policy: Do Online Consultations Favour Civil Society Participation?', *Journal of Civil Society*, **3** (3), 223–238.

Pollitt, Christopher (2006), 'Book Review: The Europeanisation of National Administrations: Patterns of Institutional Change and Persistence', in *International Public Management Journal*, **9** (1), 81–82.

Quittkat, Christine (2008), 'Wirklichnäher am Bürger? Konsultationsinstrumente der EU-Kommission auf dem Prüfstand', in Matthias Freise (ed.), *Brüssel und die Civil Society, Sonderheft Neue Soziale Bewegungen*, 64–72.

Rittberger, Berthold (2005), *Building Europe's Parliament. Democratic Representation Beyond the Nation State*, Oxford: Oxford University Press.

Rosenau, James N. and Ernst-Otto Czempiel (eds) (1992), *Governance without Government: Order and Change in World Politics*, Cambridge: Cambridge University Press.

Ruzza, Carlo and Vicent Della Sala (eds) (2007), *Governance and Civil Society: Normative Dimensions*, Manchester: Manchester University Press.

Sabel, Charles and Jonathan Zeitlin (2008), 'Learning from Difference: The New Architecture of Experimentalist Governance in the EU', *European Law Journal*, **14** (3), 271–327.

Saurugger, Sabine (2009), 'Associations and Democracy in the European Union', in Jan Beyers, Rainer Eising and William Maloney, 'Much We Study, Little We Know? The Analysis of Interest Group Politics in Europe', Special Issue *West European Politics*.

Sbragia, Alberta (2002), 'The Dilemma of Governance with Government', *Jean Monnet Working Paper*, **3** (2), 1–15.

Scharpf, Fritz W. (1999), *Governing in Europe. Effective and Democratic?*, Oxford: Oxford University Press.

Scharpf, Fritz W. (2003), 'Problem-Solving Effectiveness and Democratic Accountability in the EU', *Max-Planck-Institut für Gesellschaftsforschung Working Paper*, **3** (1), http://www.mpi-fg-koeln.mpg.de/pu/workpap/wp03-1/wp03-1.html, 12.06.2008.

Scharpf, Fritz W. (2007), 'Reflections on Multilevel Legitimacy', *MPIfSS Working Paper*, **7** (3), pp. 1–20.

Schimmelfennig, Frank und Berthold Rittberger (2006), 'Theories of European integration. Assumptions and hypotheses', in Jeremy Richardson (ed.), *European Union. Power and Policy-making*, London: Routledge, pp. 73–95.

Schuppert, Gunnar Folke (ed.) (2005): *Governance-Forschung. Vergewisserung über Stand und Entwicklungslinien*, Baden-Baden: Nomos.

Smismans, Stijn (2006), *Civil Society and Legitimate European Governance*, Northampton, MA and Cheltenham, UK: Edward Elgar Publishing.

Steffek, Jens, Claudia Kissling and Patrizia Nanz (eds) (2007), *Civil Society Participation in European and Global Governance. A Cure for the Democratic Deficit?*, Basingstoke: Palgrave Macmillan.

Tarrow, Sidney (2005), *The New Transnational Activism*, Cambridge, UK: Cambridge University Press.

Thomassen, Jacques, Abdul G. Noury and Erik Voeten (2004), 'Political Competition in the European Parliament: Evidence from Roll Call and Survey Analyses', in

Gary Marks and Marco Steenbergen (eds), *European Integration and Political Conflict,* Cambridge, UK: Cambridge University Press, pp. 141–164.

Tömmel, Ingeborg (2008), 'Governance and Policy-Making im Mehrebenensystem der EU', in Ingeborg Tömmel (ed.), *Die Europäische Union. Governance and Policy-Making, Politische Vierteljahresschrift Sonderheft,* 40/2007, Wiesbaden: VS Verlag für Sozialwissenschaften, pp. 13–35.

Treib, Oliver, Holger Bähr and Gerda Falkner (2007), 'Modes of Governance: Towards a Conceptual Clarification', *Journal of European Public Policy,* **14** (1), 1-20 (also published in *European Governance Papers (EUROGOV),* No. N-05-02).

Trenz, Hans-Jörg (2007), 'The imaginary of a European Civil Society', paper presented at RECON WP5 Kick-Off International Conference, Delmenhorst, 17-19 May.

Wallace, Helen (2005), 'An Institutional Anatomy and Five Policy Modes', in Helen Wallace, William Wallace and Mark Pollack (eds), *Policy-Making in the European Union,* 5th ed., Oxford: Oxford University Press, pp. 49–93.

Weale, Albert (2008), 'Comments on Beate Kohler-Koch "Representation, Representativeness and Accountability in EU-Civil Society Relations"', Paper presented on the CONNEX final conference, 6th-8th March 2008, Mannheim, http://www.mzes.uni-mannheim.de/projekte/typo3/site/fileadmin/Final_Conference /papers/Comments_Weale.pdf.

Zürn, Michael (1998), *Regieren jenseits des Nationalstaates. Denationalisierung und Globalisierung als Chance,* Frankfurt: Suhrkamp.

2. Travelling Concepts: EU Governance in the Social Sciences Literature

Joan O'Mahony and Jim Ottaway

INTRODUCTION

In his 1995 book *The Elements of Social Scientific Thinking*, Kenneth Hoover poses the question of the origin of concepts. The origin of concepts, their beginning, their source, in short what causes them, is an important question. Concepts move reality, Hoover argues. They are able to do so because how we conceive of a thing, the way in which a thing is presented, means that we 'ask certain questions [of it] and not others' (Diez, 2001:30). This property of concepts, their capacity to organise onto the agenda, and off it, some issues and not others, has consequences for the individuals and societies who benefit or lose from that particular way of seeing.

Concepts originate in and are made through agreement. Such agreement depends on the extent to which a consensus can emerge about the degree to which the concept in question 'captures or isolates some significant and definable item in reality' (Hoover, 1992:18). As such, concepts are inherently tentative because it is in their nature to be subject to an ongoing process of confirmation. Concepts, we said, are critical, because concepts are consequential. We should then ask not only 'where do concepts come from?', but 'where do they go to?', and also, 'how do concepts get to where they are going?' Not all concepts travel equally well. The concept of civil society, for example, spread rapidly through Eastern Europe in 1990 but at a much slower pace in the west. Why so? Presumably because the particular aspect of reality that the concept of civil society sought to capture was of much greater significance to the eastern european citizens at that time, than it was to western citizens for whom the legal constitution of the civic sphere had for long a taken-for-grantedness about it. Concepts spread, 'travel', and the question of how they do so is also of relevance. Civil society, for sure, would have arrived more slowly in the West were it not for the existence of a strong anti-Communist post-Marxist left in American Universities composed of many who had fled the Soviet bloc in the 1970s. It was they who, facing one way east and one west, provided the transmission belt for the concept. Academic communities are one significant factor in the promulgation of ideas and theories.

THE CONCEPT OF GOVERNANCE AND GOVERNANCE IN THE EUROPEAN UNION

Governance describes processes of rule-making within boundaries that are non-territorial and non-hierarchical. While Government is seen as old – as old at least as the modern state – governance is considered 'new'. The largest on-line social-scientific bibliographic collection in the world, the International Bibliography for the Social Sciences (IBSS),[1] shows 6 574 uses of the word 'governance' in book or journal titles in the almost 50 years between 1958 and 2006. But the first 30 of those years (1958–88) account for a mere 76 of such usages, with the latter 16 years from 1990 to 2007 accounting for the remaining 6 498.

A look at some of these early uses of governance tells us something of the appropriateness of the term, or the affinities the term offers for current day usage. Governance in these years was often used to refer to the activity of governors – post-colonial unelected appointed elites. *The Governance of Burma* and *The Governance of Berlin* are the two earliest titles from 1958 and 1959 respectively. While then, both Governors and Government ruled, it was only Government who was able to claim electoral legitimacy. University governance, mainly universities in the United States, follows as a popular topic in the 1960s, continuing as the lead topic throughout the 1970s and early 1980s. Corporate governance makes its first appearance in 1981 and dominates the publication scene for the following decade.

European Governance

And what of European Governance? IBSS credits Helen Wallace with the earliest mention of the term. In 1993, she published the article 'European governance in turbulent times' in the *Journal of Common Market Studies*. Between then and 2000, a mere four articles explicitly referring to European Governance followed: one in 1997, two in 1998, and one in 1999;[2] But despite what most regard as an energetic debate on the topic, European Governance nevertheless seems to be something of a timid or shy concept. Between 1951 and 2007 the term European Governance is used only 47 times as a title of a book or article (65 times, if you include EU Governance or European Union Governance). In the same period, the term corporate governance is used 1 001 times, and global governance 363 times. For sure, the term 'European Union Governance' scarcely trips off the tongue with the same phonological ease as corporate governance, or global governance, nevertheless the differences in the frequency of use are striking.

At the outset of this chapter, we said that the establishment of a concept depends on the strength of the consensus about whether the concept does in fact encapsulate or portray a significant thing. For most authors European Governance is 'a thing' that defines what Diez (2001:10) has succinctly summarised as the process 'whereby policies are made in a complex web of interaction by territorially as well as functionally differentiated actors'. This web is held to have a number of ideal typical features such as that it is non-hierarchical and regulatory, but there are disagreements about the extent to which European Governance in general or in any particular instantiation approximates these features. Indeed, Kohler-Koch and Rittberger argue that "despite the omnipresence of 'governance' in the study of the EU, governance is still ambiguous and under-specified as a concept, let alone as a theory." (2006: 43–44).

This chapter is a first attempt to track the development of the concept. We base our analysis upon a collection of bibliographic records gathered together in the GovLit database.[3] GovLit was developed as a bibliographic resource for research on EU governance. It brings together bibliographic information about publications on EU governance from a variety of sources, including the Social Sciences Citation Index (SSCI), the International Bibliography of the Social Sciences (IBSS), Google Scholar, and the British Library. Publication records from these sources were merged together into a common bibliographic record format and indexed according to keywords used for the CONNEX GovData[4] database of research projects on EU Governance. The principal keywords applied to the records are:

1. democratic theory
2. political participation
3. EU institutions
4. governance
5. integration
6. interest intermediation
7. international organization
8. legal framework
9. legitimacy
10. member states
11. non-state actors
12. policy
13. decision-making
14. social space
15. subnational level
16. transformation

Each of these keywords has some sub-keywords associated with it, but these are only used in the following account when we discuss the details of different aspects of the governance keyword.

THE JOURNEY OF EU GOVERNANCE: QUANTITATIVE AND QUALITATIVE CHANGES IN EU GOVERNANCE RESEARCH

In this section, we describe changes in the publication output on EU governance over time. We show too how the thematic concerns of EU governance researchers have changed, and finally we provide the example of the particular changes in the use of one central keyword: multi-level governance.

Publication output and counts of publications over time

Publication output on European governance has grown rapidly from the 1990s onwards. For the 1970s the mean number of records per year in the database is barely greater than one; in the 1980s it is 3.7 records per year. It is in 1990 that the number of records in the GovLit database reaches double figures: the mean number of records for each year in the 1990s is 82.4. Indeed, 1994 to 1995 could be described as EU governance's period of lift-off, when the number of records jumped from 48 to 97. There were further jumps in this decade between 1996 (97 records) and 1997 (157 records). 2000 saw another jump to 202 records; the 2000s as a whole show a marked increase on the 1990s, with a mean of 333.67 records for each year.[5]

Figure 2.1 Growth in volume of records 1995 to 2005, IBSS and GovLit

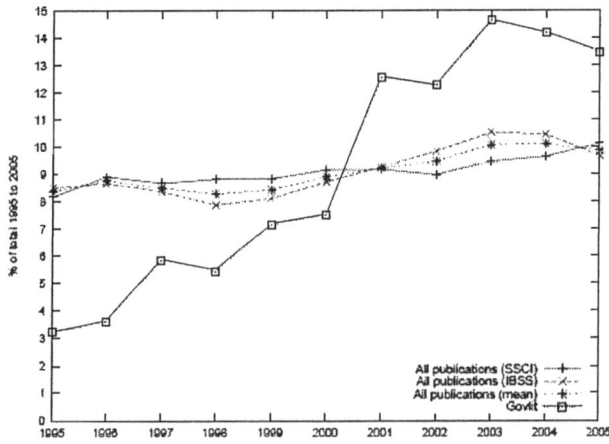

These features add up to a growth rate of publication outputs on EU governance that is ten times that of the base growth rates of publications represented in both IBSS and SSCI, as can be seen in figure 2.1.[6] The large difference in these growth rates is partially explained by the fact that the total number of records gathered annually by IBSS and SSCI are several orders of magnitude greater than the numbers involved in records of publications on EU governance. IBSS, for example, contains 102 838 records for 2005, while the GovLit database contains 361 for that year. Never the less, it is a remarkable growth rate, and one that is consistent with the advent and growth to maturity of a new field of knowledge (Beattie and Davie, 2006).

Changes in emphasis across the keywords

Here, we examined how the thematic concerns of governance researchers have changed over time by looking at the rise and decline of keywords used to classify publications for each of the years 1995 to 2005. Space precludes the inclusion of a chart for each year, but we comment on the significant changes. The total number of records in the database is currently 2 997, of which 2 510 are 'primary' publications, rather than reviews.[7] Figure 2.2 shows the overall volumes of keywords in the database.

Figure 2.2 Overall keyword counts 1995 to 2005

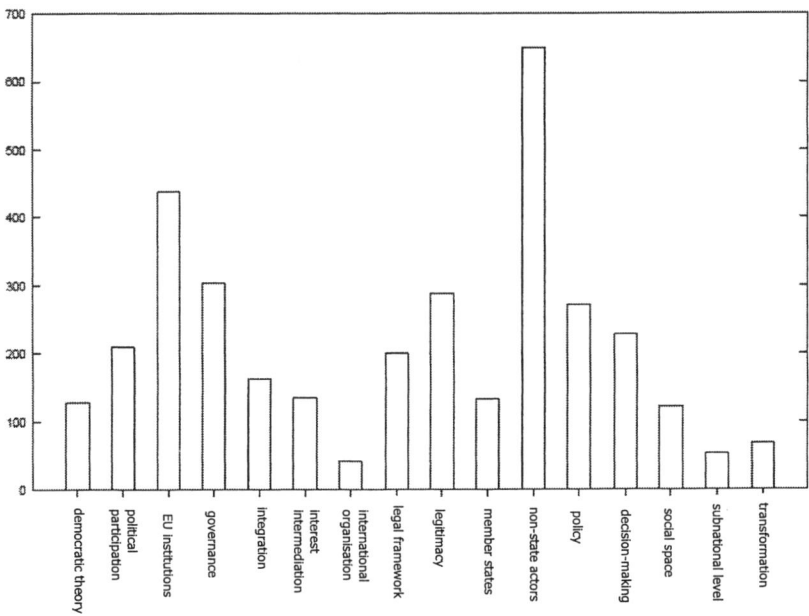

The keyword 'non-state actors' is overall for the ten years the highest scoring keyword with 649 records, followed by 'EU Institutions' with 439.

Of course, 'non-state' is a negating adjective and it embraces easily, perhaps too easily, all of that which is not the state. Nevertheless, given that '*not* the state' or '*not* the government' is much of what governance is about, it is reasonable that the word is so readily applied as a descriptor of many articles. While the 'non-state actors' keyword is the highest scorer over time, the distribution of keywords has since broadened significantly. Other keywords have grown more rapidly, as can be seen in figure 2.3, which shows the volumes of keywords at the beginning, middle and end of the decade.

Figure 2.3 Numbers of keywords 1995, 2000 and 2005

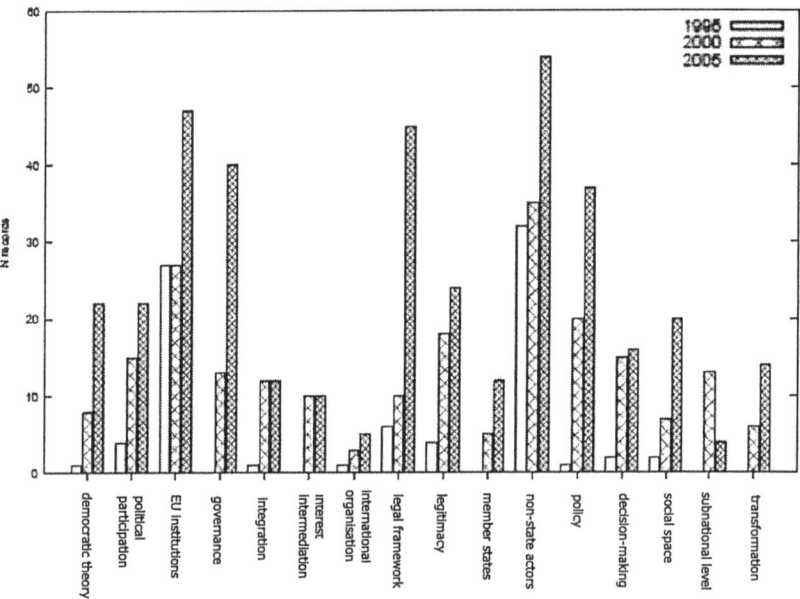

Certainly, compared to 1995 and 1996, which shows a very small number of thematic concerns, the overall picture by 2005 is much more differentiated. Crucially, if we look at the results for 2005 many of the differences between keywords have evened out, and we see that 'non-state actors' and 'EU institutions' no longer dominate, but are more a case of first amongst equals. This can be seen graphically in figure 2.4, which shows the proportions of keywords for each year. In short, research on EU governance is no longer dominated by a few thematic concerns, suggesting that research on EU governance has come of age.

Figure 2.4 Keyword proportions 1995 to 2005

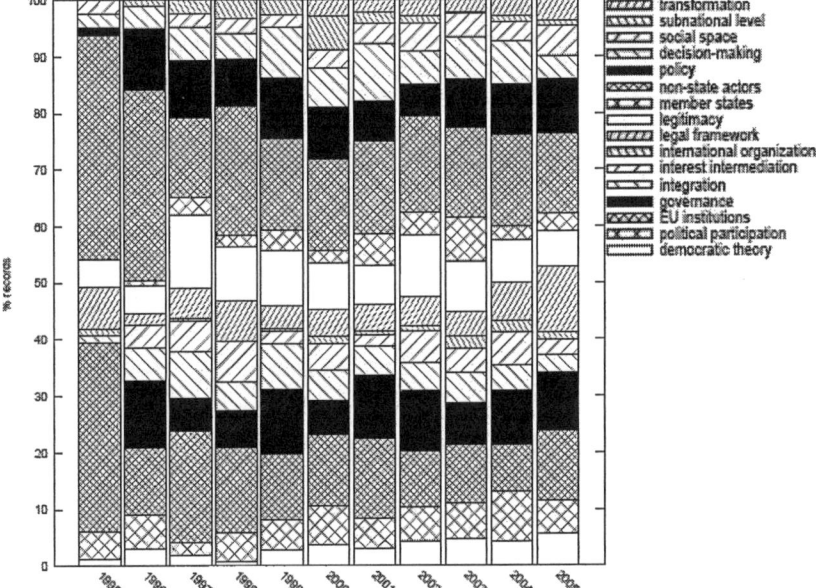

The network of keywords

Another view of the relationships between keywords in the collection is provided by thinking of them as the nodes of a network, where an edge between two keywords in the network represents a document where both keywords are present. Any two keywords may, in this case, have an arbitrary number of edges connecting them, and the number of co-occurrences of keyword pairs represents the number of links between two different keywords. This count provides a simple measure of the strength of the connections between any two keywords. The sum of the counts for a keyword with any other keyword than itself provides a measure of the 'network centrality' of that keyword: it shows how many links there are between that keyword and all of the others. We also calculate a measure that is the ratio of the sum of the counts of each keyword to the number of documents having that keyword: the proportional network centrality. Together, these two measures give an indication of what we term the 'sociability' of a concept represented by a keyword within the collection; that is keywords with a higher sum network centrality have more connections than those with lower ones; keywords with a higher proportional network centrality have more connections per document than those with lower ones.

Table 2.1 shows the network centrality figures for the principal keywords in the whole collection; the table is ordered by the sum network centrality figure. The first row in the table, for example, shows that there is a total of 363 links between the keyword 'decision-making' and other keywords and that this represents 1.59 times as many links as there are documents with the 'decision-making' keyword in the collection.

Table 2.1 Network centralities of keywords 1995 to 2005

keyword	sum	prop	keyword	sum	prop
decision-making	363	1.59	legal framework	138	0.69
policy	334	1.23	social space	131	1.07
governance	277	0.91	interest intermediation	108	0.80
EU institutions	238	0.54	transformation	106	1.56
legitimacy	233	0.81	political participation	76	0.36
integration	218	1.34	subnational level	65	1.20
non-state actors	189	0.29	democratic theory	43	0.34
member states	182	1.37	international organization	37	0.90

The relationships between keyword pairs in the network is illustrated graphically in figure 2.5, which shows the result of a hierarchical cluster analysis of the network.[8]

Figure 2.5 Keyword clusters

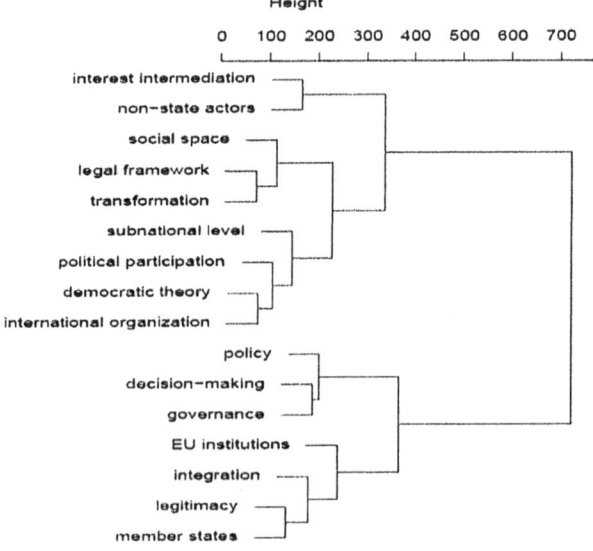

The relevance of the multi-level dimension to writings on EU governance

Finally, there is not enough space here to analyse all of the sub-keywords. However, we looked at one: multi-level governance. We chose this sub-keyword to look at because multi-level governance has been identified as a key research area on EU governance (Kohler-Koch and Rittberger 2006: 27). The proponents of the term, Liesbeth Hooghe and Gary Marks are amongst the highest scoring authors.[9] As an overall topic of research, governance has remained popular, comprising on average ten percent of keywords for each year of the decade. Amongst the governance sub-keywords, 'multi-level governance' has the highest score by a long margin (Table 2.2). It has strong links with 'decision-making' (42) and 'policy' (38), and a significant number of links with 'legitimacy' (19), 'integration' (18), 'non-state actors' (14) and 'transformation' (12). Amongst the governance sub-keywords, 'multi-level governance' has the greatest number of links with 'open method of coordination'.

Table 2.2 Network centralities of governance sub-keywords

keyword	sum	prop
multi-level governance	191	1.19
comitology	43	0.91
open method of coordination	41	0.68
network governance	8	1.33
private-public network	8	1.00
private-public partnership	0	—

Across the whole keyword space, including sub-keywords, 'multi-level governance' is one of the most 'sociable' of the keywords, interconnecting with an unusually high number of other keywords: 64 in total, one half of all distinct keywords in the collection. And not only is 'multi-level governance' influential in this way, we can see that it is influential across disciplines, as is illustrated in Table 2.3, which shows counts and proportions for 'multi-level governance' broken down by discipline. Here we can see, for example, that 65 per cent of all documents with at least one of the governance keywords have 'multi-level governance' as a keyword and politics as a discipline.

Table 2.3 Multi-level governance by discipline: totals and proportional to all governance keywords

discipline	sum	% of governance
Politics	138	65
Economics	27	42
Sociology	15	48
Environmental Studies	5	71
International Relations	5	36
Planning and Development	5	57
Public Administration	4	29

DIVERSE APPLICATIONS ACROSS DISCIPLINES

In the preceding sections we examined the increase in publications on EU governance and changes in keywords that occurred over time. In this section, we are primarily concerned with differences among disciplines. We look at which disciplines are concerned with EU governance and which disciplines dominate the field. We then look at what the thematic concerns are within each discipline (measured by keyword emphasis within each discipline). Finally, we ask whether there exists a cross-disciplinary debate on EU governance.

The disciplines of EU governance research and thematic concerns within disciplines

The chief disciplines involved in research on EU governance are in the following order, (ranked by number of individual articles) politics (1673), economics (601), sociology (532), international relations (78), public administration (56), anthropology (50) and law (42).

Using the same network approach as we did for keywords, it can be seen that the network for disciplines is much sparser than the keyword network, since many records in the collection are indexed to a single discipline. The centrality measures may, therefore, be taken as an index of the interdisciplinarity of each discipline. Table 2.4 shows the centralities of all disciplines with a sum network centrality of greater than 20.

Table 2.4 Disciplinary network centralities

discipline	sum	prop
Economics	135	0.27
International relations	97	1.26
Politics	93	0.07
Sociology	55	0.14
Law	26	0.63
Anthropology	24	0.63
Environmental studies	24	1.04

Table 2.5 shows the number of links between individual disciplines where there are greater than ten links. It shows that there are two strongly interconnected disciplinary sub-networks: the one joining international relations, politics and economics, the other joining together economics, sociology and anthropology.

Table 2.5 Keyword pairs where n links > 10

discipline pair	n links
international relations, politics	42
economics, politics	41
economics, international relations	38
economics, sociology	34
anthropology, sociology	16
law, international relations	16

Importantly, the subject of EU governance is of concern for *all* disciplines. However an examination of the proportions of keywords for each of the main disciplines shows that the disciplines are not concerned with EU governance in the same way nor to the same extent. The 'non-state actors' keyword, for example, dominates anthropological publications on governance, and is represented strongly within sociology, economics and politics. Conversely, this keyword barely appears in international relations, public administration and law, all of which show a stronger interest in legitimacy and legal frameworks.

Figure 2.6 Proportions of keywords for the main disciplines

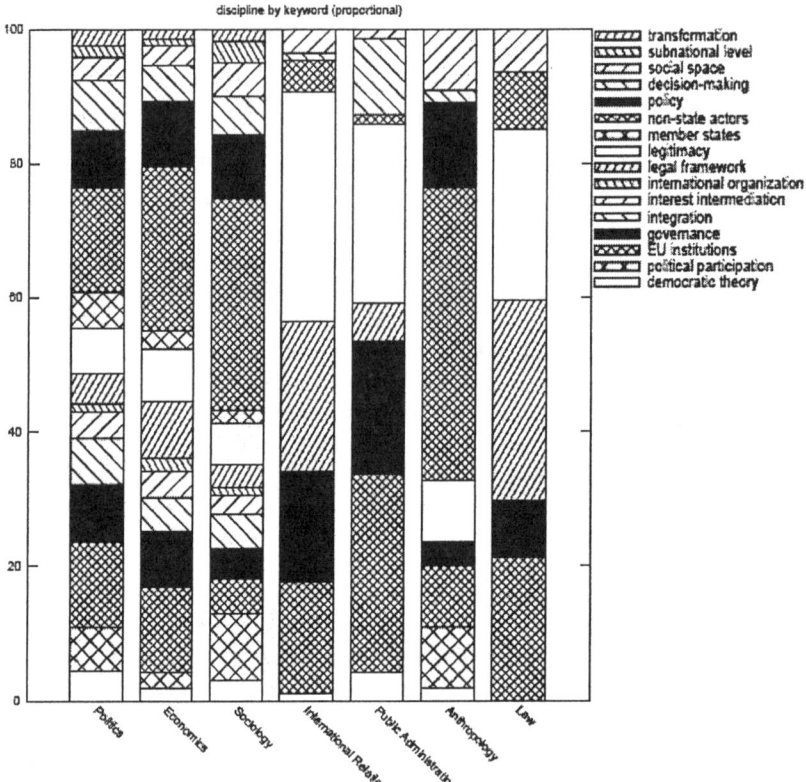

Cross-disciplinary debate: EU Governance Journals

Another way of examining how concepts travel is to look at the extent to which cross-citation takes place amongst journals of different disciplines. The top eight journals from the database are, in the following order: 1. *Journal of European Public Policy*, 2. *Journal of Common Market Studies*, 3. *West European Politics*, 4. *Regional and Federal Studies*, 5. *European Law Journal*, 6. *European Journal of Political Research*, 7. *Governance*. We examined journal cross-citation in the ISI web of knowledge which shows the following. Governance is a popular subject of debate in political science journals and in public administration journals, but less so in law journals. Unlike journals of political science or public administration, law journals are predominantly American, so this may explain the relatively small number of journals that deal with issues of European governance. Indeed the two main law journals which publish frequently on the topic of European Governance – the *Common Market Law Review*, and the *European Journal of Migratory Law* – are both published in the Netherlands, and both edited in Europe (the Netherlands and England respectively). Both are also multi-disciplinary journals (International Relations and Demography respectively). In terms of citations, both these law journals are most closely related to each other, each citing the other most frequently. Nevertheless, there is evidence of a cross-disciplinary debate; the JCMS is the third most commonly cited journal by contributors to the *European Journal of Migratory Law*, and the fifth by contributors to the *Common Market Law Review*.

When it comes to Political Science and Public Administration, cross-disciplinary debate is in earnest among contributors to the popular governance journals in both political science and public administration. Contributors to the public administration journal *Journal of European Public Policy* are more likely to cite journals of political science or international relations, than they are other Public Administration Journals. For example, articles in the *Journal of Common Market Studies* or in *European Union Politics* are more likely to be cited than articles in the Public Administration Journal *Governance*. The journal that seems to promote most cross-disciplinary debate is the multi-disciplinary *Journal of Common Market Studies* (Economics, Political Science, International Relations). In terms of citations, it is most closely related to the *Journal of European Public Policy* (Public Administration), and then to *European Union Politics* (Political Science), then to *International Organization* (International Relations), and then to *European Journal of Migratory Law* (Demography, Law). *The Journal of European Public Policy* and the *Journal of Common Market Studies* have a close relationship. Each has the other as its closest relative in terms of cross-citations. Of note, the *Journal of European Public Policy* is classed as a public administration journal and the *Journal of Common Market Studies* as a multi-disciplinary one (Economics, Political Science, and International Relations), suggesting that disciplinary boundaries are no barrier to the contemporary governance debate. Both journals are published in England.

CONCEPT TRAVELLING THROUGH ACTORS

It is also useful to think about the role of editorial actors in the promotion of concepts across disciplines. With respect to European Governance, the constitutions of the editorial boards[10] of the key journals are marked by a number of distinctive features. First, their membership comes predominantly from a small number of countries. The *Journal of European Public Policy* has 37 editorial members (that is, editor, editorial board, or editorial advisory board): eleven from the USA, eleven from the UK, six from Germany, two from France, two from Italy, and two from the Netherlands, and the remaining three from Sweden, Switzerland, and Austria. The *Journal of Common Market Studies* on the other hand is almost entirely Anglo-American in its constitution of editors. Of 31, only one comes from Germany, 19 from the UK, and four from the USA, and three from the EUI in Italy. Both journals include many of the leading theoreticians on governance. JEPP has Berthold Rittberger, Frank Schimmelfennig, Beate Kohler-Koch, and Jeremy Richardson, the editor, while the board of JCMS includes Thomas Diez, Helen Wallace, Wolfgang Wessels, and Gary Marks. Interestingly, there is no cross-over in the editorship.

However, 'link authors', that is people who spread themselves across a number of journals, are in evidence on other editorial boards. Kohler-Koch, Hooghe and Marks have all promoted the concept of 'multi-level governance', Hooghe and Marks in separate and joint articles. Hooghe and Marks held a joint post of 'Chair in Multi-Level Governance' in 1994 at the Vrije Universiteit Amsterdam. Both are on the editorial boards of Regional and Federal Studies. Hooghe is on the editorial board of *West European Politics*, of *Governance*, and of the *European Journal of Political Research*. Marks is on the editorial board of *Journal of Common Market Studies*. Of the seven leading journals, that leaves but two that they do not have a direct involvement in. Beate Kohler Koch was on the Editorial Board of the *Journal of European Public Policy* and the Advisory Board of the *European Law Journal*, the remaining two.

CONCLUSION

The delineation of a concept has methodological and normative implications (Hix, 1998). However, while there has been much discussion of the actual concept of European Governance, its origin and its development have yet to be subjected to a systematic investigation. We see this chapter as a useful starting point that tracks the evolution of the term to date, and raises a number of directions for future research that might be usefully pursued.

Based largely on the GovLit bibliographic resource, we argue that the study of European Governance is established during the 1990s, with 1994–5 being its period of lift-off. By 2005, research on European Governance had come of age: research in the field has broadened from a concentration on a few topics to cover a wide field. We also attempted a measure and analysis of what we describe as the 'sociability' of a concept. We showed for example how certain keywords 'multi-level governance', for example, are remarkably well-connected with others, indicating the emergence of clusters of affinities around a few key concepts.

There are differences amongst disciplines too. Importantly however, all disciplines are concerned with EU governance albeit not in the same way or to the same extent. We suggested too that an examination of journal cross-citation can provide useful insights into how a concept 'travels' across disciplines, and here we established that disciplinary boundaries are no barrier to the contemporary governance debate. Finally, we touched on the constitution of editorial boards suggesting that the role of editorial actors has a critical role in the promotion of a concept. For example, there is a substantial number of leading governance theoreticians on the boards of European Governance journals. And a group of journals are marked by what we call 'link authors'; that is authors who connect together a number of different governance journals by their involvement in them.

The time-scale of this analysis is relatively short, but it captures the emergence and organisation of studies on governance around a few key themes and it distinguishes important differences in concerns across different disciplines. These changes are, as we have noted, characteristic of a field that is at an early and promising stage of consolidation. It will be interesting to revisit this analysis in another decade to establish whether these patterns have crystallised still further, and indeed whether they are the early indications of the emergence of a new discipline.

NOTES

1. http://www.lse.ac.uk/collections/IBSS/
2. Thomas Christiansen, (1997) 'Tensions of European governance: politicized bureaucracy and multiple accountability in the European Commission', *Journal of European Public Policy*, 4 (1) 73–90. John Peter & Mark McAteer, (1998) 'Subnational institutions and the new European governance: UK local authority lobbying strategies for the IGC', *Regional and Federal Studies*, 8 (3) 104–124. Beate Kohler-Koch, (1998) 'The evolution and transformation of European governance. A evolucao e transformacao da governacao, *Analise social*, XXXIII (148), 659–684. Marcus Horeth, (1999) 'No way out for the beast? The unsolved legitimacy problem of European governance, *Journal of European Public Policy*, 249–268
3. http://connex-network.org/govlit. Thanks go to Thomas Schneider, Fabrice Larat, and Beate Kohler-Koch for their assistance in the construction of the database.
4. http://connex-network.org/govdata
5. We only use data up to 2005 in this account, since at the time of writing the records for 2006 are not complete in the main online database sources.
6. For comparison the figure shows annual volumes as a proportion of the total number of records for the period 1995 to 2005. The slope for the data derived from IBSS and SSCI is 0.0019 ($r = 0.89$); for GovLit, the slope is 0.0126 ($r = 0.91$).
7. In this analysis, we exclude all reviews and also the parent record for special issues.
8. For this analysis and graphic, we used the R language's hclust function with the complete linkage option (R Development Core Team, 2007).
9. The Social Sciences Citation Index is the only bibliographic resource that includes citations in its records. But its coverage of European publications, particularly of documents in languages other than English, is not broad enough to use it exclusively. Therefore, we have forgone the possibility of citation analysis of records the database. We have, however, extracted information about the numbers of citations for a large proportion of the collection using Google Scholar (www.google.com/scholar). These numbers were used as the basis of

a rating for publications in the collection and of their authors. Liesbeth Hooghe, for example, has a count of 212 citations and Gary Marks has 153.
10.   All data on the editorial boards was gathered in February 2007

REFERENCES

Beattie, Vivien and Elizabeth Davie (2006), 'Theoretical studies of the historical development of the accounting discipline: a review and evidence', *Accounting, Business & Financial History*, **16** (1), 1–25

Diez, Thomas (2001), 'Europe as a discursive battleground: Discourse analysis and European integration studies', *Cooperation and Conflict*, **36** (1), 5–38

Hix, Simon (1998), 'The study of the European Union II: the "new governance" agenda and its rival', *Journal of European Public Policy*, **5** (1), 38–65

Hoover, Kenneth R. (1992), *The Elements of Social Scientific Thinking*, New York: St Martin's Press.

Kohler-Koch, Beate and Berthold Rittberger (2006), 'Review article: The "Governance Turn" in EU studies', *Journal of Common Market Studies*, 44, 27–49

R Development Core Team (2007), 'R: A Language and Environment for Statistical Computing', Vienna, *http://www.r-project.org*.

PART II

REFLECTING THE DIVERSITY OF RESEARCH
TRADITIONS

3. United Kingdom and Ireland: Leading in Governance Research

Simon Bulmer[1]

The United Kingdom represents a strong base for research on European Union (EU) governance. CONNEX data on the period 1995–2005 indicate that the UK was the member state hosting the largest number of research projects on the subject: 187 (or 11.9 per cent of the total). Ireland is also strongly represented with 48 projects (or 3.1 per cent of the total). In seeking to outline the prominent contribution to the 'governance turn' in EU studies, as suggested by these data, the chapter follows the common understanding of EU governance deployed in this volume, namely 'efficient and democratic governance in a multilevel Europe'.

Why treat the UK and Ireland together? There are quite strong links between the social science communities in the two states. For example, the University Association for Contemporary European Studies (UACES) in the UK includes members from Ireland because of its resources and 'reach' within the English-speaking academic community. Indeed, UACES held its 2006 annual conference in Limerick as an indication of the close links with scholars in Ireland. Geographical proximity and the English language are consequently the most important factors.

CONTEXT CONDITIONS

Across both, academic communities projects on EU governance are predominantly located in political science, with law and then economics some way behind. Accordingly, in what follows the political science literature will be given stronger consideration than that in the other disciplines.

Research on EU governance is strongly influenced by the institutional context of the higher education systems within which it takes place. The UK has a number of distinctive characteristics which go some way to explaining its strong contribution to the study of EU governance. First, from the early 1970s the UK pioneered 'European Studies' as a programme of undergraduate as well as postgraduate study. This development led to the clustering of inter- or multi-disciplinary groups of scholars in academic units which were predominantly located in universities created in the 1960s; for example, Bath, Loughborough and Sussex. It ran alongside the growth of European integration studies embedded within the individual disciplines of politics, law and economics across many other higher education institutions. This twin-track approach continues to this day in the UK funding council's Research Assessment Exercise (RAE), which determines an important part of universities' research income. Academics working on EU governance may be submitted to separate sub-panels on European Studies or to their discipline depending upon the organisation of their university or upon their calculation of which route is more advantageous.

Secondly, and linked to this development, UACES was set up in 1969 and provided an intellectual arena dedicated to the subject, and with politics strongly represented. However, scholars of EU governance do not confine themselves to this academic forum. Many prefer to be most active in the conferences of discipline-based organisations. To take the case of politics these arenas are: at national level (the Political Studies Association and the British International Studies Association); at European-level (the European Consortium for Political Research); or American-based organisations such as the American Political Science Association. Amongst the community working on EU governance there are some scholars who prioritise their identity as a Europeanist and others, particularly those whose understanding of political science is as the application of formal theory-testing, who reject such an identity outright. This division is less obvious in other disciplines. There is a limited amount of research on EU governance outside the universities organised under the auspices of think-tanks, such as the Royal Institute for International Affairs or the Federal Trust, but often conducted by academics with positions at universities.

Thirdly, attention needs to be paid to the UK's role in publishing work on EU governance. The longest-established journals offering a venue for publications on EU governance are located in the UK. The *Journal of Common Market Studies* (JCMS) (which is part-owned by UACES) was first published in 1962 and the *Journal of European Public Policy* in 1994. *European Union Politics*, the *European Foreign Affairs Review* and the *Journal of European Integration* are amongst other journals where UK-based scholars have played a prominent role at particular times. Established journals, such as *West European Politics*, or newer ones, such as *Comparative European Politics* have strong roots in the UK system, although editorial teams are subject to change. Only in journals concerned with EU legal studies is there something comparable, but these journals have much less of a UK base in terms of editorial team or publishers. Several presses have given prominence to EU governance, notably in book series at Palgrave, Oxford University Press and Manchester University Press. Of course, the act of publishing does not enable the UK to appropriate all the resultant output.

However, the internationalisation of academia has turned the UK into the pre-eminent publishing location for (political science) work on EU governance as a result of the English-language's centrality to academia and the USA's disadvantage of not being in Europe. There may be some resultant positive stimulus for UK-based academics as well, for instance because of commissioning strategies. Given the strong publication incentives embedded in the RAE, UK-based scholars are expected not simply to publish, but to do so at international levels of quality.[2]

Fourthly, the UK higher education system has been a comparatively open one, and in two senses. It is open in terms of recruiting postgraduate students from different parts of Europe. Ph.D. research is the norm in politics and economics; less so in law. It is also open in terms of recruiting academic staff. This situation makes it important to indicate that research on EU governance in the UK does not equate to research undertaken by British scholars. For example, there are North American academics who have established themselves in the UK system and who work on EU governance. Even a cursory survey of the academic population identifies the importance of other European nationalities, including Germany and Greece, but also other southern European states, central Europe, not to omit the contribution of Brits working in Ireland and vice versa.[3]

The UK system is open in another sense. It is not as hierarchical as, notably, the German system, where academic resources traditionally have been concentrated in a relatively small number of university professors or counterparts in research institutes, such as the Max-Planck Institute for the Study of Societies. In the UK some limited internal research resources are in principle open to academics at any grade, providing they hold a permanent position and are located in a unit with a good RAE ranking for their discipline. Modest research projects may not therefore require external funding. External funding sources are available for small grants, such as from foundations, in addition to larger awards from the research councils. The consequence of the openness is that the academic agenda is less structured around leading figures in the profession. Thus, it is much less likely that a particular theoretical position on the EU becomes associated with a large programme of research based at a particular institution. Senior academics may have influential ideas but they normally lack sufficient financial or power resources to create a particular 'brand' of EU governance at their institution.

Lastly, reference needs to be made to the role of the Economic and Social Research Council (ESRC), the UK's main funding agency for social science research projects. Its single market research programme in the early 1990s and, in particular from the late-1990s its 'One Europe or Several Programme', directed by Helen Wallace,[4] had an impact on UK-based scholarship on EU governance. However, the ESRC's impact may have been even greater as a result of its wider agenda-setting role. Governance was one of its thematic priorities in the 1990s. In particular, the ESRC commissioned the 'Local Governance' research programme. Influential in this were Rod Rhodes, who chaired the programme's steering group, and Gerry Stoker, who was programme director. The programme ran from 1992–98. Together with publications by Rhodes and Stoker the research programme had a significant impact on the governance 'turn' in British political science. One final general point about ESRC-funded research; the expectation that research projects engage with 'user groups' tends to privilege applied over basic research.

The Irish system is, of course, much smaller than that of the UK. Thus the importance of individual institutions (and, by extension, of individual academics) is much greater. However, there are some echoes of these features of the UK system. The two institutions with the largest engagement in research on EU governance, as measured in CONNEX data, are University College Dublin (UCD) and the University of Limerick (Auer and Shaw 2006). UCD follows the model of integrating research on EU governance within discipline-based departments, whereas Limerick has pursued interdisciplinarity in a Centre for European Studies. As in the UK, research on EU governance has been concentrated in the seven national universities, although the Institute of European Affairs has also been active in its capacity as a Dublin think-tank, with a strong interest in sponsoring research on Irish engagement with EU governance. The small size of the academic community has certain consequences for the conduct of academic debates. The Irish European Studies Association is 'currently dormant' and only one Europe-related journal – the *Irish Journal of European Law* – has local roots (Auer and Shaw 2006, p. 5). Perhaps more significantly, it is only since 2000 that the Irish Research Council for the Humanities and Social Sciences has been in operation to support research projects and doctoral training. The infrastructural resources for developing a distinctive Irish approach to EU governance have therefore been more limited than in the UK. English-language debates – whether they emanate from the UK or the US – have had a comparative advantage over continental European counterparts in influencing Irish scholarship on governance (Auer and Shaw 2006, p. 5). Contributions on EU governance from the academic community in Ireland have tended to be more empirically-oriented than in the UK.

It is in this institutional setting that research on the EU has developed in the two academic communities. With both states acceding to the European Communities in 1973, there are some parallels in the development of EU studies. However, the contested nature of UK membership – two failed attempts to join, a divisive ratification process, a referendum on continued membership in 1975, and persistent policy disputes, notably over the budget – created a distinctive context within which UK research on the EU has taken place (see for example, George 1992; George 1998; Young 1998; Young 2000). The dissection of UK European policy and the related party debates have been a focal point for British scholars as well as for politicians in their memoirs (on party debates, see for example Baker and Seawright 1998; Forster 2002). In Ireland, by contrast, accession to, and membership of the EC were much less contested, apart from at the time of the initial rejection of the Nice Treaty in a referendum held in June 2001.

Against this background what has been the genesis of the use of the term governance in the EU context? Has there been a governance 'turn' in EU studies? It is argued here that there has indeed been a governance 'turn' but that it was not brought about by a seminal piece of work or a prominent advocate or exponent but, rather, arose piecemeal over a period of several years. The use of the term governance has been driven by two principal factors: developments in the real world of the EU and in other political systems, notably the UK; and the changes in associated academic debates. The two are, of course, inter-related.

First, the consolidation of the European construction itself gathered pace with the Single European Act (SEA) and the single market programme from the mid-1980s. With an unprecedented succession of constitutional reform agreements – the SEA (1986), the Treaty on European Union (1992), the Amsterdam Treaty (1997) and the Nice Treaty (2000) – it became clear that the EU had to be understood as a political system rather than as a process of integration or as an international organisation. By 2001 the European Commission had explicitly used the terminology in its White Paper on European Governance (CEC 2001). This trend in development impacted on academia. The changing 'nature of the beast' as well as the perceived shortcomings of integration theories shifted the focus of the literature. Arguably the most prominent UK response was that of Simon Hix, who in 1994 called for an analytical focus in EU studies based upon the comparative politics toolkit (Hix 1994; also see Hurrell and Menon 1996). Hix did not use the terminology of governance at this stage – and, indeed subsequently did so in a particular way (see Hix 1998) – but I would argue more broadly that the burgeoning of the comparative politics literature on the EU was very significant to the developing analysis of EU governance.

Changes in the character of UK and Irish politics contributed undoubtedly to emerging research agendas. In particular, the privatisation and de-regulation of British industrial and service sectors, particularly under the Thatcher governments (1979–90), led to changes in the character of economic management: a reduction of the interventionist state and the growth of the regulatory state. In Ireland the impact of the EU itself had considerable significance, in particular that of the structural funds upon economic development. An economic turnaround was achieved from the late-1980s on the basis of a number of factors, prominent amongst which was a strategy of local social partnerships: arrangements which were particularly well-attuned to the absorption of the significant flows into the economy from the EU structural funds (O'Donnell 1998). These real-world developments in the EU, the UK and Ireland transformed the subject of study. 'Government' had never been a term suited to the analysis of the EC and EU. The shift from traditional 'command-and-control' instruments in national public policy to more permeable boundaries between the public and private realms also called for a new terminology. In the specific context of study of the EU, these developments also forced analysis out of a somewhat self-referential branch of international relations into the mainstream of political science and into greater prominence in other sub-disciplines, such as regional economics and socio-legal studies.

The second development has already been alluded to, namely the developing orientation of social science analysis towards the concept of governance. Seen in terms of its theoretical and analytical origins, this new direction came about primarily because of advances in comparative politics and public policy, albeit influenced by international developments. Guy Peters and Jon Pierre (1998, 223) identified a number of explanations for the emergence of the term governance as follows.[5]

- The impact of the international environment in restricting state power. UK-based scholarship was prominent in revealing this impact, notably work by Paul Hirst and Graeme Thompson (1996) and by Susan Strange (1996) on globalisation.
- The changing relationship between government and the private sector, alluded to earlier, was reflected in particular at this time in the work of Rod Rhodes (1994; 1996; 1997). He had already utilised the policy network literature to explain central–local relations in British politics (Rhodes 1988).

However, it is worth mentioning two other sources behind the term's emergence that are not referred to explicitly by Peters and Pierre:

- Chris Hood's work on the new public management had already identified the changing policy instruments available in the British public sector (see, for example, Hood 1991). Hood's work may be seen as pre-figuring the governance turn in the study of British public administration.
- In work on urban governance Gerry Stoker had explored public–private partnerships (Stoker 1997). This strand of work took on its own dynamics as part of the ESRC Local Governance programme. Stoker later made a much broader statement of the merits of 'governance as theory' (1998). This article was juxtaposed with a more critical approach to governance by the sociologist Bob Jessop (1998).

One point underlined by Peters and Pierre (1998: 224) is that the emergence of governance represented a 'direct challenge to the Whitehall model of strong, centralised government'. This challenge was doubtless a stimulus to

UK-based scholars such as Rhodes and Stoker to study the phenomenon of governance in the first place.

In the case of scholarship in the UK and Ireland on *EU governance* an important point to make is that CONNEX data reveal that such research started much earlier in the UK than in Ireland.[6] The term governance entered usage without particular conceptual examination (Wallace 1993). One explanation for this was that governance was being used as a vehicle to advocate other analytical propositions. Thus, a frequently-cited article on 'The Governance of the European Union' (Bulmer 1993) advocated a new institutionalist understanding of the EU. New institutionalism, with its emphasis upon the formal and informal components of politics, obviously fitted well with the changing patterns of public authority that are captured by the term governance. Governance also featured strongly in the work of John Peterson and Elizabeth Bomberg but their emphasis on the crucial private–public interface of EU decision-making was to advocate the use of the policy network literature (see Peterson 1995; Peterson and Bomberg 1999).[7] To summarise: the emergence of governance as a theme in UK and Irish research on the EU governance did not come about in my view as a deliberate 'turn' but rather as a consequence of several inter-related developments: the emergence of a European Union political system; the growth in comparative politics analysis of the EU; broader developments in the political science discipline; and the advocacy of new institutionalism and policy networks as vehicles for understanding EU governance. Of course, the impact of the work of non-UK scholars such as Liesbet Hooghe, Gary Marks and collaborators on *multi-level* governance also had an impact from the mid-1990s (Marks 1993; Marks, Hooghe and Blank 1996; Marks et. al. 1996).

THE PROFILE OF EU GOVERNANCE RESEARCH IN THE UK AND IRELAND

In attempting to profile research on EU governance it is necessary to adopt an inclusive approach. EU governance – as defined earlier in this book – extends beyond the literature that explicitly uses the terminology of governance and is very encompassing. It comprises theoretical and analytical work as well as a wide range of empirical research. Amongst the social sciences the tradition in British political science has tended to emphasise empirical analysis over formal theory. Empirical studies of institutions and policy have been prominent strengths but, reflecting the English-language influence of American political science, there has more recently been a small but growing rationalist or rational-choice strand in research. One might therefore anticipate some replication of this pattern in the profile of EU governance research.

One observation is in order at the outset. Simon Hix has argued that two distinct approaches have emerged in respect of analysing the EU (1998). One is a view that 'the EU is transforming politics and government at the European and national levels into a system .... best understood as a *sui generis* phenomenon'. The system's characteristics are 'its multi-level, non-hierarchical, deliberative and apolitical governance, via a web of public or private networks and quasi-autonomous executive agencies'. This so-called 'new governance' view sees institutional and structural factors [as] more influential than calculated rational action in determining policy outcomes (Hix 1998, 54). Hix contrasts this new governance approach with a rival approach, which asserts 'that "traditional politics and government" *do* exist in the EU'. The (unnamed) rival camp is concerned with competition over the input side of politics and is more likely to involve rational choice explanations. Hix admits that, whilst these may be seen as two rival camps, it is through the combined forces of the two approaches that a better understanding will emerge of how the EU works and how it may be improved (Hix 1998, 55). The understanding of governance in this review includes input-oriented research and is therefore not the same as the term 'new governance' as defined by Hix. However, his distinction has some organisational value for the account that follows; input-oriented approaches are treated after those he terms new governance.

The academic *acquis* in the UK until the debates began to move forward from the late-1980s was centred around understanding European Community *policy-making* (notably Wallace, Wallace and Webb 1977 and successor editions); some attention to integration theory (for instance, Taylor 1971) and institutional analysis (for example, Coombes 1970; Herman and Lodge 1979). As elsewhere, from the mid-1980s there was a large growth in the literature on EU governance. In what follows I give more attention to theory and analysis over empirical studies.

THEORETICAL AND ANALYTICAL ADVANCES

UK-based academics have made significant analytical contributions to middle-range theory that explores EU governance. These contributions have been made in several areas of governance: new institutionalism, constructivism, policy network analysis, multi-level governance, integration through law/constitutionalism, other comparative politics approaches and Europeanisation. Although predominantly political science categories, it is possible to include relevant developments in legal and economic analysis under these headings as well.[8] There have also been contributions made in respect of the input side of governance: both in relation to normative political theory as well as to more formal understandings of legislative politics.

New institutionalism emerged in political science as a reaction to the behaviouralist revolution that had taken place in American political science, with its emphasis upon rationality in political action. But there was no such reaction needed in studies of the EU because that revolution had not taken place. Indeed, the reverse dominance came to apply and this is at the heart of Simon Hix's plea for more theorised work on the input side of EU politics (Hix 1998). The broad hypothesis articulated in new institutionalism is that institutions matter in explaining political outcomes. More detailed analysis is then required to identify *how* institutions matter. The first contribution essentially set down a marker in arguing that institutions matter in the EU context, identifying the different institutions and instruments of EU governance (Bulmer 1993). This paper further argued that the profile of instruments and institutions differed within discrete 'governance regimes' situated within an overarching EU structure that had pronounced regulatory characteristics. This paper served as an intellectual prospectus for an ESRC-funded project on the single market and was applied to a number of cases of governance regimes, for instance on merger control (Bulmer 1994; Armstrong and Bulmer 1998). From the mid-1990s new institutionalism was becoming more prevalent in the literature on EU governance, both in the UK and in the USA.[9] Research undertaken by Laura Cram revealed insights into institutional entrepreneurship in the contexts of social policy and information technology (1994; 1997). Insights from new institutionalism influenced Dan Wincott in his critique of liberal intergovernmentalism for neglecting the legal dynamics of integration (Wincott, 1995a; 1995b). More positively, such insights were being utilised to advocate a closer integration of the legal and political analysis of EU governance (Armstrong 1998; Armstrong and Shaw 1998; Shaw and More, 1995). Developments in new institutionalism within the UK thus gave further momentum to an established literature on 'integration through law', particularly from a socio-legal perspective, and to what might be called the new constitutionalism (on which, see below).[10]

Greater differentiation within the new institutionalism – into rational choice, historical and sociological variants – led to some fragmentation in the literature, as different arguments were advanced on *how* institutions impacted upon political outputs (Aspinwall and Schneider 2000). The rational choice institutionalism (RCI) also concerned itself with how institutions impact upon political *inputs*. RCI has been most strongly represented in continental European and US studies of EU governance. Nevertheless, this is an area of scholarship that is represented in the UK, notably in the work of Fabio Franchino, specifically on the delegation of powers to the EU (2000; 2004).

New institutionalism had originally been applied to identify how the EU's institutional configuration impacted on policy. This approach has been developed recently by deploying institutionalism as an underpinning to the concept of policy transfer. In this work a set of hypotheses has been developed to test the circumstances under which policy ideas, policy content, administrative arrangements and institutions may be transferred via the medium of the EU (Bulmer and Padgett 2005; for empirical application, see Bulmer et al. 2007). Historical institutionalism has also been operationalised in the context of EU-member state relations, for example in connection with the Europeanisation literature (see below).

Sociological institutionalism has been utilised in EU studies in a rather limited way by UK and Irish-based academics. It has gone hand-in-hand with the development of the literature on constructivism, so will be treated jointly. The common ground between the two approaches lies in the emphasis upon 'the social' (Wiener 2006). Sociological institutionalism is a structural approach, regarding the social dimension of institutions as shaping political action.[11] Constructivism, by contrast, regards the *interaction* between structure and agency as of crucial importance. Constructivist approaches therefore assume that interests, identities and institutions are mutually constitutive.

Sociological institutionalism has influenced the work of Claudio Radaelli, notably on policy transfer (2000) and the politics of expertise in the EU (1999). However, constructivism has received more attention and, interestingly, major protagonists in the UK have been scholars of German origin: Thomas Christiansen, Thomas Diez and Antje Wiener. Constructivist insights into the EU were brought to the fore with a special issue of the *Journal of European Public Policy* (Christiansen, Jørgensen and Wiener 1999). Many of the contributors to this volume – beyond Christiansen and Wiener – were not based in the UK. However, Ben Rosamond contributed a valuable article considering discourses of globalisation and their impact on identitive politics (Rosamond 1999). Indeed both constructivism and sociological institutionalism have facilitated the integration of discourse analysis into the study of EU governance (see Diez 2001). Another example of this work is the set of case studies developing out of initial work by US academic Vivien Schmidt, but largely conducted by UK-based academics, on policy change and discourse in the EU (Schmidt and Radaelli 2004). These case studies offer insights into the role of discourse in EU governance but do so in a manner closer to sociological institutionalism rather than constructivism.

Policy network analysis emerged in the mid-1990s as a competing analytical framework to new institutionalism. Advocated in particular by John Peterson (1995; Peterson and Bomberg 1999) and Jeremy Richardson (1996), policy network analysis gave greater attention to policy actors (or agency) than the more structuralist accounts offered by institutionalism. Its affinity to the 'governance turn' arose from its emphasis upon 'the mutuality and interdependence between public and non-public actors' (Peterson 2004, p. 119). Policy network analysis proved particularly useful to the examination of policy sectors and policy issues. Bomberg and Peterson applied the policy network framework systematically across a number of case studies: the internal market, agricultural, trade, cohesion and environmental policies amongst others (Peterson and Bomberg 1999). However, they did so within an eclectic understanding of the EU that suggested liberal intergovernmentalism be deployed for understanding so-called history-making decisions (for example, on institutional reform); new institutionalism for understanding 'policy-setting' decisions; and policy network analysis for interpreting 'policy-shaping' analysis (Bomberg and Peterson 1999, p. 9). Links were not developed between policy network analysis and the 'network governance' approach being pursued in Germany by Beate Kohler-Koch and associates (see, for instance, Eising and Kohler-Koch 1999).

Multi-level governance (MLG) emerged over the last two decades as an important reference-point in the analysis of EU governance. Major contributions came from the USA (for example, Marks, Hooghe and Blank 1996; Hooghe and Marks 2001) as well as from Germany (for example, Kohler-Koch 1996). Contributions from the UK and Ireland were more empirical in nature, although Bache and Flinders's collection (2004) brings together several of the key Anglo-Saxon protagonists in the debates as well as exploring some of the new domestic manifestations of multi-level governance within the UK. Charlie Jeffery (2000) offered a mild critique of the MLG of Hooghe and Marks, arguing that it has an overly top-down approach. Instead a 'European domestic politics' model of sub-national mobilisation is offered, that emphasises the options available for influencing policy from the bottom-up. Jeffery thus proposed a model for comparing the political resources available to sub-national authorities (2000, 11–20). Alex Warleigh (2006) suggests that the MLG and policy network literatures could profitably be used in harness, chiming with arguments also put by Maura Adshead (2002).

A substantial amount of empirical research has been conducted into multi-level governance, whether explicitly using that as an analytical framework or not. Given the framework's suitability for analysing territorial policy, notably the structural funds, it is not surprising to find that there has been significant application in the Irish academic community (Adshead and Quinn 1998; Rees, Quinn and Connaughton 2006). The same applies in the UK, for example Ian Bache's work on the structural funds (1998; 2000). Following devolution of power within the UK in 1999 a number of scholars have been concerned with the multi-level governance of European policy (see, for instance Bulmer et al. 2002).

The 'new constitutionalism' has been a prominent concern of scholars working at the interface of law with political theory. As Neil Walker has put it, constitutionalism seeks to 'provide an explanatory nexus between constitutional doctrine and institutions on the one hand, and the broader socio-political dynamics of European Union on the other' (Walker 1996, 266). These constitutional 'meta-issues' surrounding EU governance have received considerable attention. For example, Jo Shaw has explored the notion of 'postnational constitutionalism' (Shaw 1999, 579–97). A normative debate about constitutionalism developed in the run-up to the Convention on the Future of Europe (see Shaw 2003; Wiener 2003).[12] In parallel, contributions were being made from the perspective of political theory (see Bellamy, Buffachi and Castiglione 1995; and Bellamy and Castiglione 1996). With the formal opening of the constitutional debate Jo Shaw led a project on 'Constitutionalism, Federalism and EU Reform', based at the Federal Trust and funded by the James Madison Trust. The project examined constitutionalism in the context of the evolving discussions among politicians during the Convention.[13] The debate on European constitutionalism has thus found much expression in the UK academic community including a distinctive normative or reflective approach to the subject-matter.

Attention is now turned to the analysis of the input side of EU governance. Political theorists have also contributed to questions concerning the EU's legitimacy, democratic accountability and the related concept of citizenship (for example, Lehning and Weale 1997; Nentwich and Weale 1998; Beetham and Lord 1998; Lord 2004; Bellamy and Warleigh 2001; Weale, 2006). The increasing salience of the identitive dimension of EU governance has received attention from the Irish Brigid Laffan (1996; also see Laffan et al. 1999). These contributions offer a normative approach to understanding the input side of the EU system of governance. More empirically-focused contributions have been made on interest groups (Greenwood and Aspinwall 1998; Greenwood 2003; Mazey and Richardson 1993); corporate lobbying (Coen 1998); and political parties (Hix and Lord 1997). Given the divisions on Europe within UK political parties, it is perhaps not surprising to see considerable attention devoted to the issue of Euro-scepticism (Taggart and Szczerbiak 2008a; 2008b).

These studies complement the 'politics like any other approach' of Simon Hix (see Hix 2005). This work includes several studies of voting alignments in the European Parliament (for example, Hix 1999; 2001; 2004); MEPs' relations with their voters (Bowler and Farrell 1993; Farrell and Scully 2007); Roger Scully's analysis of the socialisation of MEPs (2005); Scully's lively debate with American counterparts George Tsebelis and Geoffrey Garrett concerning the Parliament's co-decision powers (for example, Scully 1997); and work on party incentive structures in the Parliament's committee system (Whitaker 2001). Michael Marsh and Richard Sinnott are notable Irish contributors to the literature on the input side of governance.

Europeanisation has been another area where important contributions have been made; in this case to the EU's impact on *national* governance. Hix and Goetz (2001) and Featherstone and Radaelli (2003) assembled important early collections of contributions on this topic. There have also been detailed empirical studies of the impact of Europeanisation deploying a range of analytical frameworks. For example Andrew Jordan employed double-loop learning to explore changing policy in the UK Department of the

Environment under the EU's influence (Jordan 2003; see also 2002). Simon Bulmer and Martin Burch utilised historical institutionalism to explain the impact of the EU on UK central government (1998) and comparatively with German experience (2001). Hussein Kassim has been engaged in long-term work on national institutional adaptation to the challenges of EU membership (for example, Kassim 2005). Hay and Rosamond (2002) have taken these studies of Europeanisation into a more sociological, discourse-oriented direction. Major collections of the impact of Europeanisation on Germany and the UK have been coordinated by, respectively, Kenneth Dyson and Klaus Goetz (2003) and Ian Bache and Andrew Jordan (2006). Brigid Laffan has explored the impact of Europeanisation on Ireland (2003) as well as leading a major cross-national project on how smaller states organise for EU enlargement.[14]

EMPIRICAL CONTRIBUTIONS: POLICY AND INSTITUTIONS

There has been a vast contribution from scholars in the UK and Ireland towards understanding the practice of EU governance. Some of this literature has been organised by institution; some by policy area; and some by the process of policy-making or governance itself. It is possible only to pick out some of the major contributions.

An important area of research has been economic governance. The governance of the single market has received considerable attention. Some of this work has been organised specifically as relating to governance issues (Armstrong and Bulmer 1998; Bulmer et. al. 2007). Other work has focused strongly on regulatory politics in the EU or the EU as a 'regulatory state' (McGowan and Wallace 1996; Young and Wallace 2000; Coen 2005; Coen and Thatcher 2005; Thatcher 2002). Despite non-participation in the single currency, two British scholars, Kenneth Dyson and Kevin Featherstone, produced a very comprehensive study of the negotiation of monetary union (1999) that has been followed by analysis of the euro-zone (for example, Dyson 2002). The *economic governance* of monetary union is specifically addressed by Schelkle and other contributors to a journal special issue (2006). Economic coordination and the emergence of the EU's Lisbon Agenda for economic competitiveness have also received considerable attention (for example, Hodson and Maher 2001) as part of the trend towards exploring the Open Method of Coordination (see, for example, Radaelli 2003).

Another policy area especially deserving of attention, is the EU's international role. Here an important analytical contribution has been made by Christopher Hill and more empirical contributions by a wider group of scholars. Hill's important paper on the 'capability–expectations gap' formed an important reference point for evaluation of the performance of the Common Foreign and Security Policy (Hill 1993). It served as the intellectual framework for a wider empirical application (Peterson and Sjursen 1998). Michael Smith has undertaken many empirical studies of the EU's international role, including foreign economic policy (see for example, Smith 2001). From Ireland, Ben Tonra has contributed on the Europeanisation of foreign policy (2001). Jolyon Howorth has been one of the key contributors to the analysis of the emergent European Security and Defence Policy (Howorth 2001).

Amongst many major studies of other policy areas there have been significant analyses of policing (Anderson et. al. 1996), environmental policy (Jordan and Liefferink 2004; Jordan and Schout 2006); competition policy (Cini and McGowan 1998); the EU's finances (Laffan 1997); transport policy (Stevens 2004) and the Common Agricultural Policy (Grant 1997; Greer 2005). Of book-length institutional studies there have been several contributions on the European Commission (Cini 1996; Nugent 2001; Stevens and Stevens 2000) but fewer on the others (but see Judge and Earnshaw 2003 on the European Parliament; and Hayes-Renshaw and Wallace 2006 on the Council). The national coordination of European policy has received greater attention, albeit in edited collections (Kassim, Peters and Wright 2000; Jordan and Schout 2006).

ACCUMULATED KNOWLEDGE AND SUMMARY

As can be seen from this survey, there have been important contributions to the governance literature from UK- and Ireland-based scholars. There was, as argued, a 'governance turn', but it did not centre on using a theoretical interpretation based around governance. Instead, the terminology of governance was employed as a platform for other approaches that moved away from more formal institutional studies on the one hand, and the integration literature, on the other. To this development, socio-legal scholars and political theorists have introduced a normative dimension to studies of (largely) the input side of EU governance, but this is not the only approach taken, as indicated by Hix's 'politics like any other' approach. Political science has been the most prominent discipline, with legal scholarship also notable, whilst the contribution by economists has been handicapped by the discipline's incentives to publish technical pieces that are difficult to classify as work on governance.

The contribution of UK- and Ireland-based scholars to the study of EU governance has been diverse. It has followed diverse analytical and theoretical approaches: from constructivism to the techniques of electoral analysis. It has been cosmopolitan in nature, with many contributions coming from academics based in the two states but originating from elsewhere. Contributions to theory and analysis have arguably been disproportionately large in light of the general intellectual tradition of empiricism in the two states. Nevertheless, there have been many empirical contributions that have not been discussed here, not least because it is more difficult to structure a review of disparate empirical studies across policy areas and institutions. The governance turn has undoubtedly played a role in bringing some legal scholars into closer inter-disciplinary engagement with political scientists. The more recent focus on Europeanisation has brought about a different change, namely close attention to the EU's impact on *domestic* governance.

British- and Irish-based studies of European governance have made important contributions. Nevertheless, through exchanges and collaboration on a European level, such as through the CONNEX network of excellence, there remains ample scope for developing closer understanding of the sometimes different conceptions of EU governance deployed elsewhere in Europe.

NOTES

1. I am grateful to Mick Moran, Rod Rhodes and Gerry Stoker for exchanges enabling me to situate the EU governance literature within wider trends in British political science.
2. The demonstration of international excellence differs between social science disciplines. In economics, excellence is associated with a very small number of academic journals. In political science there is a more catholic approach to the choice of journals in which to publish. Those with a European focus are not disadvantaged. Research monographs with the top presses are also favoured.
3. This situation can raise problems where individuals move between national systems (or to the European University Institute) as the employment market becomes more fluid across the EU. Another issue that creates some difficulties in what follows is international collaboration by scholars based in the UK or Ireland.
4. Helen Wallace gives an indication of the earlier point about the UK system's openness by reporting that the 'One Europe or Several?' research programme comprised 'scholars of more than twenty nationalities (all based in British research institutions)' (Wallace 2003, 6).
5. It is interesting in the context of the present volume that, while noting it is in Europe where the main discussion of 'governance without government' has taken place, they hold that it is in the UK and the Netherlands where it has been concentrated (Peters and Pierre 1998, 224). Paradoxically, an early use of the term in the EU context (Bulmer 1993) derived from its usage by American academics working on the governance of the American economy and deploying social network theory (Campbell et al. 1991).
6. The first Irish project on governance in the CONNEX database is dated as starting in 2000, whereas a significant number pre-dated 1994 in the UK.
7. In fact, it was precisely the variant of the policy network literature that had been deployed by Rod Rhodes, Peterson's one-time colleague at the University of York.
8. Excluded from coverage are studies of substantive law in particular areas as well as areas of economic theorising which do not intersect with the concerns of governance.
9. Notable contributors in the USA were Paul Pierson (1996) and Mark Pollack (1996; 2002). Pierson's historical institutionalist analysis was part of his work towards a *magnum opus*

on the role of time in politics (Pierson 2004). Both Pierson's and Pollack's work entailed a more formalised approach, characteristic of US political science.

10.   For a review of the 'integration through law' literature, see Haltern (2004).
11.   This approach is broadly in line with UK historical institutionalists, that is to say, with those proponents who emphasise the role of norms. It is less compatible with Paul Pierson's thinner conception of institutions that downplays norms. Historical institutionalists of both kinds are typically concerned with the temporal dimension of politics.
12.   Also see the ConWeb papers, available at: http://www.bath.ac.uk/esml/conWEB/, accessed 1 June 2007.
13.   Numerous on-line papers are available on the Federal Trust's website: www.fedtrust.co.uk/default.asp accessed 20 February 2007.
14.   For papers arising from the comparative project, see http://www.oeue.net/.

REFERENCES

Adshead, Maura (2002), *Developing European Regions: Comparative Governance, Policy Networks and European Integration*, Aldershot, UK: Ashgate.

Adshead, Maura and Bríd Quinn (1998), 'The move from government to governance: Irish development policy's paradigm shift', *Policy and Politics*, **26** (2), 209–26.

Anderson, Malcolm; Monica den Boer; Peter Cullen; William Gilmore; Charles Raab and Neil Walker (1996), *Policing the European Union: Theory, Law and Practice*, Oxford: Clarendon Press.

Armstrong, Kenneth (1998), 'Legal integration: Theorizing the legal integration of European integration', *Journal of Common Market Studies*, **36** (2), 155–74.

Armstrong, Kenneth and Simon Bulmer (1998), *The Governance of the Single European Market*, Manchester: Manchester University Press.

Armstrong, Kenneth and Jo Shaw (eds) (1998), 'Integrating Law', special issue of *Journal of Common Market Studies*, **36** (2).

Aspinwall, Mark and Gerald Schneider (2000), 'Same menu, separate tables: The institutionalist turn in political science and the study of European integration', *European Journal of Political Research*, **38** (1), 1–36.

Auer, Stefan and Colin Shaw (2006), 'Research on EU multilevel governance in Ireland: A state of research', available at http://www.connex-network.org/govdata/reports/Report-Ireland.pdf, accessed 26 January 2007.

Bache, Ian (1998), *The Politics of the European Union Regional Policy: Multi-level Governance or Flexible Gate-keeping?*, Sheffield: Sheffield Academic Press.

Bache, Ian (2000), 'Government within governance: Network steering in Yorkshire and the Humber', *Public Administration*, **78** (3), 575–592.

Bache, Ian and Matthew Flinders (eds) (2004), *Multi-level Governance*, Oxford: Oxford University Press.

Bache, Ian and Andrew Jordan (eds) (2006), *The Europeanization of British Politics*, Basingstoke: Palgrave.

Baker, David and David Seawright (eds) (1998), *Britain for and against Europe: British Politics and the Question of European Integration*, Oxford: Oxford University Press.

Beetham, David and Christopher Lord (1998), *Legitimacy and the European Union*, London: Longman.

Bellamy, Richard and Dario Castiglione (eds) (1996), *Constitutionalism in Transformation: European and theoretical perspectives*, Oxford: Blackwell.

Bellamy, Richard and Alex Warleigh (eds) (2001), *Citizenship and Governance in the European Union*, London: Continuum.

Bellamy, Richard, Vittorio Bufacchi and Dario Castiglione (eds) (1995), *Democracy and Constitutional Culture in the Union of Europe*, London: Lothian Foundation Press.

Bowler, Shaun and David Farrell (1993), 'Legislator shirking and voter monitoring: Impact of European parliament electoral systems upon legislator–voter relations', *Journal of Common Market Studies*, **31** (1), 45–69.

Bulmer, Simon (1993), 'The governance of the European Union: A new institutionalist approach', *Journal of Public Policy*, **13** (4), 351–80.

Bulmer, Simon (1994), 'Institutions and policy change in the European communities: The case of merger control', *Public Administration*, **72** (3), 425–446.

Bulmer, Simon and Martin Burch (1998), 'Organising for Europe – Whitehall, the British State and the European Union', *Public Administration*, **76** (4), 601–28.

Bulmer, Simon and Martin Burch (2001), 'The Europeanization of central government: the UK and Germany in historical institutionalist perspective', in Gerald Schneider and Mark Aspinwall (eds), *The Rules of Integration*, Manchester: Manchester University Press, pp. 73–96.

Bulmer, Simon and Stephen Padgett, (2005), 'Policy Transfer in the European Union: an Institutionalist Perspective', *British Journal of Political Science*, **35** (1), 103–26.

Bulmer, Simon, David Dolowitz, Peter Humphreys, and Stephen Padgett (2007), *Policy Transfer in European Union Governance: Regulating the Utilities*, Abingdon: Routledge.

Bulmer, Simon, Martin Burch, Caitríona Carter, Patricia Hogwood, and Andrew Scott (2002), *British Devolution and European Policy-Making: Transforming Britain into Multi-Level Governance*, Basingstoke: Palgrave.

Campbell, John, J. Rogers Hollingsworth, and Leon Lindberg (eds) (1991), *Governance of the American Economy*, New York and Cambridge: Cambridge University Press.

CEC (Commission of the European Communities) (2001), 'European Governance: A White Paper', COM(2001) 428, accessed at http://ec.europa.eu/governance/white_paper/en.pdf, 6 February 2007.

Christiansen, Thomas, Knud-Erik Jørgensen, and Antje Wiener (1999), 'The Social Construction of Europe', special issue of *Journal of European Public Policy*, **6** (4).

Cini, Michelle (1996), *The European Commission: Leadership, Organisation and Culture in the EU Administration*, Manchester: Manchester University Press.

Cini, Michelle and Lee McGowan (1998), *Competition Policy in the European Union*, Basingstoke: Palgrave Macmillan.

Coen, David (1998), 'The European business interest and the nation state: Large–firm lobbying in the European Union and member states', *Journal of Public Policy*, **18** (1), 75–100.

Coen, David (2005), 'Redefining the regulatory space', in David Coen and Adrienne Héritier (eds.), *Refining Regulatory Regimes: Utilities in Europe*, Cheltenham: Edward Elgar.

Coen, David and Mark Thatcher (2005), 'Business-Regulatory Relations: Learning to play regulatory games in European Utility Markets', special issue of *Governance*, **25** (3).

Coombes, David (1970), *Politics and Bureaucracy in the European Community: a portrait of the Commission of the E.E.C.*, London: Allen & Unwin.

Cram, Laura (1994), 'The European Commission as a multi-organization: Social policy and IT policy in the EU', *Journal of European Public Policy*, **1** (2), 195–217.

Cram, Laura (1997), *Policymaking in the European Union: Conceptual Lenses and the Integration Process*, London: Routledge.

Diez, Thomas (2001), 'Europe as a discursive battleground', *Cooperation and Conflict*, **36** (1), 5–38.

Dyson, Kenneth (2002), *The Politics of the Euro-zone: Stability or Breakdown?*, Oxford: Oxford University Press.

Dyson, Kenneth and Kevin Featherstone (1999), *The Road to Maastricht: Negotiating Economic and Monetary Union*, Oxford: Oxford University Press.

Dyson, Kenneth and Klaus Goetz (eds) (2003), *Germany, Europe and the Politics of Constraint*, Oxford: Oxford University Press; British Academy.

Eising, Rainer and Beate Kohler-Koch (eds) (1999), *The Transformation of Governance in the European Union*, London: Routledge.

Farrell, David and Roger Scully (2007), *Representing Europe's Citizens?: Electoral Institutions and the Failure of Parliamentary Representation*, Oxford: Oxford University Press.

Featherstone, Kevin and Claudio Radaelli (eds) (2003), *The Politics of Europeanization*, Oxford: Oxford University Press.

Forster, Anthony (2002), *Euroscepticism in Contemporary British Politics: Opposition to Europe in the Conservative and Labour Parties Since 1945*, London: Routledge.

Franchino, Fabio (2000), 'Control of the Commission's executive functions: Uncertainty, conflict and decision rules', *European Union Politics* **1** (1), 59–88.

Franchino, Fabio (2004), 'Delegating powers in the European Community', *British Journal of Political Science*, **34** (3), 269–93.

George, Stephen (ed.) (1992), *Britain and the European Community: The Politics of Semi-Detachment*, Oxford: Clarendon Press.

George, Stephen (1998), *An Awkward Partner: Britain in the European Community*, 3rd edn, Oxford: Oxford University Press.

Grant, Wyn (1997), *The Common Agricultural Policy*, Basingstoke: Palgrave.

Greer, Alan (2005), *Agricultural Policy in Europe*, Manchester: Manchester University Press.

Greenwood, Justin (2003), *Interest Representation in the European Union*, Basingstoke: Palgrave Macmillan.

Greenwood, Justin and Mark Aspinwall (1998), *Collective Action in the European Union*, London: Routledge.

Haltern, Ulrich (2004), 'Integration through law', in Antje Wiener and Thomas Diez (eds), *European Integration Theory*, Oxford: Oxford University Press, pp. 177–96.

Hay, Colin and Ben Rosamond (2002) 'Globalization, European integration and the discursive construction of economic imperatives', *Journal of European Public Policy*, **9** (2), 147–67.

Hayes-Renshaw, Fiona and Helen Wallace (2006), *The Council of Ministers*, 2nd edn, Basingstoke: Palgrave Macmillan.

Herman, Valentine and Juliet Lodge, (1979), *The European Parliament and the European Community*, London, Macmillan.

Hill, Christopher (1993), 'The Capability–Expectations Gap or Conceptualizing Europe's International Role', *Journal of Common Market Studies,* **31** (3), 305–28.

Hirst, Paul and Grahame Thompson (1996), *Globalization in Question: the International Economy and the Possibilities of Governance,* Cambridge: Polity Press.

Hix, Simon (1994), 'The study of the European Community: the challenge to comparative politics', *West European Politics* , **17** (1), 1–30.

Hix, Simon (1998), 'The Study of the European Union II: the "new governance" agenda and its rival', *Journal of European Public Policy,* **5** (1), 38–65.

Hix, Simon (1999), 'Dimensions and alignments in European Union politics', *European Journal of Political Research,* **35** (2), 69–106.

Hix, Simon (2001), 'Legislative behaviour and party competition in the Euroepan parliament: An application of nominate to the EU', *Journal of Common Market Studies,* **39** (4), 663–88.

Hix, Simon (2004), 'Electoral systems and legislative behaviour: Explaining voter-defection in the European parliament', *World Politics,* **56** (1), 194–223.

Hix, Simon (2005), *The Political System of the European Union,* 2nd edn, Basingstoke: Palgrave.

Hix, Simon and Klaus Goetz (eds.) (2001), *Europeanized Politics? European Integration and National Political Systems,* London: Frank Cass.

Hix, Simon and Christopher Lord (1997), *Political Parties in the European Union,* Basingstoke: Palgrave Macmillan.

Hodson, Dermot and Imelda Maher (2001), 'The Open Method as a new mode of governance: The case of soft economic policy co-ordination', *Journal of Common Market Studies,* **39** (4), 719–745

Hood, Christopher (1991), 'A public management for all seasons', *Public Administration,* **69** (1), 3–19.

Hooghe, Liesbet and Gary Marks (2001), *Multi-Level Governance and European Integration,* Lanham, MD: Rowman and Littlefield.

Howorth, Jolyon (2001), 'European Defence and the Changing Politics of the European Union: Hanging Together or Hanging Separately?' *Journal of Common Market Studies,* **39** (4), 765–789.

Hurrell, Andrew and Anand Menon, (1996), '"Politics like any other?" Comparative politics, international relations and the study of the EC', *West European Politics,* **19** (2), 386–402.

Jeffery, Charlie (2000), 'Sub-national mobilization and European integration: Does it make any difference?', *Journal of Common Market Studies,* **38** (1), 1–23.

Jessop, Bob (1998), 'The rise of governance and the risks of failure: the case of economic development', *International Social Science Journal,* **50** (155), 29–45.

Jordan, Andrew (2002), *The Europeanization of British Environmental Policy: A Departmental Perspective,* Basingstoke: Palgrave Macmillan.

Jordan, Andrew (2003), 'The Europeanization of national government and policy: A departmental perspective', *British Journal of Political Science,* **33** (2), 261–82.

Jordan, Andrew and Duncan Liefferink (eds) (2004), *Environmental Policy in Europe,* Abingdon: Routledge.

Jordan, Andrew and Adriaan Schout (eds) (2006), *The Coordination of the European Union,* Oxford: Oxford University Press.

Judge, David and David Earnshaw (2003), *The European Parliament,* Basingstoke: Palgrave Macmillan.

Kassim, Hussein (2005), 'The Europeanization of member state institutions', in Simon Bulmer and Christian Lequesne (eds), *The Member States of the European Union*, Oxford: Oxford University Press, pp. 285–316.

Kassim, Hussein, Guy Peters and Vincent Wright (eds) (2000), *The National Co-ordination of EU Policy*, Oxford: Oxford University Press.

Kohler-Koch, Beate (1996), 'Regionen im Mehrebenensystem der EU', in Thomas König, Elmar Rieger and Hermann Schmitt, (Hrsg.), *Das europäische Mehrebenensystem*, Frankfurt am Main: Campus Verlag, pp. 201–227.

Laffan, Brigid (1996), 'The politics of identity and political order in Europe', *Journal of Common Market Studies*, **34** (1), 81–101.

Laffan, Brigid (1997), *The Finances of the European Union*, Basingstoke: Palgrave Macmillan.

Laffan, Brigid, (2003), 'Ireland: Modernisation through Europeanisation', in Wolfgang Wessels, Andreas Maurer and Jürgen Mittag (eds), *Fifteen into One? The European Union and its Member States*, Manchester: Manchester University Press, 248–70.

Laffan, Brigid, Rory O'Donnell, and Michael Smith (1999), *Europe's Experimental Union: Rethinking Integration*, London: Routledge.

Lehning, Percy and Albert Weale (eds) (1997), *Citizenship, Democracy and Justice in the New Europe*, London: Routledge.

Lord, Christopher (2004), *A Democratic Audit of the European Union*, Basingstoke: Palgrave Macmillan.

McGowan, Francis and Helen Wallace (1996), 'Towards a European regulatory state', *Journal of European Public Policy*, **3** (4), 192–211.

Marks, Gary (1993), 'Structural Policy and Multi-Level Governance in the EC', in Alan Cafruny and Glenda Rosenthal (eds.), *The State of the European Community Volume 2: Maastricht Debates and Beyond*, Harlow: Longman, pp. 391–410.

Marks, Gary; Hooghe, Liesbet and Kermit Blank (1996), 'European integration from the 1980s: State–centric v. multi–level governance', *Journal of Common Market Studies*, **34** (3), 341–78.

Marks, Gary; Scharpf, Fritz; Schmitter, Philippe; and Wolfgang Streeck (eds.) (1996), *Governance in the European Union*, London: Sage Publications Ltd.

Mazey, Sonia and Jeremy Richardson (eds) (1993), *Lobbying in the European Community*, Oxford: Oxford University Press.

Nentwich, Michael and Albert Weale (1998), *Political Theory and the European Union: Legitimacy, Constitutional Choice and Citizenship*, London: Routledge.

Nugent, Neill (2001), *The European Commission*, Basingstoke: Palgrave Macmillan.

O'Donnell, Rory (1998), 'Ireland's Economic Transformation: Industrial Policy, European Integration and Social Partnership', University of Pittsburgh European Union Centre Working Paper, no 2, http://www.ucis.pitt.edu/euce/pub/workingpapers/ODonnell_1998.pdf, accessed on 6 February 2007.

Peters, B. Guy and Jon Pierre (1998), 'Governance without government: Rethinking public administration?', *Journal of Public Administration and Theory*, **8** (2), 223–43.

Peterson, John (1995), 'Decision-making in the European Union: Towards a framework for analysis', *Journal of European Public Policy*, **2** (1), 69–93.

Peterson, John (2004), 'Policy networks', in Antje Wiener and Thomas Diez (eds), *European Integration Theory*, Oxford: Oxford University Press, pp. 117–35.

Peterson, John and Elizabeth Bomberg (1999), *Decision-Making in the European Union*, Basingstoke: Macmillan.

Peterson, John and Helen Sjursen (eds.) (1998), *A Common Foreign Policy for Europe? Competing Visions of the CFSP*, London: Routledge.

Pierson, Paul (1996), 'The path to European integration: A historical institutionalist analysis', *Comparative Political Studies*, **29** (2), 123–63.

Pierson, Paul (2004), *Politics in Time: History, Institutions, and Social Analysis*, Princeton, NJ: Princeton University Press.

Pollack, Mark (1996), 'The new institutionalism and EU governance: The promise and limits of institutionalist analysis', *Governance*, **9** (4), 429–58.

Pollack, Mark (2002), *The Engines of European Integration: Delegation, Agency and Agenda-Setting in the EU*, New York: Oxford University Press.

Radaelli, Claudio (1999), *Technocracy in the European Union*, London: Longman.

Radaelli, Claudio (2000), 'Policy transfer in the European Union: Institutional isomorphism as a source of legitimacy', *Governance*, **13** (1), 25–43.

Radaelli, Claudio (2003), 'The Open Method of Coordination: A new governance architecture for the European Union?', Rapport No. 1, Swedish Institute for European policy Studies, at: http://www.sieps.se/publ/rapporter_en.html, accessed 23 February 2007.

Rees, Nicholas, Bríd Quinn, and Bernadette Connaughton (2006), 'The challenge of multi-level governance and Europeanization in Ireland' in Christos Paraskevopoulos, Panayotis Getimis and Nicholas Rees (eds), *Adapting to EU Multi-Level Governance: Regional and Environmental Policies in Cohesion and CEE Countries*, Aldershot: Ashgate, pp. 53–78.

Rhodes, **R. A. W.** (1988), *Beyond Westminster and Whitehall*, London: Unwin Hyman.

Rhodes, R. A. W. (1994), 'The hollowing out of the state: The changing nature of the public service in Britain', *Political Quarterly*, **65** (2), 138–51.

Rhodes, R. A. W. (1996), 'The New Governance: Governing without Government', *Political Studies*, **44** (5), 652–67.

Rhodes, R. A. W. (1997), *Understanding Governance: Policy Networks, Governance, Reflexivity and Accountability*, Buckingham: Open University Press.

Richardson, Jeremy (1996), 'Actor-based models of national and EU policy-making', in Hussein Kassim and Anand Menon (eds), *The European Union and National Industrial Policy*, London: Routledge.

Rosamond, Ben (1999), 'Discourses of globalization and the social construcition of European Identities', *Journal of European Public Policy*, **6** (4), 652–68.

Schelkle, Waltraud (2006), 'The theory and practice of economic governance in EMU revisited: what have we learnt about commitment and credibility in particular?' *Journal of Common Market Studies*, **44** (4), 669–85.

Schmidt, Vivien and Claudio Radaelli (2004), 'Policy change and discourse in Europe: Conceptual and methodological issues', *West European Politics*, **27** (2).

Scully, Roger (1997), 'The EP and the co-decision procedure: A reassessment', *Journal of Legislative Studies*, **3** (3), 58–73.

Scully, Roger (2005), *Becoming Europeans? Attitudes, Behaviour, and Socialization in the European Parliament*, Oxford: Oxford University Press.

Shaw, Jo (1999), 'Postnational constitutionalism in the European Union', *Journal of European Public Policy*, **6** (4), 579–97.

Shaw, Jo (2003), 'Process, responsibility in EU Constitutionalism', *European Law Journal*, **9** (1), 45–68.

Shaw, Jo and Gillian More, (eds) (1995), *New Legal Dynamics of European Union*, Oxford: Oxford University Press.

Smith, Michael (2001), 'The European Union's commercial policy: Between coherence and fragmentation', *Journal of European Public Policy*, **8** (5), 787–802.

Stevens, Anne and Handley Stevens (2000), *Brussels Bureaucrats*: The Administration of the European Union, Basingstoke: Palgrave.

Stevens, Handley (2004), *Transport Policy in the European Union*, Basingstoke: Palgrave Macmillan.

Stoker, Gerry (1997), 'Public–Private Partnerships and Urban Governance', in J. Pierre (ed.), *Partnerships in Urban Governance: European and American experience*, London: Macmillan, pp. 34–51.

Stoker, Gerry (1998), 'Governance as theory: Five propositions', *International Social Science Journal*, **50** (155), 17–28.

Strange, Susan (1996), *The Retreat of the State: The Diffusion of Power in the World Economy*, Cambridge: Cambridge University Press.

Taggart, Paul and Aleks Szczerbiak (eds) (2008a), *Opposing Europe?: The Comparative Party Politics of Euroscepticism: Case Studies and Country Surveys*, Oxford: Oxford University Press.

Taggart, Paul and Aleks Szczerbiak (eds) (2008b), *Opposing Europe?: The Comparative Party Politics of Euroscepticism: Comparative and Theoretical Perspectives*, Oxford: Oxford University Press.

Taylor, Paul (1971*), International Co-operation Today: the European and the Universal Pattern*, London: Elek.

Thatcher, Mark (2002), 'Regulation after delegation: independent regulatory agencies in Europe', *Journal of European Public Policy*, **9** (6), 954–972.

Tonra, Ben (2001), *The Europeanisation of National Foreign Policy: Dutch, Danish and Irish Foreign Policy in the European Union*, Aldershot: Ashgate.

Walker, Neil (1996), 'European constitutionalism and European integration', *Public Law*, Summer, 266–90.

Wallace, Helen (1993), 'European governance in turbulent times', *Journal of Common Market Studies*, **31** (3), 293–303.

Wallace, Helen, William Wallace and Carole Webb (1977), *Policy-Making in the European Communities*, London: Wiley.

Wallace, Helen (2003), 'Contrasting Images of European Governance', in Beate Kohler-Koch (ed.), *Linking EU and National Governance*, Oxford: Oxford University Press, pp. 1–9.

Warleigh, Alex (2006), 'Conceptual combinations: multilevel governance and policy networks', in Michelle Cini and Angela Bourne (eds), *Palgrave Advances in European Union Studies*, Basingstoke: Palgrave, pp.77–95.

Weale, Albert (2006), *Democratic Citizenship and the European Union*, Manchester: Manchester University Press.

Whitaker, Richard (2001), 'Party control in a committee-based legislature? The case of the European parliament', *Journal of Legislative Studies*, **7** (4), 63–88.

Wiener, Antje (2003), 'Editorial: Evolving norms of constitutionalism', *European Law Journal,* **9** (1), 1–13.

Wiener, Antje (2006), 'Constructivism and sociological institutionalism', in Michelle Cini and Angela Bourne (eds), *Palgrave Advances in European Union Studies*, Basingstoke: Palgrave, pp. 35–55.

Wincott, Daniel (1995a), 'Institutional interaction and European integration: Towards an everyday critique of liberal intergovernmentalism', *Journal of Common Market Studies*, **33** (4), pp. 597–605.

Wincott, Daniel (1995b), 'Political Theory, Law and European Integration', in Jo Shaw and Gillian More (eds), *New Legal Dynamics of European Union*, Oxford: Oxford University Press, pp. 293–311.

Young, Alasdair and Helen Wallace (2000), *Regulatory Politics in the Enlarging European Union*, Manchester: Manchester University Press.

Young, Hugo (1998), *This Blessed Plot: Britain and Europe from Churchill to Blair*, London: Macmillan.

Young, John (2000), *Britain and European Unity, 1945–1999*, 2nd edn, Basingstoke: Palgrave Macmillan.

4.   German Governance Research: Advanced but Mono-Disciplinary

Beate Kohler-Koch

In Germany, EU governance came into focus with the expansion of the regulatory activities that established the Single European Market. Governance research advanced with the launch of a national research programme on 'Governance in the European Union' (1996).[1] It aimed at reinvigorating research on European integration and bridging the disciplinary divide that is so typical of German academic research. The chapter will start with the context conditions of German governance research and then ask whether or not there has been a governance turn in EU studies. Subsequently, it will present a profile of German EU governance research in the past two decades and assess the empirical findings.

CONTEXT CONDITIONS

The distinctive characteristics of the German research context become particularly apparent when compared to the United Kingdom. Whereas British universities pioneered 'European Studies' as early as the 1970s (see Chapter 3), curricula at German universities were up to very recently strictly defined along disciplinary lines. 'European integration', 'European law', or the 'Monetary and Economic Union' were just one field among others in the respective disciplines of Political Science, Law or Economics. Only with the implementation of the Bologna Process and the introduction of BA and MA studies, have multi-disciplinary curricula been introduced and many MA programmes in the social sciences offered as 'European studies'. Despite this multi-disciplinary re-orientation of teaching, a university career is still mono-disciplinary. Thus, the incentives to engage in inter-disciplinary research are limited, even though national and above all EU research funding encourages cross-disciplinary approaches.

Another characteristic feature for German research is a distinct division of labour between basic and applied research. Basic research is mainly located in universities and the Max Planck Institutes whereas specialised institutes have been established for applied research and policy advice. They, nevertheless, also pursue basic research and are often linked to universities. Particularly prominent are the six German institutes for economic research. [2] In addition to a strong policy orientation, they also engage in more theory-oriented research. Hence, their research concentrates on the economic impact of individual EU policies and only irregularly takes up fundamental issues of regulation and governance. Four mainly Political Science oriented centres exercise a similar bridging function between academic research and policy advice; two of them are primarily focused on EU affairs. [3]

In the first decades of European integration, Law was the 'leading discipline' in European studies. A 'European Law Association' and a 'European Law Journal' supported intra-disciplinary communication and textbooks were published long before 'Europe' attracted the attention of other disciplines. For scholars of Law, European law constituted a genuine object of research very early on, whereas for political scientists the European Communities sat uneasily between International Relations and Comparative Government, and until the early 1990s was of interest only to a small group of scholars not well integrated in the mainstream of German Political Science (Kohler-Koch 2008). With the Treaty of Maastricht the image of the EU changed from an economic community to a political system and this increasingly attracted the attention of political scientists. A parallel shift occurred in Economics. Whereas in the past only a few specialists interested in external trade theory, economic integration or agriculture engaged in research on the common market, the monetary union provoked a vivid and highly controversial debate among German scholars of Economics (Wegner 2008: 97). For both disciplines the 1990s were a turning point in European studies, bringing more scholars into the field and focusing research on broader issues, such as the future of the EU, enlargement, and questions concerning polity and governance.

In History and Sociology, researchers interested in European integration are still in a minority position. The history of Europe was never a main subject, and only very recently a very small, but internationally well connected group of historians have taken an interest in the history of European integration (Kaelble 2008: 193). Even their communication with Political Science or Law is less than could be expected. Sociology has been a latecomer, too, and only in the last decade has it shifted attention to three main issues; firstly, to the impact of EU integration on the re-structuring of national identities and the formation of a European identity; secondly, to the likely and factual emergence of a European public sphere; and thirdly, to the transformation of the European welfare states (Münch 2008).

Several initiatives set out to modify the disciplinary orientation of European studies but were not particularly successful. The European Studies Association (Arbeitskreis Europäische Integration; AEI), which was set up in 1969, and the journal 'integration', initiated by the AEI and first published in 1969, provided a platform for exchange between disciplines and between academia and practitioners. But compared to UACES and the Journal of Common Market Studies, both had only a limited impact. In contrast to some European countries, the German Research Foundation (DFG), the central public funding organisation responsible for promoting research in Germany, has no agenda-setting role. It promotes interdisciplinary research by distinct 'Coordinated Programmes'[4] but leaves the thematic initiative to academia. It is noteworthy that since the early 1990s, the time of increased research interest in EU affairs, the DFG funded only one large research programme with an EU focus. The respective 'Priority Programme'[5] on 'Governance in the EU' was a major effort for bringing the disciplines engaged in EU research together. Though heavily biased in favour of Political Science, it achieved a broad disciplinary participation, and it succeeded in putting 'governance' on the research agenda of different disciplines. However, it did not generate sustainable multi-disciplinary cooperation.[6] The main reason for this is the decentralised approach of the Priority Programmes. The individual research projects are located in the respective departments of different universities and researchers only communicate on the occasion of joint conferences. Thus, the institutional context conditions and the disciplinary career perspectives quite obviously pave the way for disciplinary persistence. It is worth noting, however, that even research centres renowned for European research, and which facilitate long-term research in a given institutional framework, such as the Mannheim Centre for European Social Research (MZES), the Max-Planck Institute for the Study of Societies, Cologne, or the former Max-Planck Group for the Research on Collective Goods, Bonn, are marked by a disciplinary divide.

A GOVERNANCE TURN IN EU STUDIES?

'Governance' was the common focus of more than 60 research projects which were funded by the DFG in the national Priority Programme 'Regieren in der Europäischen Union'.[7] In order to take several disciplines on board, the programme was not theory-oriented but problem-based and the conceptual framework which was submitted for application refrained from a theoretical definition of the key term of 'Regieren' (governance).

The main ambition was to analyse and assess the functioning of the EU.[8] Furthermore, the detailed and thorough empirical analysis of political interaction and co-operation in the EU was presumed to provide a better understanding of governing beyond the nation state (Kohler-Koch 1998). Research should not only address the particularities of supra-national governance but also explore the impact of the EU on governance in member states. The EU was conceptualised as a system of multi-level and penetrated governance, so that attention was directed to the interdependence of regulatory systems and the interaction of public and private actors across levels of jurisdiction and diverse functional arenas. From a normative perspective, the efficiency and democratic legitimacy of multi-level governance was put under scrutiny.

It is worth remembering that when the programme was launched, it was difficult to persuade scholars in Law and Economics to join the initiative and only very few colleagues from history and sociology were interested. The experts on European law very convincingly argued that from a lawyer's point of view, governance needs a government and because the EU is a system without government, research on EU governance is a futile attempt. Consequently, research projects in 'Governance in the EU' was a major effort for bringing the disciplines engaged in EU research together. Though heavily biased in favour of Political Science, it achieved a broad disciplinary participation, and it succeeded in putting 'governance' on the research agenda of different disciplines. Therefore, research should concentrate on the institutional setting; a 'governance' approach would come close to advocate political interference that mostly works to the detriment of competition and growth. Consequently, economic scholars turned to the more fundamental question of the scope and depth of European regional integration and the adequate distribution of competence between the national and the supranational level. A prominent contribution, emanating from the research of the Max Planck Institute of Economics, Jena, was the juxtaposition of the 'Rome model' with the 'Maastricht model'. It was argued that the treaty that had established the European Economic Community came closest to a constitution for a market system, whereas the Maastricht Treaty introduced further non-market elements and has been dominated by traits which are characteristic of modern welfare states (Streit and Mussler 1994). The majority of German economists shared the sceptical view concerning the compensation of market failures by political intervention. Thus, they supported the pre-Maastricht liberal market constitution and propagated it as a model to cope with the challenges of globalisation. Concerning the theoretical orientation, 'constitutional economics' took the lead in designing optimal institutional models that would incite self-interested rational actors to act for the public good (Wegner 2008: 100).

The DFG-funded research programme on governance put the 'real world' phenomenon of EU governance on the agenda, but it did not ignite a theoretical debate and particularly not an interdisciplinary exchange on the development of a governance theory. One reason is the growing distance between disciplines in European research in the 1970s and 1980s (Haltern 2005: 65). Another reason is that the research framework was problem-based and not theory-oriented. This attracted researchers who took an interest in EU affairs, and they imported the dominant theoretical approaches of their own disciplines. In the 1990s, the governance approach in Economics was restricted to the sub-field of 'corporate governance', a discipline that did not link with the European Union, but which was well established and attracted a renewed interest in 2001 after the collapse of a number of large corporations in the USA. But the transfer of the governance approach to the macro-level of economic politics remained singular (Priddat 2005). In the discipline of Law the concept of governance was unknown in the early 1990s, though legal scholars also addressed the phenomenon of changing patterns of governing. The interest in flexible regulation and public–private interaction was concentrated in Administrative Law and went hand in hand with a methodological re-orientation of the field in Germany (Voßkuhle 2006). It was a response to the transformation of the state to an 'enabling state' ('Gewährleistungsstaat'; Hoffmann-Riem 2005) and a change in administrative behaviour which entailed an increased openness of public administrations to collaboration with private actors ('informales Verwaltungshandeln'). It was further stimulated by the adaptation of new public management models by local administrations and, last, not least, by the Europeanisation of the national regulatory systems. Though Administrative Law became more involved in the inter-disciplinary exchange with Political Science (Hoffmann-Riem and Schmidt-Aßmann 1990), the term 'governance' was met with reservations. Prominent authors (Voßkuhle 2006: 59) argue that Law has more to lose than to gain by introducing the governance terminology. Apart from the fuzziness of the concept, governance draws attention to systems of regulation and the interdependent interactions of private and public actors. Thus, from their point of view, the central focus of legal analysis, namely the attribution of competence and responsibility to distinct actors moves out of sight. In the meantime, the governance approach in Law has found a strong advocate in Gunnar Folke Schuppert (2005a). From his perspective, governance has the potential of a 'bridging concept' that is well suited for interdisciplinary discourse. He sees the specific contribution of a law approach to governance in the systematic analysis of the (normative) regulatory structures; these constitute the framing context of governance and it is the role of the law to provide a cooperation-friendly infrastructure (Schuppert 2005a: 384–390). Furthermore, he claims that research on Europe, by necessity, needs to be governance research analysing the structures and processes of the EU polity (Schuppert 2005b: 13).

In Political Science the interest in a governance approach and in the EU coincided in several aspects. The development of the EU into a political system with multiple layers of jurisdiction and close interaction between public and private actors became inter-related with the theoretical interest in new modes of political 'steering'. In past years, German Social Science had engaged in a thorough debate on the state's steering capacity. Different theoretical strands developed and had a strong impact both, on the theory of the state and on comparative politics. The system-theory approach of Niklas Luhmann was far less influential for EU studies than the 'actor centred' approach developed by Renate Mayntz and Fritz Scharpf (Mayntz 1987; 2005; Mayntz and Scharpf 1995). They drew attention to new forms of exerting public power[9] and the importance of institutions that structure the interaction of decision-makers and thus impact on policy outputs (Scharpf 1997; 1999).

Another input came from policy-analysis, an import from the US which was already well-established in German research on comparative politics. The rapidly evolving empirical research on individual EU policies followed the idea that EU politics is about 'problem-solving' and that public actors are no longer in command of autonomous policy-formulation and policy-outcome. The theoretical debate paved the way for exploring the distinct features of co-operative forms of decision-making in the EU and of the policy networks of state and non-state actors in which the distinction between steering subjects and steering objects become increasingly blurred. With the neo-institutionalist turn, the interdependence of EU institutions and modes of EU governance were brought into focus. It was argued that the distinct features of the EU system promote a system of 'network governance' which attributes to the state the role of mediator and activator, encourages joint problem-solving, brings about multiple overlapping negotiating arenas where state and private actors meet on more equal footing, and accommodates rival interests by encouraging the participation of stakeholders (Kohler-Koch 1999: 20–26).

Another strong impetus on German governance research came from scholars of International Relations. Whereas an early strand of the debate acclaimed the anachronism of sovereignty and an international system of 'governance without government' linking the concepts of governance, democracy and peace (Czempiel 1969; Czempiel 1992), the later focus shifted to the problem-solving capacity of international governance arrangements and the role of non-governmental actors in trans-national relations (Risse-Kappen 1995). 'De-nationalisation' (Zürn 1998) and 'governing without borders' (Kohler-Koch 1998) drew attention to the limits of effective national policy making and, above all, to the erosion of democratic representation and accountability.

Especially when compared to the UK, where normative questions entered EU research rather late with the Constitution on the Future of Europe (see Bulmer in this volume), it is noteworthy that from early on the issue of EU democracy figured prominently on the German agenda.[10] The exploration of the empirical legitimacy of the EU profited from a strong tradition in survey and electoral studies (Niedermayer and Schmitt 2005). Research concentrates on electoral participation and voting behaviour, but also looks at citizens' perceptions and the evolution of an EU political community.[11] The vivid discourse between different strands of theories of democracy also stimulated a distinctly normatively oriented empirical research. Research mostly followed either the liberal democracy approach or was inspired by the writings of Jürgen Habermas. The proponents of the theory of deliberative democracy argue that this approach offers an attractive alternative to dominant approaches for curing the democratic deficit of the EU (Schmalz-Bruns 2007: 286–287) and, I would add, can easily be related to a governance approach of EU politics.

Looking back on German EU research in the last two decades, one can conclude that there has been a 'governance turn'. The attention of researchers shifted away from the process of integration to the ways and means of governing the EU and addressed the issues of efficiency and democratic quality. The governance turn was also a response to changes in the 'real world', namely the successive transformation of the EU into a 'regulatory state' (Majone 1995) as it was spurred by developments in social science theory and methodology. In Political Science it benefited from the growing interest in policy-analysis and the theoretical debate on the 'steering' capacity of the state. Undoubtedly, the turn gained momentum through the launch of the national research programme, but also individual contributions from scholars who did not participate in the programme had an international impact, such as Fritz W. Scharpf's book on 'Governing in Europe' (1999).[12] The term 'governance' slowly replaced the German 'Regieren', not least through the international (and that is English) debate on the Commission's White Paper on Governance. However, despite the high degree of attention paid to EU governance, no German governance community evolved aiming at designing an interdisciplinary EU governance approach, let alone developing a governance theory.

THE THEMATIC PROFILE OF EU GOVERNANCE RESEARCH IN GERMANY

Since German academia refrained from developing a distinct governance approach, the field of research on European governance is far broader than the use of the terminology would suggest. Therefore, for our stock-taking exercise we opted for an inclusive approach.[13]

The framing of German EU governance research

Apart from divergent theoretical orientations, the framing of research questions reveals a pronounced difference in the conceptualisation of the research objective. The German research as documented in GOVDATA and known to the author by 'participant observation' reflects three fundamentally different approaches:

(1) A *sui generis* approach. For some authors the EU represents a system *sui generis* that inherently calls for new forms of governance as the traditional procedures of political steering and of democratic legitimacy of the nation states are not suitable. In the original terminology of legal scholars

the term used to emphasise the uniqueness of European integration, the Community was characterised as being neither a federal state nor an international organisation. Today, *sui generis* refers to the character of the EU as a laboratory for the study of general changes in the political and social system of the Western world. This renders the EU a particular attractive object when studying the development of alternative structures of political order and new forms of governance that are not yet as clearly discernible elsewhere.

(2) The 'politics like any other' approach[14]. Another group of authors regard the EU as merely one field of study among others. Although they will admit that it is always necessary to take into account distinctive context factors, they insist that these factors do not fundamentally change the general logics of action.

(3) A moderate 'specific context' approach. The majority of researchers are positioned somewhere in-between; that is they focus on studying the peculiarities of the EU and the conditions of multi-level governance in this specific political system. Research aims at exploring the differences and similarities of the social, economic and political organisation of the EU compared with those of national systems and the international system. Since researchers start by assuming systemic differences, they seek to explore the conditions and chances of preserving national diversity in the process of European community building.

A *sui generis* perspective on EU governance and democracy

For those who conceive of the EU as a *sui generis* phenomenon, the issue of democratic legitimacy receives utmost attention. Empirical research follows the different theoretical approaches and consequently turns up with divergent diagnoses and remedies. For those who see the main function of legitimacy in securing the voluntary support of authority, the main weakness of multi-level governance is that '(…) the unrestrained pursuit of economic and legal integration may weaken the political legitimacy of member states (…).' Consequently, Fritz W. Scharpf calls for '(…) creating a defense for politically salient national concerns that avoids the disruptive consequences of open non-compliance (…)' (Scharpf 2007: 16).

From the perspective of normative democratic theory it has been argued that the EU lacks the necessary conditions, above all a collective identity that turns it into a representative democracy. The prominent dictum by Peter Graf Kielmansegg that a 'viable' European identity will not come into being soon because the EU is not a community of communication, of memory, and of experience (Kielmansegg 1996: 55) has been mainly criticised in the abstract. When Stefan Seidendorf scrutinised it empirically in a longitudinal analysis of French-German elite and media communication, he found that over time, the 'Europeanisation of national identities' becomes quite apparent

(*Europeanization of Nation-State Identities? A Franco-German Comparison of Identity Discourses*, 2002–2005). A critical approach to the unitary model of identity is common place in German research. It has been the starting point for the empirical analysis of the social construction of 'Europe' and 'Europeans'. It revealed persistent cross-country divergence but also that over time, 'Europe' has become increasingly associated with the polity of the EU whereas the associations related to 'Europeans' are still quite diverse (*Identity conditions of European citizenship,* 1999–2001). Another pertinent question relates to the type of public spheres that might provide democratic legitimacy to EU governance. Klaus Eder and Hans-Jörg Trenz developed a concept of 'sectoral publics' and explored the resonance of EU policies in empirical case studies. Though media coverage differs between countries, the empirical findings confirm the emergence of trans-national 'sectoral public spaces' (*Governance in Europe – Beyond public legitimacy?*, 1997–1999; *From the emergence of a European elite public to the Europeanization of the national public,* 1999–2001; *Trans-national public spaces and the structuring of political communication in Europe*, 2001–2004). An even more radical approach to advance democracy in a polity that lacks a system-wide public sphere and identity is presented in the concept of 'multiple demoi'. Starting from the persuasive no-demos hypothesis, Heidrun Abromeit and her team have explored alternative approaches to safeguard equal and effective democratic participation. They have identified 'trans-national sectoral demoi' as the most likely societal base of a European democracy that may be granted political power through referenda (*Democracy within a multi-dimensional supra-national decision making system,* 1997–2001).

For some researchers the *sui generis* character of the EU also becomes manifest in the institutional and legal integration of the member states, through which they are 'deeply enmeshed in the multi-level governance system'. Compared to the national and international level, this results in a surprisingly high degree of compliance (*Compliance in modern political systems,* 1997–2001). Legal scholars, as well as political scientists generally agree that in Europe a system of integrated administration has evolved. It is a 'European administrative compound' ('Verwaltungsverbund'; Schmidt-Aßmann/Schöndorf Haubold 2005) which comes close to a 'fusion' of state levels (Wessels 2000: 123). The procedures of integrated law-making and legal frameworks channelling the information flows between the various units of the EU system of multi-level governance have created what von Bogdandy calls 'a communicative universe' (*Integrated law making between EU and the Federal Republic of Germany,* 1999–2001; see also Sommer 2003).

The question of how changes in governance are linked to system transformation attracted particular attention in German research with respect to the role of regions.[15] Central issues included whether the regions will be able to establish themselves as a relevant third decision making level and whether the EU indeed fosters a development towards a 'Europe of the regions'. The political emancipation of regions was often linked to the Union's support of a 'Europe of the regions' but empirical research offers evidence that the demand for regional autonomy and the differential treatment of regions across Europe has been less a reflection of EU-induced policies than of domestic constitutional and cultural traditions, economic interests and (party) political power games (Between Regionalism and European Integration –1998). Concerning the political empowerment of regions, the empirical results are equally sobering: regions in command of efficient administrative capacities profit most from becoming partners in EU policies and although the idea of a 'Europe of the regions' attracts wide support from all strands of political life, network analysis reveals a continuous high level of inner-regional exchange relations (*Regions as Political Actors in the Process of European Integration (REGE)*, 1992–1996).

Concerning foreign and security policy, the EU is mostly considered a special case in which, first and foremost, its quality as an actor has to be clarified. Especially in relation to international Great Powers, the tendency towards 'national reflexes' can be discerned. EU foreign policy shows a greater coherence only when the EU's common self-image as a 'peace-keeping power' is a common reference in peace-keeping interventions (*The Common Foreign and Security Policy (CFSP) of the EU – intergovernmental network or collective actor*, 1999–2001). This complements the finding that national identities still form the dominant frame of reference for foreign policy discourses and that a common European foreign policy is possible only when a compatible discourse can be constructed (*Conditions and factors for success of national foreign policy in the European multi-level system*, 1999–2001).

The 'politics like any other' approach

The advocates of the generalist approach are interested in wide-ranging insights in the decision-making processes of and between the various levels of the EU. Based on expert interviews and applied game theory, the influence of the leading ministries in domestic pre-negotiations could be ascertained. At the EU-level, influence over legislative output is spread out; winners and losers vary with time and policy issues and, despite a growing heterogeneity of interests in the course of enlargement, the decision-making capacity has not decreased greatly (*EU Decisions at the National Level: A Comparative Analysis of Cleavages and Interest Intermediation*, 2001–2004).

The patterns of interaction and cooperation within and between EU institutions have been a preferred research area of the 'generalists'. To them, empirical findings look familiar; complex and contested issues are dealt with by a piecemeal strategy. The differentiation of arenas of bargaining, consultation and decision-making, furthers the development of common criteria of rationality and thus promotes consensus building (*Interactive structures and cooperative patterns of networks of executives and experts within the 'committee regime' of the European multi-level system*, 1997–2002; *Interest representation in multi-level systems*, 1997–1999).

Governance in the specific context of the EU

The majority of German governance projects apply a *moderate context approach*, that is the characteristics of the EU as a multi-level system with segmented arenas of action are regarded as constitutive for European governance, but they are not seen as so unique that they defy any comparison. The resulting research questions address: (1) the optimal allocation of governance competence; (2) the prevailing patterns of multi-level governance; (3) how to cope with the democratic deficiencies of EU governance; and (4) the compatibility of national and EU governance and the Europeanisation of national governance systems.

The optimal allocation of governance competence

Projects in the field of Law have been concerned predominantly either with the structural features of the federal legal order (*Legal cohesion in the European Union*, 1999–2001), or with the interdependence of national and international constitution building in the sense of a 'multi-level constitutionalism' (The Foundation of European Constitutional Law, 1999–2001). Programmatically, economic research has dealt with the federal architecture of the EU. Economic scholars have examined the optimal design of an institutional framework regulating budgetary decisions of EU member states (*Coordination of public budgets and fiscal discipline in the EU*, 1996–1999), questioned the appropriateness of the still national competence for banking supervision and suggested alternative solutions (*EU Banking Supervision and Increasing Integration of Financial Markets*, 2001–2003) or developed normative criteria for an efficient allocation of regulatory competencies between the EU and member states in areas such as the management of trans-European networks (*The responsibilities of the European Union for trans-European networks*, 1997–1999).

The prevailing patterns of multi-level governance

A wealth of information is contained in the DICE-Database of the Ifo-Institute (*Ifo's Database for Institutional Comparisons in Europe*, 1999–ongoing) which includes institutional regulations of all EU member states in a broad range of policy fields. It does not contain, however, any comparative analysis of regulatory patterns, neither across countries nor concerning EU regulations compared to national regulations. Yet, the database can be well utilised by others for a comparative evaluation of patterns of governance or for an exploration of the characteristics of multi-level governance. Economic research mostly concentrated on the impact of distinct regulations and did not engage in a meta-analysis. Political scientists, for their part, mostly take an interest in the impact of EU regulation on policy convergence (*Environmental Governance in Europe: The Impact of International Institutions and Trade on Policy Convergence,* 2003–2006). When they turn to governance, they are predominantly interested in the evolution of particular governance patterns and in causal explanations. Consequently, they prefer a case study approach and their comparative investigations are restricted to a small selection of policy fields.

German political scientists are as interested in the input side of EU governance as in the regulatory output. A preferred subject in the past was the changing patterns of public–private interest intermediation.[16] It covered the issue of the 'co-evolution' of polity and interest associations in the EU (*Co-evolution of statehood and interest associations in the European Union,* 1997–1999); the dominant rationale and patterns of European interest intermediation; and the conditions of interest group influence. The empirical findings reveal a structural bias towards intense though informal public–private relations and the emergence of policy related networks and communities that are self-regulatory and oriented towards problem-solving (*Economic order, policy-framing, and regime competition,* 1999–2002). Concerted interests are most successful in exerting influence; partly because they command more resources, partly because their interest is more focused and, above all, because they have control over outcome (*The Europeanization of Economic Interests,* 1993–1996; *State–Society Relations in European Trade Policy: The Civil Society Dialogue of the European Commission,* 2004–2007; *The determinants of European climate policy in the perspective of New Political Economy,* 1996–2001). The Commission supports interest associations that find it difficult to become organised at EU level by providing funds and granting privileged access to consultations, without being able to compensate for their structural weakness (*Trans-national co-operation in the European Research and Technology Policy,* 1997–1999). The importance of resources and administrative efficiency also explains why certain actors – territorial as well as economic actors – rather bypass forums of collective interest representation such as the Committee of the Regions and trade associations and go it alone (*The Committee of the Regions: Limits of and opportunities for institutionalizing a third level of decision making in the European Union,* 1997–1999; *Package Deals between the European Commission and Large Firms,* 2000–2003).

Another focus of German governance research has been the multi-level interplay in the field of regional and structural policy. In particular the upgrading of regional actors as 'partners' in programming and implementation has attracted attention to the multi-level interplay in EU governance (*State regulation and European integration: Regional policy of the EC and its implementation in Italy*). A primary interest concerned the question of how consensus on successive policy reforms could be achieved. Using the development of the EU Structural Funds as an example, the original hypothesis that the extraordinary adaptability was related to the close connection between decision-making and implementation networks was empirically not supported. Research revealed other mechanisms, such as loose coupling, and organisational and functional differentiation together with the sequencing of decisions. Informal norms of negotiation and shared beliefs in appropriate problem-solving strategies turned out to be the mechanisms of coherence (*The development of the European Structural Funds as cumulative policy process*, 1998–2001).

Another special characteristic of the EU is the development of 'parallel links' of co-operation between different levels of governance – an attempt to govern complexity in policy fields such as employment, where the national varieties in policy network structures are not reconcilable with simple implementation strategies (*Territorial employment pacts in the European multi-level system,* 2001–2003). Overall, the European multi-level system is deeply penetrated by massive interventions, even if only with soft instruments such as 'benchmarking', while heeding formal national competences (*Employment as a new policy field in the dynamic multi-level system of the EU?* 1997–1999, *Economic constitution, Policy-Framing and Regime competition*, 1999–2002). Studies using cognitive approaches have clearly shown that the linkage of formal and informal discourses fosters the generation of shared rationality criteria and paves the way for common problem-solving strategies (*The Institutionalization of European Research Policy*, 1998).

How to cope with the democratic deficiencies of EU governance?

Multi-level governance has raised concerns regarding the sustainability of parliamentary democracy. In the early 1990s, it was common knowledge that the long chain of delegation and accountability is not compatible with effective democratic participation and that the executive escapes parliamentary control. Empirical analysis of the complex interplay between intergovernmental negotiations, co-operation in policy networks and decision-making in parliaments, tells a different story. National and even sub-national parliaments have developed effective strategies to preserve their influence. Though the approach varies with the national constitutional context, a common feature is that parliamentary control is informal and hence not visible to the public. This undermines democratic accountability (*The Politics of National Parliaments in the EU*, 2001–2003; *Democratic legitimacy of regional policy in the multi-level system of the European Union*, 1997–2001; *Accountability in multi-level governance systems*, 2004–2005). Also, the European Parliament is far more effective than normally assumed in exerting influence on the policy-making process (*Parliamentary democracy in the European Union: The Contribution of the European Parliament and national parliaments*, 1998–2001). But again, it escapes public awareness and thus contributes less than expected to democratic accountability.

The intensive theoretical debate on 'deliberative democracy' stimulated a new approach to analysing the trans-nationalisation and the transformation of political mobilisation and communication in European public spheres (*The Trans-nationalization of Public Spheres and its Impact on Political Systems*, 2003–2007; *EUROPUB.com – The Transformation of Political Mobilisation and Communication in European Public Spheres*, 2001–2004). Empirical analysis reveals that media coverage of EU institutions and EU policies has increased, but the resonance of EU related debates across national borders is at a very low level and has not changed significantly over the years. Thus, the empirical findings underscore the stability of a nation-centred public sphere and give little hope for the emergence of a well-informed democratic European public.

The discourse on deliberative democracy in the tradition of Jürgen Habermas also activated research on the role of civil society. As proclaimed by the Commission in the White Paper on Governance, the extended participation of citizens and civil society organisations (CSO) was perceived as a promising input to strengthen both the EU's input and output legitimacy. The theoretical debate stimulated empirical research investigating the conditions of civil society engagement, the role and performance of CSO in EU governance and their potential contribution to render EU policies more democratic (*Democratic Legitimacy via Civil Society Involvement?*, 2003–2008; *Legitimation and Participation in International Organizations*, 2003–2010). Those with a strong background in Third Sector research concentrated on the importance of CSO for the efficiency of European multilevel governance and explored the potential in the new post-communist member states in Central and Eastern Europe (*Junior Research Group European Civil Society and Multilevel Governance*, 2004–ongoing).

Systematic comparative analysis confirmed the persistence of biased representation, despite efforts of EU institutions to establish a more open and inclusive consultation regime. The institutional support adds little to the trans-national visibility of EU associations and, consequently, their input to a European public sphere is marginal. Their role is first of all that of a 'watchdog' which does not correspond to the expected enhancement of the deliberative quality of EU governance.

Political Sociology has turned to a bottom-up perspective, and survey-based comparative research provides evidence for the difficult relation between EU level organisations and the grass roots. Those who presumably command a high level of social capital, namely citizens active in grass-root associations, take little interest in the EU. Even more relevant is the perception of what makes a good citizen: on average, political engagement and, above all, participation in an association rates very low (*Citizenship, Involvement, Democracy,* 2000–2004)

Compatibility and Europeanisation of systems of governance

The term 'Europeanisation' subsumes the core of a number of research projects investigating the adaptation of structures and procedures of governance to EU regulations and examining the different 'compatibility' of national systems and the EU system. There are copious studies in the field of Law, often dissertations, which research the effects of EU secondary law or the rulings of the European Court of Justice on member state procedures (*The effect of the jurisdiction of the European Court of Justice on the member-national procedure in public disputes,* 1998).[17] Over the years, the complexity of the process of Europeanisation has been revealed in numerous single projects. The preferred fields of study were environmental protection (*Environmental Governance in Europe: The Impact of International Institutions and Trade on Policy Convergence*); transport policy, research- and innovation policy (*Trans-national cooperation in the European R&D policy,* 1996–2000); and energy policy (*The Europeanization of Economic Interests,* 1993–1996). Although the studies have been very illuminating, by necessity, they focus on the peculiarities of their respective cases and, consequently, it is difficult to draw general conclusions. This underlines the need for a systematic research programme, such as the one conducted by Adrienne Héritier and her team of the Max-Planck-Research Group, Bonn from 1999–2003. As they aptly summarised their findings: the outcome of Europeanisation is not convergence, but a 'differential Europe' (Héritier 2001). This diagnosis reflects the variety of the empirical reality, as well as the methodological limitations of comparative research. The specific contexts which affect Europeanisation can be discerned only by conducting broad comparative studies in international research networks. Whenever this approach has been tried, the results have confirmed the findings of the individual research: in regard to the Economic and Monetary Union, for example, the national political and administrative operation schemes prove to be rather persistent; there is no sign of a unitary adaptation model, despite the intensified coordination efforts on all levels (*Governance in the economic and monetary union after 1999,* 1999–2002).

Likewise, also the research on regional and structural policy documents that EU regulations meet with the resistance of national context conditions. Many comparative empirical studies present evidence for the dominance of country-specific developments, despite the formation of European policy-networks which encompass all levels of governance. Adaptations follow an incremental logic and seek to defend political and administrative autonomy (*The Transformation from Nationalism. Europeanization and Bureaucratization in an Organised Society*, 1996–2000). However, Europeanisation is not a one-way-street. Some sub-national actors are using European politics for their own means or to enhance their own capacity to act (*EU Policy at Regional Level. How Adaptive and Resistant is Regional Governance?* 1993–1997). Employing varied strategies, their success is related to differentiated constellations of interests and power. Since administrative actors have to comply with diverging interests of European, national and local levels and with the different rationality criteria of administrations, politics and the public, an 'administrative opportunism' is emerging to cope with the complexity of the system (*Bureaucratization through Europeanization?*, 1999–2003).

Nevertheless, some factors actually do foster the transposition of EU policies even in a situation of structural 'misfit'. A broad comparative study on EU policy on gender equality demonstrates that despite marked variations in legal and administrative arrangements in the member states, implementation was successful because the domestic gender discourse was backed by a strong European discourse and because trans-national networks supported gender equality 'advocacy coalitions' (*Public policy discourses and gender equality in European governance*, 1999–2001). A glance at other policy areas confirms the importance of international agenda setting and emphasises that trans-national interest groups can make a great difference when it comes to pushing a certain issue. If an issue is perceived of as a national competence and as domestically contentious, the willingness to accept EU regulations diminishes. Despite the extensive transfer of competence in the field of asylum and migration policy to the EU, the readiness for the Europeanisation of national migration policy is met with strong resistance (*Asylum and migration politics in the European Union*, 1999–2001). In sum it can be stated that local political contexts remain highly relevant. For example, the fact that EU-induced networks have not gained a foothold in the East German states can only be explained by the characteristic dynamics the German re-unification process has taken (*Networks induced by the EU in East German states ('Länder')*, 1999–2001).

Applying the concept of Europeanisation of governance to the readiness of political elites to act in favour of European politics, the question that arises is why Germany has actively promoted the extension of EU competences in matters of asylum and refugee policy as well as in security and defence policy but is increasingly reluctant to support the progressive implementation of the policy agreements. This change is explained, on the one hand by the costs of implementation and, on the other hand, by an obvious change of attitudes; that is the trust of German political elites in the European integration project has gradually been replaced by a more instrumental approach (*De-Europeanisation by Default? Germany's EU Policy in Defence and Asylum*, 2001–2004).

Transformation in governance and system change

Research emanating from the DFG-funded Collaborative Research Centre on the 'Transformation of the Nation State' at the University of Bremen underscores the persistence of the action capacity of the state in spite of shifting patterns of governance.

Nation states have not transferred their political responsibilities, despite increasing EU competences and the obvious internationalisation of many policy areas. Instead of out-sourcing state functions to international organisations, including the EU, the state chooses the path of privatisation and joins trans- and supranational co-operations that enlarge its competency to act. The paradoxical result of this is that the nation state's capacity to solve problems is strengthened while at the same time its autonomy to make decisions is restricted. The state distributes responsibility and actively supports the universalisation of legal norms and norms of action, from which it cannot withdraw.

Taking the opposite point of view, the focus turns to the compatibility of member state and EU governance. Empirical findings vitiate the widespread assessment that centralisation furthers the ability of a member state to prevail at the European level and that there are institutional models for success. Thus, the expectation that the transformation-states could have been prescribed a 'successful' adaptation model is entirely unfounded (*Governance in the European Union 'after' Maastricht*, 1997–2000). Rather, specific national cultures have penetrated EU governance. The most obvious case is in monetary affairs where the culture of stability has been transmitted through the entire European Central Bank system, so that one might speak of a 'national path-dependency in European central banking' (*The EMU and Different National Stability Cultures*, 1997–1998; 2004–2005).

CONCLUSION

Summarising the findings of German research we can state that EU governance is researched from many perspectives. A consensus has been formed concerning chief characteristics; that is, the boundaries between levels of governance are disappearing and a European system of integrated governance and administration is evolving. The national systems have consistently proven a high degree of adaptability; mostly, however, Europeanisation occurs in 'national colours' and has not provoked noticeable raptures or shifts in the national systems' architectures. The policy-making and implementation process is linking elements of hierarchy and co-operation in a way that furthers consensus building. The challenge of the increasing complexity of EU governance has been met with great flexibility and consequently patterns of interaction on the European as well as between the EU and the national level have multiplied. EU governance is evolutionary and not a uniform system, rather, governance arrangements vary by policy area. The strive for more efficiency has increased the flexibility of procedures and the proliferation of soft modes of governance, such as the Open Method of Coordination. Likewise, the attempt to intensify the integration of 'stakeholder' groups into the European policy process has furthered the trend towards a 'de-formalisation of politics'. Increased participation has produced mixed results: The plurality of societal interests is better represented in EU policy-making than a decade ago. But increased networking between a multitude of actors and informal public–private agreements obstruct democratic accountability and, thus, endanger the democratic legitimacy of European governance.

German research has analysed variations in EU governance in comparative perspective both with regard to its impact on different countries and its implementation in different policy fields. In depth empirical investigations are theory driven and use all the available tools of state-of-the-art methods. In more recent years, German research has become more occupied with the problems of democratic legitimacy. The deficiencies of the democratic infrastructure, the problem of constituting a European demos and a transnational political public, along with the lack of institutional safeguards ensuring democratic representation and accountability in the complex system of network governance have come to the fore.

German governance research in Political Science, Economics and Sociology is well integrated in the international academic community, not least due to the readiness of German scholars to publish in English. By contrast, the wealth of knowledge produced in Law is far less visible beyond national and disciplinary borders because research results are published almost exclusively in law journals and in the German language. The German presence in international interdisciplinary research networks is equally unbalanced, with Political Science outnumbering all other disciplines. The international visibility of German Political Science research is further enhanced by the many young German scholars holding positions abroad and importing research findings from German publications into their country of residence.

Trying to summarise the distinctiveness of German research on EU governance, one can say that the disciplinary divide is still discernible. Europeanisation in terms of being present in international conferences, European research networks and peer review journals is well advanced in the generation of young scholars though with disciplinary variations. All disciplines have in common the focus on real world issues, and research is mainly geared towards theory-based empirical investigations. The international competitiveness of German Social Science research is reflecting both organisational structures and the availability of resources. Social Science research is still mainly located in universities which put great emphasis on research performance and provide basic resources for research that is sufficient for small projects or to apply for external funds for larger research endeavours. Funds are available from different sources on the basis of strict peer review assessment; the most prestigious source is the German Research Foundation. The advantage of the German system, from a scholar's point of view, is that it gives the individual researcher full autonomy concerning the thematic orientation of her or his research. Consequently, the future of German governance research is difficult to predict. The problem is not the availability of research money but the intellectual attractiveness of investigating EU governance that will attract future research. Even though a wealth of knowledge has accumulated over the past years, puzzles concerning the emergence and differentiated impacts of distinct modes of EU governance remain to be explored. Last, but not least, also the ambitious goal of developing a governance theory is still on the agenda.

NOTES

1. 'Regieren in der Europäischen Union', see: http://gepris.dfg.de or http://www.mzes.uni-mannheim.de/projekte/reg_europ/dfg.htm.
2. See the membership list of the Leibnitz Gemeinschaft http://www.wgl.de.
3. These are the Institute for European Politics, Berlin (IEP), http://www.iep-berlin.de; The Center for Applied Policy Research (C·A·P) at the University of Munich, http://www.cap-lmu.de. The German Institute for International and Security Affairs, Berlin (SWP), http://www.swp-berlin.org and the Research Institute of the German Council on Foreign Relations (DGAP), http://www.dgap.org/fi, have a more international orientation.
4. These are 'Priority Programmes' supporting research projects emanating from different universities, 'Research Units' embracing a small number of researchers working together at one university, and 'Collaborative Research Centres' bringing together a larger number of researchers for a longer period of time.
5. To be successful, a 'Priority Programme' (Schwerpunktprogramm) has to pass not only the peer review but also the interdisciplinary assessment by the Senate of the DFG; the main criteria is that the programme promises to advance knowledge in an emerging field of research.
6. See the evaluation report by the programme co-ordinator (Kohler-Koch 2007: 7). http://www.connex-network.org/govdata/reports/Kohler-Koch_2007_DFG.pdf.
7. The programme was funded for six years (1996–2003) but research projects lasted up to 2006.
8. For the programmatic intentions of the programme see Kohler-Koch and Jachtenfuchs 1996.
9. In the terminology of Renate Mayntz: 'Formwandel staatlicher Machtausübung' (Mayntz 1995: 163).
10. The relevant contributions from the German governance research programme are presented and commented in Kohler-Koch and Rittberger 2007.
11. The European Elections Studies (EES), co-ordinated by Hermann Schmitt, MZES, University of Mannheim, started with the first EP election in 1979 and continued to the

present day; http://www.europeanelectionstudies.net.
12. The book was first published in English and then translated in German, Italian and French.
13. For the delineation of the governance research see the introduction.
14. For the terminology see Bulmer in this volume.
15. For a presentation of the German research on regions and on regional- and structural policy see the volume edited by Thomas Conzelmann und Michèle Knodt (2002).
16. For a presentation of the numerous German empirical research projects see Eising and Kohler-Koch 2005.
17. Since Germany has no register for dissertations and only few universities and faculties have a public register of dissertations, the wealth of doctoral research cannot be assessed properly.

REFERENCES

Conzelmann, Thomas and Michèle Knodt (eds) (2002), *Regionales Europa - Europäisierte Regionen*, Mannheimer Jahrbuch für Europäische Sozialforschung Nr. 6, Frankfurt, New York: Campus Verlag.

Czempiel, E.-O. (ed.) (1969), 'Die anachronistische Souveränität. Zum Verhältnis von Innen- und Außenpolitik', *Politische Vierteljahresschrift*, Sonderheft 1.

Czempiel, Ernst-Otto (1992), 'Governance and Democratization', in Ernst-Otto Czempiel and James N. Rosenau (eds), *Governance without Government: Order and Change in World Politics*, Cambridge: Cambridge University Press, pp. 250–271.

Eising, Rainer and Beate Kohler-Koch (eds) (2005), *Interessenpolitik in Europa*, Baden-Baden: Nomos.

Haltern, Ulrich (2005), 'Rechtswissenschaft als Europawissenschaft', in Gunnar F. Schuppert, Ingolf Pernice and Ulrich Haltern (eds), *Europawissenschaft*, Baden-Baden: Nomos, pp. 37–87.

Héritier, Adrienne (2001): *Differential Europe. The European Union Impact on National Policymaking*, Boulder, CO: Rowman & Littlefield.

Hoffmann-Riem, Wolfgang (2005), 'Governance im Gewährleistungsstaat – vom Nutzen der Governance-Perspektive für die Rechtswissenschaft', in Gunnar F. Schuppert (ed.), *Governance Forschung. Vergewisserung über Stand und Entwicklungslinien*, Baden-Baden: Nomos, pp. 195–219.

Hoffmann-Riem, Wolfgang and Eberhard Schmidt-Aßmann (eds) (1990), *Konfliktbewältigung durch Verhandlungen – Informelle und mittlerunterstützte Verhandlungen in Verwaltungsverfahren*, vol. 1, Baden-Baden: Nomos.

Kaelble, Hartmut (2008), 'Die Europaforschung der Historiker', in Hans Joas and Friedrich Jaeger (eds), *Europa im Blick der Kulturwissenschaften*, Baden-Baden: Nomos Verlag, pp. 183–203.

Kielmansegg, Peter G. (1996), 'Integration und Demokratie', in Markus Jachtenfuchs and Beate Kohler-Koch (eds), *Europäische Integration*, Opladen: Leske + Budrich, pp. 47–71.

Kohler-Koch, Beate and Markus Jachtenfuchs (1996), 'Regieren in der Europäischen Union – Fragestellungen für eine interdisziplinäre Forschung', *Politische Vierteljahresschrift*, 37 (3), 537–556.

Kohler-Koch, B. (ed) (1998), 'Regieren in entgrenzten Räumen', *Politische Vierteljahresschrift*, Sonderheft 29, Opladen: Westdeutscher Verlag.

Kohler-Koch, Beate (1999), 'The evolution and transformation of European governance', in Beate Kohler-Koch and Rainer Eising (eds), *The Transformation of Governance in the European Union*, London: Routledge, pp. 14–35.

Kohler-Koch, Beate (2007), *DFG Schwerpunktprogramm 1023 Regieren in der Europäischen Union. Abschlussbericht*, Mannheim. http://www.connex-network.org/govdata/reports/Kohler-Koch_2007_DFG.pdf.

Kohler-Koch, Beate (2008), 'Die Europäisierung der politikwissenschaftlichen Europaforschung', in Hans Joas and Friedrich Jaeger (eds), *Europa im Blick der Kulturwissenschaften*, Baden Baden: Nomos Verlag: pp. 17–43.

Kohler-Koch, Beate and Berthold Rittberger (eds) (2007), *Debating the Democratic Legitimacy of the European Union*, Lanham: Rowman & Littlefield Publishers.

Mayntz, Renate (1987), 'Politische Steuerung und gesellschaftliche Steuerungsprobleme Anmerkungen zu einem theoretischen Paradigma', *Jahrbuch zur Staats- und Verwaltungswissenschaft*, 1, Baden-Baden: Nomos: pp. 89–110.

Mayntz, Renate and Fritz W. Scharpf (1995), 'Der Ansatz des akteurzentrierten Institutionalismus', in Renate Mayntz and Fritz W. Scharpf (eds), *Gesellschaftliche Selbstregelung und politische Steuerung*, Frankfurt: Campus: pp. 39–72.

Mayntz, Renate (2005), 'Governance Theory als fortentwickelte Steuerungstheorie?', in Gunnar F. Schuppert (ed.), *Governance-Forschung. Vergewisserung über Stand und Entwicklungslinien*, Baden-Baden: Nomos, pp. 11–20.

Majone, Giandomenico (1995), 'The European Community as a Regulatory State', *Series of Lectures of the Academy of European Law*, Leiden: Nijhoff.

Niedermayer, Oskar und Hermann Schmitt (eds) (2005), *Die Europawahl 2004*. Wiesbaden: Verlag für Sozialwissenschaften.

Münch, Richard (2008), 'Von der Familie europäischer Nationen zur europäischen Gesellschaft – Soziologische Zugänge zur Europaforschung', in Hans Joas and Friedrich Jaeger (eds), *Europa im Blick der Kulturwissenschaften*, Baden-Baden: Nomos Verlag, pp. 73–96.

Priddat, Birger (2005), 'Economic Governance', in Gunnar F. Schuppert (ed.), *Governance-Forschung. Vergewisserung über Stand und Entwicklungslinien*, Baden-Baden: Nomos, pp. 173–194.

Risse-Kappen, Thomas (ed.) (1995), *Bringing Transnational Relations Back in: Non-State Actors, Domestic Structrures and International Institutions*, Cambridge: Cambridge University Press.

Scharpf, Fritz W. (1997), *Games Real Actors Play. Actor-Centered Institutionalism in Policy Research,* Boulder, CO, Oxford: Westview Press.

Scharpf, Fritz W. (1999), *Governing in Europe. Effective and Democratic?*, Oxford/ New York: Oxford University Press.

Scharpf, F. W. (2007): *Reflections on Multilevel Legitimacy*, MPIfG Working Paper 7/, Max Planck Institute for the Study of Societies, Cologne, July.

Schmalz-Bruns, Rainer (2007), 'The Euro-Polity in Perspective: Some Normative Lessons from Deliberative Democracy', in Beate Kohler-Koch and Berthold Rittberger (eds), *Debating the Democratic Legitimacy of the European Union*, Lanham: Rowman & Littlefield, pp. 281–203.

Schmidt-Aßmann, Eberhard and Bettina Schöndorf-Haubold (eds) (2005), *Der europäische Verwaltungsverbund: Formen und Verfahren der Verwaltungszusammenarbeit in der EU*, Tübingen: Mohr Siebeck.

Schuppert, Gunnar F. (2005a), 'Governance im Spiegel der Wissenschaftsdisziplinen', in Gunnar F. Schuppert, (ed.), *Governance-Forschung*.

Vergewisserung über Stand und Entwicklungslinien, Baden-Baden: Nomos, pp. 371–469.

Schuppert, Gunnar F. (2005b), '"Theorizing Europe" oder Von der Überfälligkeit einer disziplinübergreifenden Europawissenschaft', in Gunnar F. Schuppert, Ingolf Pernice and Ulrich Haltern (eds), *Europawissenschaft*, Baden-Baden: Nomos, pp. 3–35.

Sommer, Julia E. (2003), *Verwaltungskooperation am Beispiel administrativer Informationsverfahren im Europäischen Umweltrecht*, Berlin: Springer Verlag.

Streit, Manfred E. and Werner Mussler (1994), 'The Economic Constitution of the European Community – From "Rome" to Maastricht', *Constitutional Political Economy*, **5** (3), 319–353.

Voßkuhle, Andreas (2006), 'Neue Verwaltungsrechtswissenschaft', in Wolfgang Hoffmann-Riem, Eberhard Schmidt-Aßmann and Andreas Voßkuhle (eds), *Grundlagen des Verwaltungsrechts*, vol. 1, München: C. H. Beck Verlag, pp. 1–61.

Wegner, Gerhard (2008), 'Integrationsalternativen für Europa – Kontroversen in der ökonomischen Theorie', in Hans Joas and Friedrich Jaeger (eds), *Europa im Blick der Kulturwissenschaften*, Baden-Baden: Nomos Verlag, pp. 97–116.

Wessels, Wolfgang (2000), *Die Öffnung des Staates. Modelle und Wirklichkeit grenzüberschreitender Verwaltungspraxis 1960–1995*, Opladen: Leske + Budrich.

Zürn, Michael (1998), *Regieren jenseits des Nationalstaates. Denationalisierung und Globalisierung als Chance*, Frankfurt: Suhrkamp.

5. The Netherlands and Norway: Strong in Governance Research

Nico Groenendijk, Martin Rosema, Jacques Thomassen and Ramses Wessel; Ulf Sverdrup

The Netherlands and Norway are quite different countries in terms of size and in their relation to the EU. The Netherlands is a founding member whereas Norway decided not to join the EU. Nevertheless, both are strong in EU governance research and their scholars are involved in many international academic networks. In order to facilitate a comparative assessment of the reasons for success and their specific profiles the two countries are put together in one chapter though written by different authors.

* * *

THE NETHERLANDS RESEARCH ON EU GOVERNANCE

Nico Groenendijk, Martin Rosema, Jacques Thomassen and Ramses Wessel

In this sub-chapter we present an outlook on a decade of Dutch research on EU multi-level governance. Given the wide range of disciplines involved and given the large capacity of the governance concept to absorb different research topics, the outlook presented here is limited by nature. Still, three main characteristics of Dutch research on EU governance can be made out clearly:

a) multi-disciplinary research cooperation, strongly encouraged by public actors providing research funding;
b) strong orientation towards empirical research;
c) strong international orientation.

These characteristics are rooted in the Dutch social sciences in general, which is why we first deal with the broader context of social science research in the

Netherlands (section 2). In section 3 the standing of research on the EU in the Netherlands is discussed, including the relationship between the research agenda and the political agenda. Section 4 deals with the 'governance turn' in EU research. Section 5 focuses on the 'Dutch profile' with regard to research content and in section 6 we present our conclusions.

SOCIAL SCIENCE RESEARCH IN THE NETHERLANDS

In the Netherlands, throughout all fields of social science (economics, law, political science, public administration, sociology), research is very well-developed and generally of high quality. The Netherlands has a strong tradition of multi-disciplinary cooperation, especially of comparative empirical research. An important element in that regard is that in the Netherlands, public administration studies are very well-developed as a multi-disciplinary academic field (and according to some as a discipline in its own right) with its own programmes, institutions and journals.

National research is fairly well accessible to foreign scholars, as the number of publications in international journals by Dutch researchers has always been rather high. Besides, the presence of Dutch scholars at international conferences is very high and always has been. To the extent that this is possible, it is still increasing.

Institutional incentives for social science research at universities

The two main institutional incentives for social science research at universities are (external) funding and the existence of national research schools.

In addition to the basic resources supplied to the universities by central government (largely depending on the numbers of graduates and comprising 70 per cent of total university funding), external research funding is provided by research councils and similar organisations (comprising 9 per cent of total university funding) and through specific funding for research commissioned by government authorities or the private sector (21 per cent of total university funding). Compared to other countries, the basic grant is relatively high and the share of funding by research councils is relatively low (Centraal Planbureau, 2002). However, because the basic grant is to a large extent used to cover teaching costs, external funding is very important for research and is successfully used by funding authorities to promote large-scale national cooperation and multi-disciplinary projects. The Netherlands' Organisation for Scientific Research (NWO) is the most important organisation in this respect. The competition between social science researchers to attract NWO funding for PhD and/or post-doc positions and for large-scale research projects is rather fierce (approximately 10 per cent of all NWO proposals in this field are successful). Funding is increasingly sought from EU programmes like the EU Framework Programmes for Research and Development.

Besides funding, institutionalisation of research cooperation is important. The Netherlands is a relatively small country in which cooperation in research projects across universities has traditionally been high. Over the last two decades, part of this cooperation has been institutionalised by means of inter-university research schools. Based on their performance, these schools are officially accredited by the Royal Netherlands Academy of Arts and Sciences (KNAW). Participation as a (senior) fellow in research schools has become a must for social scientists. It also plays an important part in the recurrent national peer review of research and teaching programmes.

PhD research

The Dutch PhD system is still based on individual supervision. It involves a 4-year period in which PhD students generally follow a limited number of courses offered by a research school or institute in their field. There are no full-time PhD programmes. A PhD position is a hybrid one, as PhD students have the legal status of employees and are expected to participate to a certain extent in teaching and other activities.

Today, most dissertations are written in English. PhD candidates are increasingly encouraged to present papers at international conferences and to publish in international journals. Building a strong track record in (international) research has become extremely important for PhD students in terms of their academic career opportunities.

Non-university social science research

The bulk of social science research is conducted in (fourteen) universities but there are some very strong research institutions as well. These include governmental advisory bodies, three of which have to be mentioned. First, the Netherlands Scientific Council for Government Policy (Wetenschappelijke Raad voor het Regeringsbeleid – WRR) is an independent think-tank for the Dutch government. The WRR advises the government – asked and unasked – about a variety of themes in a long-term perspective. Secondly, the Netherlands Bureau for Economic Policy Analysis (Central Planbureau – CPB) is an independent research institute within the central government, that is mainly involved in economic analyses. Thirdly, the Social and Cultural Planning Office of the Netherlands (Sociaal en Cultureel Planbureau – SCP) is a government agency which conducts research of the social aspects of all areas of government policy. Its reports are widely used by the government, civil servants, local authorities and academics.

The value added to university research by these advisory bodies does not only pertain to the (applied) research as such (which generally is of a high academic standard), but also to data collection and dissemination. Moreover, there are strong personal links between universities and these advisory bodies, for instance through joint appointments of research staff. In addition, publications by the WRR and SCP are often based on background studies carried out by universities.

THE STANDING OF EU (GOVERNANCE) RESEARCH

From a historical perspective, research on the EU (and its legal precursors) has always been linked to the actual developments of European integration. For decades, the interest in the Netherlands was clearly infused by the practice of integration and was directed at:

a) issues of economic integration (conditions for and effects of the establishment of the customs union and later, the single market);
b) the emerging European legal system (the relationship between EC regulation and national legal systems, importance of European Court of Justice case law);
c) decision-making processes (the role of various institutions, lobbying), issues of political representation, and the legitimacy of the European Union, mainly from the perspective of political science.

In fact, there is a strong disciplinary focus on economics, political science and law. As in other countries, the interest of the discipline of sociology in the EU and European integration is a fairly recent phenomenon.

Major research institutes on international and European affairs

The strong international tradition in the Netherlands (in economics, in international relations theory and in law) is reflected in renowned international institutes that are also engaged in European research. The most prominent are:

*   the Netherlands Institute of International Relations, better known as *Clingendael*, which is a think-tank in the field of international and European affairs;
*   the *T.M.C. Asser Institute* in The Hague, which is a research institute that focuses on Private and Public International Law, International Commercial Arbitration, and European Law. Academic research is conducted in collaboration with participating organisations which include law faculties from universities, as well as other institutes;

- the *European Institute of Public Administration* (EIPA) in Maastricht, which carries out research on public administration and European policies, but mostly is involved in training specifically aimed at public officials; and

- *the Hague Institute for the Internationalisation of Law* (HiiL), which was founded in 2005. HiiL is an international research institute focusing on the internationalisation of law in the context of globalisation. HiiL is both a research organisation in its own right and a funding body for (multi-disciplinary) university research projects.

Obviously, EU (governance) research is not only linked to actual developments in terms of European integration but also to teaching activities and to specific issues on the national public and political agendas.

Research and teaching

In the Netherlands, there are two fully-fledged multi-disciplinary programmes in European Studies that focus on governance issues. These (English-language) programmes are currently offered in Twente and in Maastricht (both at the BA and MA level). These two universities also have specialised institutes (Centres for European Studies). Besides these two programmes, the University of Groningen offers a Dutch BA programme and an English MA programme in international affairs, and other universities offer numerous possibilities to specialise in European Studies as part of their regular curricula in economics, law, political science or public administration.

The research agenda and the public and political agendas

There is a striking similarity between the major themes on the academic research agenda and the development of the political and public agenda. This similarity is largely due to the high level of interaction (through seminars, guest lectures, advisory work) between academics, politicians and government officials, made possible by the relatively small scale of Dutch society.

On all three agendas the legitimacy and the democratic quality of EU institutions and decision-making processes seem to be the most prominent issues. To some extent the major research questions with regard to these issues are very classical ones and developed from traditional state-oriented normative views on democracy. From this perspective the relationship between the several institutions of the European Union in terms of accountability and democratic control is an important topic, in particular the relationship between politics and administration. Equally important are issues in the broad context of political representation, like the development of a

European party system, the representativeness of the European parliament, and the involvement of citizens across Europe in European politics. Ever since the debate on the draft constitution and the rejection of it by a referendum the legitimacy of the Union has become a major item both in the public debate and in academics.

A second major theme is the relationship between the EU and 'lower' levels of government, that is, not only the national level but also the regional and local levels of government. The increasing academic interest in this relationship parallels with an increasing public concern about a shift of power towards 'Brussels'. In law and public administration, the relationship between national and European law is a major research theme, encompassing issues like the enforcement of European rules and the transposition of European Union directives into national law. In political science there is an increasing interest in the question to what extent Europeanisation has an impact on national political systems. In economics, the theoretical perspective of fiscal federalism is an important source of inspiration.

Equally important is the developing academic interest in the patterns of influence in the other direction: to what extent can and do Dutch policy-makers influence European decision making? To what extent can and does the Dutch parliament scrutinize the input of the Dutch government in EU decision making?

GOVERNANCE, GOVERNANCE EVERYWHERE

Over the last decade, EU governance has become a major research theme in the Netherlands in both political science and public administration. A similar development can be observed in economics and law, although in these disciplines the term 'governance', and especially the term 'multi-level governance', might be less common.

To a large extent this development is the result of the interests of individual researchers and research groups in these topical issues, triggered by actual developments in European governance. For instance, the establishment of the multi-level European System of Central Banks has sparked a huge interest among Dutch economists into issues of independence and accountability of central bankers within the EU. Similarly, within the science of law, new EU modes of governance (like the open method of coordination) have led to an increased interest in the (de)merits of soft law. We would argue that in the Dutch case, in all disciplines involved, the actual changes regarding the location of governing capacities within the EU system and regarding the modes of governance have led researchers to go beyond the traditional analysis of EU integration mentioned in section 3. Actual developments in terms of upward, downward and vertical shifts in governance, and new problems of efficiency, effectiveness, accountability and legitimacy have spurred the governance turn in research rather than path-breaking theoretical developments or paradigm shifts within the various disciplines. Interestingly enough, because the different disciplines have been dealing with the same empirical phenomenon, the governance turn in research has clearly contributed to a stronger multi-disciplinary orientation.

Besides that, there has been a *strong institutional impetus* in which the *Netherlands Organisation for Scientific Research* (NWO) played an important part. The Social Science Research Council (MAGW) of NWO developed and funded a special research programme called *Shifts in Governance: Problems of Legitimacy and Accountability*, which started in 2001. One of the most important themes of this multi-disciplinary programme was the development of multi-level governance, its causes and consequences for the legitimacy of national and European governance.

The governance turn was also present at the level of *national research schools*. The *Netherlands Institute of Government* (NIG) is a national research school in which all departments of public administration and political science but one cooperate. In the period from 2000–2005, one of the school's five research programmes was entitled 'Governance in the European Union'. Approximately 70 researchers were involved in that programme. In the current research programme (2006–2010), two of the main themes are citizenship and governance, and the future of the nation state. Both themes have sub-programmes that deal with EU governance issues.

A focus on the legal dimension of multi-level governance may be found in the research programme of the *Ius Commune* research school, in which the Law Faculties of Amsterdam, Leuven, Maastricht and Utrecht participate. This programme focuses, *inter alia*, on constitutionalization processes at the national, regional (EU) and global level and the interaction between these processes.

In the field of economics, the *Tinbergen Institute* is one of the main inter-university networks for economic research. The better part of the research programme of this institute deals with the analysis of markets (especially financial and labour markets) and governance structures at various levels (global, European, regional).

Among the research programmes that are directed at *(single) universities or institutions*, several can be identified that focus more or less explicitly on multi-level governance in Europe. One of them is 'Multi-layered governance in Europe and beyond', directed by Hans Keman from the Free University in Amsterdam (Keman, 2001–2005). The research programme directed by Jacques Thomassen of the University of Twente, entitled 'Governance in a complex society' (Thomassen, 2003–2005), stands out as one of the few in which researchers from the same university but from different disciplinary backgrounds participate (political science, law, economics). This programme is one of the research programmes of the Institute for Government Studies (IGS) of the University of Twente. In 2001, at the Radboud University,

Nijmegen, the research programme 'Governance and Places' (GaP) has been introduced. This programme deals with multi-level governance issues of spatial planning and the environment, involving different spatial units (cities, regions, nations, transboundary units, and Europe). Harry Garretsen from the Utrecht School of Economic together with Wil Hout (Institute for Social Studies, The Hague) has conducted a programme entitled 'Between adjustment and rigidity: an international political-economic analysis of internationalisation, institutions and economic performance', in collaboration with the Radboud University, Nijmegen (Bob Lieshout) and the Free University, Amsterdam (Kees van Kersbergen). Frans Stokman (University of Groningen) has coordinated a project on 'Explaining EU Decision Making' in cooperation with the universities of Leyden and Nijmegen. The increased attention for non-state actors as well as for the blurring of boundaries between legal orders has resulted in a stronger focus on the interplay between global, European and national legal orders in the research programmes of almost all law faculties. A prime example can be found in the research programmes of the Amsterdam Center for International Law.

All these programmes have provided the organisational framework for the emergence of numerous PhD thesis and research projects gathering one or more scholars around related topics. On a meta-level, such national or collaborative programmes instigate fruitful intellectual debates between scholars from different universities, departments and disciplinary backgrounds and contribute to the emergence of a vivid community dedicated to EU governance research.

A DUTCH PROFILE?

Due to the traditionally strong international orientation of Dutch researchers, it is difficult to distinguish a Dutch research agenda from an international one. Still, when looking at the Dutch projects in the CONNEX GOVDATA database and at the publications of Netherlands-based researchers, as recorded in the CONNEX GOVLIT database (1995–2005), two themes seem to stand out. First, the *legal framework* is addressed in many projects. These projects concern the effect of EU rules on national law (including transposition issues), as well as the division of competences between the EU and its member states. Strikingly, this is true not only for projects conducted in the field of law, but also for those conducted in fields such as public administration, political science and economics, which clearly shows the strong impetus the governance turn has given to multi-disciplinary research. A second theme, discussed in political science and to a lesser extent within economics, concerns *legitimacy and accountability*. Within these two broad themes, some more specific topics are repeatedly dealt with:

a) the general concept of (multi-level) governance (Hooghe, 1996; Marks, 1996a, 1996b; Hooghe and Marks, 2000, 2003; Van Kersbergen and Van Waarden, 2001, 2004; Keman, 2001–2005), governance, integration theory and Europeanisation (Hosli and Börzel, 2003; Aalberts, 2004; Haverland and Holzhacker, 2006), the subsidiarity principle (Verbeek and Van Kersbergen, 2004) and fiscal federalism theory (Groenendijk, 2003);

b) issues of political representation, accountability, and legitimacy (Schmitt and Thomassen, 1999, 2000; Thomassen, Noury, and Voeten 2004; Bovens, 2006, Bovens 2005–2010; Curtin and Nollkaemper 2006; Laver, Mair and Gallagher 2001; Mair 2005), including issues of political contestation (Marks and Steenbergen 2004), and electoral behaviour, both in European elections (Van der Eijk and Franklin 1996; Van der Brug and Van der Eijk 2007) and referenda (Aarts and Van der Kolk 2006);

c) the establishment, functioning and legitimacy of the (multi-layered) European System of Central Banks (see Van der Cruijsen and Eijffinger, 2007 for a survey);

d) the development of a European Public Sphere (see for example De Vreese et al. 2006; Semetko et al. 2000; Koopmans 2001–2004);

e) lobbying, interest groups and access to European policy-making (Beyers 2002, 2004; Van Schendelen 2002);

f) EU decision-making (Steunenberg 2002, 2003; Stokman and Thomson 2004; Thomson, Boerefijn and Stokman 2004; Stokman et al. 2006; Princen 2003–2007), more specifically voting and decision rules in the Council (Hosli 1996; Hosli and Nurmi 2003; Hosli and Thomson 2006), and the role of committees and comitology (Christiansen 1996; Christiansen and Kirchner 2000; Steunenberg et al. 2000);

g) the role of the administration, especially the European Commission, in EU affairs and integration (Hooghe 2001; Curtin and Wille 2004–2006), agencies (Curtin 2005–2009), administrative governance and the CFSP (Vanhoonacker and Duke 2006) and informal governance (Christiansen et al. 2006);

h) the constitutional relation between the EU and the domestic legal order, including transposition of EU directives (Steunenberg 2004–2008, 2005–2006; Berglund 2002–2006; Mastenbroek 2001–2005), and the constitutional interplay between the global and the domestic legal orders (see Heere 2003; Nollkaemper and De Wet 2004; De Wet 2006; Wessel, Follesdal and Wouters 2007).

Not surprisingly, the Convention, the IGC and the Constitutional Treaty have recently been subjects of research (Crum 2005; Groenendijk 2007; Hosli et al. 2005; Marks and Hooghe 2006).

Obviously, even though some specific thematic foci can be observed, the range of topics covered by researchers in the Netherlands is very broad and there are only a few aspects of the EU as a multilevel system of governance that remain unexplored. In terms of research approach, the variety is large. It is hard to establish a favoured theoretical approach or favoured methodology. In other words, the impressive number of large collaborative programme and projects does not flourish at the expense of diversity and pluralism. The main common feature is that most research carried out in the Netherlands in the field of EU multi-level governance has a large empirical content and is policy-oriented.

CONCLUSION

Dutch research on EU multi-level governance is well on track. In all relevant disciplines multi-level governance and the EU in general have become an important research topic. Dutch academics in this area of research are strongly internationally oriented and are involved in many international academic networks. Because of this international orientation, Dutch academics contribute largely to the European scientific debate. As far as possible, this international orientation will become even stronger rather than weaker in the future. To some extent, this is the predictable consequence of the institutional context of Dutch universities and major research institutes. They are subject to an intensive external review system. Failing to meet the high standards that review committees are using can have very negative consequences for research groups. One of the major criteria is excellence according to international standards, which is mainly operationalised as publishing in high quality English language journals. 'Publish (in English) or perish' has become a fact of life at Dutch universities. Therefore, in addition to their intrinsic motivation to work in an international environment, Dutch academics simply have no option if they want to be professionally acclaimed. If this sounds like a negative incentive, there are strong positive motivations, as well. As mentioned, both the Netherlands Organisation for Scientific Research and national research schools, as well as local university research institutes have taken a strong interest in research on governance in general and EU multi-level governance in particular.

* * *

NORWEGIAN GOVERNANCE RESEARCH

Ulf Sverdrup

During the last decade we have seen a strong increase in governance research in Norway, and this research has also received attention in other countries. This sub-chapter gives some ideas that might explain why we have seen this remarkable shift, and why the governance research has developed in this specific direction. My starting point is the observation that scientific activity is not a borderless activity, and that scientific perspectives and approaches to a given object are often shaped by the cognitive features of the dominant paradigm, by the social organisation of the science system, and by external or contextual factors (Mayntz 2005).

Before turning to the discussion, I will make a few conceptual clarifications. By the term 'Norwegian research governance', I mean research and research projects that have been conducted primarily in Norway, or financed primarily by Norwegian authorities. By the term 'European governance', I mean research on the EU governance system, as well as the impact of EU institutions and policies on national institutions and governance structures. Moreover, I focus particularly on governance research in the field of political science.[1]

The chapter is organised in the following way. Firstly, I provide the political backdrop for EU governance research in Norway. Secondly, I examine how traditional approaches and distinct scientific traditions in the Norwegian social sciences have impacted on Norwegian EU governance research. I argue that the academic roots, more so than national political interests, have affected the research questions that have been asked, the concepts in use, the theories and approaches that have been applied, as well as the methods and research designs that have been employed. Finally, I briefly discuss the organisation of research on EU governance in Norway.

A DRAMATIC POLITICAL BACKDROP

It is difficult to understand the development and dynamics of Norwegian research on EU governance without taking into account its dramatic political backdrop. Norway has applied for membership three times, and two referendums have been held on the issue. A clear majority voted 'No' to membership both in 1972 and 1994. The issue of membership is still unsettled, and it remains one of the most contested issues in the political debate, it has created deep cleavages in most political parties and it has represented a destabilising force for every Norwegian government since 1994.

However, Norwegian non-membership does not mean that Norway is unaffected by the transformation of governance that is taking place in Europe; rather the contrary. Over time Norway has developed wide-ranging agreements with the EU linking Norway and its society closely to the European Union and its member states. The most important elements in the rather complex web of formal and informal co-operative arrangements between the EU and Norway is the European Economic Area Agreement (EEA) and the Norwegian participation in the Schengen Agreement. There is also some degree of co-operation with the EU in the field of foreign and security policy. Norway is also a full member of EU's research programmes and numerous other programme activities of the EU.

It is easy to imagine that this rather remarkable political context could have impacted on the organisation and operation of Norwegian research on European governance. For instance, the strong political contestation and the deep political and ideological divisions could have led to limited interest in funding studies of European integration and EU governance. Alternatively, the attention could primarily have been centred on issues of special interest for Norway and Norwegian interests in relation to the EU, such as fishery and energy, instead of general European issues. A third foreseeable option is that the deep political polarisation of the Norwegian membership issue could have lead to a politicisation and contestation of the research on EU governance, challenging its legitimacy, and possibly creating instability regarding its financial and organisational foundation.

None of these three options have manifested themselves. During the last decade we have seen a considerable growth in EU governance research in Norway. Rather than being concerned with issues closely related to Norwegian political or economic interests, the Norwegian researchers have addressed theoretical, methodological and conceptual issues that has been on the general European and international research agenda. Finally, rather than having to cope with unstable and shifting financial frameworks, the Norwegian research environment on EU governance has benefited from a relatively stable and long term financial framework.

This development in Norwegian EU governance research is to a large extent a result of key factors in the political context in Norway. The strong and numerous formal and informal linkages between Norway and the EU have created a functional demand for research on EU governance. Since the Norwegian society, economy and political space is so closely interlinked with the EU, research based knowledge has been regarded as important for improving the Norwegian policy towards the EU. In addition, the contested political situation with limited trust has also increased the need for independent, systematic and autonomous production of knowledge and meaning about the developments in Europe and its consequences. One could even argue that the deep political contestation regarding the membership issue has played a sobering function on the researchers and has increased the efforts among scholars to focus on scholarly activities, distance themselves from EU clichés and deliberately avoid normative biases. In short we might say that the political contestation and the distinct political backdrop have provided a push for, and a space for, scientific and academic autonomy. Of course, this gradual 'scientification' of EU governance studies is not unique to Norway. This is part of a trend in all European countries and across a variety of disciplines in the same time period. However, in the Norwegian case it seems particularly obvious that this shift was not only a result of internal academic and scholarly developments, but also to a large extent a result of changing political environments.

INCREASED ATTENTION TO EU GOVERNANCE

Compared to other European countries the Norwegian universities and research milieus were slow in establishing centres of European research and providing teaching and doctoral courses on European integration and governance. In the period from the 1970s until the early 1990s European integration and EU governance was a neglected topic in Norwegian political science. Few worked on the issue, hardly any wrote a PhD in this field, and the libraries did not hold key journals and reference books (Olsen et al 1997).

During the mid-1990s this situation changed. Research picked up in quality and quantity. There was a rapid increase in the number of publications dealing with issues related to European integration. Compared to earlier days, the research was increasingly aimed at a larger audience. Nevertheless, even in the mid-1990s the Norwegian research on European governance was still situational and primarily concerned with the political and social situation in Norway. The key element of the research reflected issues related to the referendum on Norwegian membership in the EU in 1994, as well as being concerned with specific policy effects of a possible Norwegian membership or non-membership in the EU.

At this time there were still some signs indicating a further development of the Norwegian EU governance research. One of the key indicators was that the field of European integration and EU governance started to attract attention from researchers from a variety of political science sub-fields, not just the international relation scholars. Students from public administration, comparative politics as well as sociology and industrial relations were increasingly turning their attention to the issues of European integration and governance.

Ten years later, there is no doubt that there has been a significant increase of research on EU governance. The CONNEX GOVDATA lists 36 projects on various governance issues in Norway. In the period from 1996 until 2005, researchers at just one, though prominent, institution, namely ARENA published 239 academic articles and book chapters, in addition to numerous books. Approximately 80 percent of these publications were published in English or in another non-Nordic language, and most of them dealt with issues related to EU governance in one way or another. In addition, numerous research results and ideas related to EU governance have been published and disseminated through the ARENA working paper series.

During the same period we have also seen a significant increase in the number of doctoral students working in the field of EU governance. Approximately ten PhDs have been completed in political science at the University of Oslo addressing various issues related to European integration and governance. The number is of course marginal compared to other European countries, but it still accounts for about one quarter of the total of doctoral degrees awarded in the period.[2]

ARENA has been the largest research centre and the one that most consistently has focused on issues related to EU governance, but other institutions have also made significant contributions.[3] For instance, researchers at The Norwegian School of Management BI have contributed in particular on issues related to regulatory politics, lobbying and interest representation (Andersen and Eliassen 2001; Eliassen 1998). The Norwegian Institute for International Studies (NUPI) has worked on issues related to the governance of the EU's foreign policy (Rieker 2006). The industrial relations research institute FAFO has worked on the changing role of trade unions and labour market policies in the EU (Dølvik 1997). Researchers at the University of Bergen have contributed to the fields of regulatory politics and administrative adaptations to the emerging multi-level governance system in Europe (Jacobsson et al 2003). In addition, studies at the Centre for European Law at the University of Oslo have contributed with studies of compliance with EU legalisation and governance of the internal market as well as with the legal developments of the EEA institutions.

Measuring the quality of Norwegian research on EU governance goes beyond the scope of this article. In 1999 Phillipe Schmitter argued that the 'works of Johan P. Olsen and (...) the ARENA project have been of major importance in the identification and the analysis of the impact of "Europeanization"' (Schmitter 1999). Whether other scholars agree with his impression is of course unclear. But a bibliographical data search reveals that researchers, such as Svein Andersen, Jeff Checkel, Morten Egeberg, Erik Oddvar Eriksen, Jon Erik Fossum, Andreas Føllesdal, Johan P. Olsen, and Helene Sjursen, to mention some, have had a significant production, and that their work has attracted considerable attention and has been frequently cited. For instance, an article by Johan P. Olsen (Olsen 2002a) on the concept of Europeanisation, as well as an article by Andreas Føllesdal and Simon Hix (Follesdal and Hix 2006) on the democratic deficit have both ranked high on the list of the most cited articles in the Journal of Common Market Studies.[4]

Although this development has been rather remarkable in a Norwegian setting, we should of course keep in mind that the scale and volume of the Norwegian research is still limited and the milieu is vulnerable.

THE ACADEMIC ROOTS AND ROUTES

As an integrated part of the international research community, Norwegian scholars have to a large extent related themselves to the major intellectual discussions in Europe, but there are at least two roots or traditions that have yielded a particularly strong influence on the development of the Norwegian research on EU governance.

The first tradition is represented by the legacy from Stein Rokkan and his colleagues on the emergence of the nation state system in Europe.[5] This work dealt with key questions related to processes of state-building, nation-building, democratisation and redistribution. In this perspective, the European nation states were seen as a result of a special configuration of political, administrative, cultural and religious boundaries. The works of Stein Rokkan on the emergence of the European political map have had significant impact on the Norwegian political science community, and it has been important in influencing both the research questions that were asked, as well as the conceptual and empirical approaches to dynamics of European integration and the transformation of the nation state.

There is a strong linkage between the works of Rokkan, and the related project on small states by Robert Dahl, as well as the recent Norwegian research on EU governance. Much of the research has been concerned about examining how, and to what extent, and through which processes, the stages of state-building and nation-building, which Rokkan identified as crucial in the development of the European nation state, could be rediscovered or identified in the current European transformation. The link is obvious in the concepts and problem formulation that characterised the research profile of ARENA published in 1997.

Partly as a result of this academic legacy, and partly as a result of the Norwegian political history, the Norwegian research on European governance has always been strongly related to question of the future of the nation state, its 'retreat' or 'rescue'. Much of the research has dealt with the validity of such claims. Since Norway is a small and fairly unitary state with an open economy competing in the world markets and a state with a high degree of redistribution, such issues had always been regarded as critical. In addition, since Norway is not a member of the EU, the issue related to the significance of formal membership and formal ties to the EU has continuously been a limited, but still important element of the research focus. However, in spite of these important elements of continuity regarding concepts and research questions, it is noteworthy that the recent Norwegian governance research have never been much occupied with the long historical comparisons, and the large-n studies that was typical and played such a prominent role in the Rokkanian approach.

The second key tradition for Norwegian EU governance research has been the strong link to research on organisational theory and the organisational basis of politics. The works by Herbert Simon and James G. March (March and Simon 1993) have inspired research on the role of organisations in political life and how organisational factors affect decision making, learning, and the conditions for design and change. During a period of more than thirty years, Norwegian political scientists have developed and advanced theories of organisations within this tradition and have developed strong ties across the Atlantic. It is therefore not surprising that the EU governance research has been strongly influenced by this tradition. In fact, a key motivation behind much of the Norwegian EU governance research has been to explore and exploit the possibilities of bringing concepts, theories and methods from the general public administration and organisational theory to the case of European governance. European integration has therefore to a large extent been seen as an experiment for on the one hand, to study the creation and evolution of a new multi-layered and poly-centric governing system, and on the other hand a laboratory for studying how domestic institutions adapt to changes in their tasks and environments.

The linkage to organisational and institutional theory can be easily traced in general and encompassing approaches to the EU (Egeberg 2006; Olsen 2007).[6] It can also be traced in specific studies of the roles and behaviour in EU committees (Trondal 2001; 2004; Trondal and Veggeland 2003)[7]; and in studies examining the prevalence and implications of different organizational principles in the EU (Egeberg 2006[8]; in works regarding the possibilities for institutional design in the EU, in for instance treaty revisions, as well as in the developments of a European administrative space (Olsen 2002b); in relationship to the importance of political labelling and institutional fit in EU decision making (Ugland 2003)[9]; as well in studies of national adaptation and implementation of EU policies (Sverdrup 2003).[10]

These roots have played an important role in skewing the Norwegian research into empirical research focusing primarily on explaining and interpreting the creation, developments and change of institutions and political orders. We find a clear pattern of path-dependency in the approaches and concepts that have been used, but at the same time the transfer of lessons from these traditions into the study of EU governance has also provided an opportunity for critical assessments and new innovations.

There is one significant exception to this path-dependency, namely the more recent research on political theory and the focus on evaluations and justification of the emerging EU governance system. Historically, such normative political theory has played second fiddle to empirically based studies in Norwegian political science. Parts of the normative political theory research has been strongly inspired by the works of Jürgen Habermas, and it has focused in particular on the role of formal legal rights, legal constitutions, and the particular role of deliberation in the emerging European order (Eriksen and Fossum 2000).[11] Some of this research is theoretical, but there are some studies showing how specific norms and ideas have influenced the governance of EU's polices in the field of external affairs, and in its decision to expand and to include new member states (Sjursen 2006).[12] Others have approached issues related to the democratic qualities of the EU governance system from a different analytical approach and angle (Føllesdal 2006).

ORGANISING KNOWLEDGE PRODUCTION

One of the key factors for creating a strong research milieu on EU governance was the decision in the early 1990s to develop a long-term research programme on European integration and its effects on the nation state. This initiative came from a group of researchers in political science, who argued that Norwegian social science was not adapted to the new political situation, and recommended that the Norwegian Research Council initiated a research programme focused on basic research aimed at improving the understandings of the basic dynamics of the current changes in Europe. This initiative later led to the creation of the ARENA programme.

A large part of the dynamics created by ARENA was also caused by the leadership of the centre. Johan P. Olsen, who was already a well-established scholar in public administration and organisational theory, and an experienced leader of research programmes, played a key role in setting up the research centre, designing its research profile, and not least, played a key role in implementing it.

Since 1994 ARENA has had a budget of approximately 1 million Euro per year. Compared with the money spent on EU governance research in other countries this budget is very small. But by the standards of social science research in Norway this amount was generous and significant. Perhaps equally important as the size of the budget, was the time-horizon. The programme had a long term horizon (ten years), which meant that it was possible to set up research groups, recruit researchers (several of them from universities abroad), and to develop a genuine research centre which could attract most of its attention to conducting research. The decision in Norway to set up a research programme focusing on European integration and EU governance was also noticed with interest in other European countries. The creation of the 'Regieren in Europa' programme in Germany and the UK programme 'One Europe or Several' eased the communication and exchanges between governance scholars and increased the internationalisation of the Norwegian research.

CONCLUSIONS

In this brief examination of the Norwegian case, I have highlighted three distinct features that have been particularly influential.

Firstly, the political contestation of the issue of Norway's formal relationship to the EU, and the importance of the EU to the Norwegian government and society created a functional demand for research and knowledge on European integration in the Norwegian society. The polarised political setting created a window of opportunity for academic research that was autonomous and neutral, and it also contributed to skew the research towards the international research agenda.

Secondly, Norwegian research on EU governance has been influenced and inspired by its legacy. Both the state and nation building literature stemming from the Rokkan tradition, and the organisational theory approach, have influenced the research questions that have been asked, the theories and concepts applied, as well as the methods that have been used. However, the EU governance research is not just a passive replication of former findings; instead some of the previous findings have been put to a test in a new international and European political order. With such strong path-dependencies, it is not unexpected that approaches related to for instance formal game-theory have experienced harsher growth conditions.

Thirdly, I have pointed to some elements related to the significance of the organisation of knowledge production for Norwegian research on EU governance. The creation of a research programme, with a long-term financing arrangement, combined with a strong and ambitious academic and administrative leadership has been important to shape the development of Norwegian EU governance research.

Although there are some Norwegian particularities, it is also important to note that the extensive growth of EU governance research is part of larger Pan-European development. A large part of the success of the Norwegian initiatives during the beginning of the 1990s was attributed to the fact that it coincided with initiatives and developments that were taken in other countries. Involvement in the large EU financed networks and programmes related to EU governance, like CIDEL and CONNEX and to some extent NEWGOV, has contributed to link the Norwegian governance research to the larger European research environment. It follows from this contextual approach that the issue of sustainability of the Norwegian research on EU governance is left open. It is beyond doubt that the Norwegian research milieu is limited and vulnerable, compared to the research that is going on in other countries. Although there have been significant improvements in terms of quantity and quality during the last decade, it remains to be seen how robust this research milieu is to changes in its political environment, its financial arrangements, as well as to its leadership and organisation.

NOTES

1. I have decided to focus primarily on the EU governance research that has been conducted at ARENA (Advanced Research on The Europeanization of the Nation State), now the ARENA Centre for European Studies at the University of Oslo. It follows from this that the picture I paint is not the complete picture of Norwegian EU governance research. However, I still believe that this delimitation can be justified by the fact that ARENA has been the largest research centre on European governance in Norway during the last decade, and that it has served as a node for European research in Norway. In addition, during the time of ARENA there has been considerable turnover and exchange of ideas, persons, and research projects between ARENA and other research groups in Norway. Finally, and more pragmatically, since I have been attached to ARENA for quite some time myself, I found it most convenient to focus on the research activity that I know the best.
2. For an overview of the number of PhDs and research themes see: http://www. statsvitenskap.uio.no/fag/polit/disputas/
3. This listing below is just meant as an illustration and could of course be made longer.
4. See here for the list which is continuosly changing http://www.blackwell-synergy.com/ action/showMostCitedArticles?journalCode=jcms&cookieSet=1
5. For an overview of the works of Rokkan see the book edited by Peter Flora, which was also partly financed by ARENA (Flora P. 1999. *State Formation, Nation-Building, and Mass Politics in Europe: The Theory of Stein Rokkan*. London: Oxford University Press.)
6. Project in GOVDATA: 'ARENA'.
7. Project in GOVDATA: 'Integration through Participation in EU committees'.
8. Project in GOVDATA: 'Role behaviour in the College of the European Commission' and 'Role behaviour in the European Commission services'.
9. Project in GOVDATA: 'Europeanization of Nordic Alcohol Control Policies'.
10. Project in GOVDATA: 'Compliance with EU norms – comparing the EU and EEA'.
11. Project in GOVDATA: '(CIDEL) Constitution Making and Legitimacy'.
12. Project in GOVDATA: '(CIDEL) External Security', and '(CIDEL) Justifying Enlargement'.

REFERENCES

Aalberts, Tanja E. (2004), 'The future of sovereignty in multilevel governance Europe – a constructivist reading', *Journal of Common Market Studies*, **42** (1), 23–46.

Aarts, Kees and Henk van der Kolk (2006), 'Understanding the Dutch "No": The Euro, the East, and the Elite', *Political Science and Politics* **39** (2), 243–246.

Andersen, Svein S. and Kjell A. Eliassen (2001), *Making Policy In Europe*, London: Sage Publications Ltd.

Beyers, Jan (2002), 'Gaining and seeking access: the European adaptation of domestic interest associations', *European Journal of Political Research* **41** (5), 585–612.

Beyers, Jan (2004), 'Voice and access: political practices of European interest associations', *European Union Politics* **5** (20), 211–240.

Bovens, Mark (2006), 'Analysing and Assessing Public Accountability. A Conceptual Framework', *European Governance Papers (EUROGOV)*, No. C-06-01.

Brug, Wouter van der and Cees van der Eijk (2007), *European Elections and Domestic Politics: Lessons from the Past and Scenarios for the Future*, Paris: University of Notre Dame Press.

Centraal Planbureau (2002), 'Financiering van wetenschappelijk onderzoek in internationaal perspectief', *CPB Memorandum* 28, The Hague: CPB.

Christiansen, Thomas (1996), 'Second thoughts on Europe's "third level": the European Union's Committee of the Regions', *Publius* **26** (1), 93–116.

Christiansen, Thomas and Emil Kirchner (2000), *Committee governance in the European Union*, Manchester: Manchester University Press.

Christiansen, Thomas, Andreas Follesdal and Simona Piattoni (eds) (2006), *Informal governance in the European Union*, Cheltenham: Edward Elgar.

Cruijsen, Carin van der and Sylvester Eijffinger (2007), 'The economic impact of central bank transparency: a survey', *CentER Discussion paper* 2007–06, Tilburg: CentER, Tilburg University.

Crum, Ben (2005), 'Tailoring representative democracy to the European Union: does the European constitution reduce the democratic deficit?', *European Law Journal* **11** (94), 452–467.

Curtin, Deirdre and André Nollkaemper (2006), 'Conceptualising Accountability in International and European Law', *Netherlands Yearbook of International Law*, **36**, 3–20.

Dølvik, Jon E. (1997), 'Redrawing boundaries of solidarity? ETUC, social dialogue and the Europeanisation of trade unions in the 1990s', *ARENA Report* 5/97/FAFO (report no. 238), Oslo: ARENA.

Egeberg, Morten (ed.) (2006), *Multilevel Union Administration - The transformation of Executive Politics in Europe*, London: Palgrave Macmillan.

Eijk, Cees van der and Mark Franklin (1996), *Choosing Europe? The European Electorate and National Politics in the Face of Union*, Ann Arbor: The University of Michigan Press.

Eliassen, Kjell A. (ed.) (1998), *Foreign and Security Policy in the European Union*, London: Sage Publications Ltd.

Eriksen, Erik O. and John E. Fossum (eds) (2000), *Democracy in the European Union – Integration through deliberation?*, London: Routledge.

Flora, Peter (1999), *State Formation, Nation-Building and Mass Politics in Europe: The Theory of Stein Rokkan*, London: Oxford University Press.

Føllesdal, Andreas and Simon Hix (2006), 'Why There is a Democratic Deficit in the EU: A Response to Majone and Moravcsik', *Journal of Common Market Studies*, **44**, 533–62.

Føllesdal, Andreas (2006), 'Survey Article: The Legitimacy Deficits of the European Union', *Journal of Political Philosophy*, **14**, 441–68.

Groenendijk, Nico (2003), 'Multi-level Governance, Network Governance, and Fiscal Federalism Theory', in Ari Salminen (ed.), *Governing networks*, Amsterdam: IIAS/IOS Press, pp. 349–370.

Groenendijk, Nico (2007), 'Enhanced cooperation: the way-out or a non-starter?', in Nanette Neuwahl and Stefan Haack (eds), *Unresolved Issues of the European Constitution – Rethinking the Crisis*, Montreal: Éditions Thémis, pp. 263–290.

Haverland, Markus and Ronald Holzhacker (2006), *European research reloaded: Cooperation and integration among Europeanized states*, Dordrecht: Springer.

Heere, Wybo P. (ed.) (2003), *From Government to Governance. The Growing Impact of Non-State Actors on the International and European Legal System*, Proceedings of the Sixth Hague Joint Conference held in The Hague, The Netherlands, The Hague: T.M.C. Asser Press.

Hooghe, Liesbeth (ed.) (1996), *Cohesion, policy and European integration: building multi-level governance,* Oxford: Oxford University Press.

Hooghe, Liesbeth (2001), *The European Commission and the Integration of Europe: images of governance*, Cambridge, New York: Cambridge University Press.

Hooghe, Liesbeth and Gary Marks (2000), 'Optimality and authority: a critique of neoclassical theory', *Journal of Common Market Studies*, **38** (5), 795–815.

Hooghe, Liesbeth and Gary Marks (2003), 'Unraveling the Central State, but How? Types of Multi-level Governance', *American Political Science Review*, **97**, 233–243.

Hosli, Madeleine (1996), 'Coalitions and power: effects of qualified majority voting on the Council of the European Union', *Journal of Common Market Studies*, **34** (20), 255–274.

Hosli, Madeleine and Hannu Nurmi (2003), 'Which decision rule for the future Council?', *European Union Politics*, **4** (1), 37–50.

Hosli, Madeleine and Robert Thomson (2006), 'Who has power in the EU? The Commission, Council and Parliament in legislative decisionmaking', *Journal of Common Market Studies*, **44** (2), 391–417.

Hosli, Madeleine and Tanja Börzel (2003), 'Brussels between Bern and Berlin: comparative federalism meets the European Union', *Governance*, **16** (2), 179–202.

Hosli, Madeleine, Christine Arnold, Michael Laver and Kenneth Benoit (2005), 'Measuring national delegate positions at the convention on the future of Europe using computerized word scoring', *European Union Politics*, **6** (3), 291–313.

Jacobsson, Bengt, Per Lægreid and Ove K. Pedersen (2003), *Europeanization and Transnational States: Comparing Nordic Central Government*, London: Routledge.

Kersbergen, Kees van and Frans van Waarden (2001), *Shifts in Governance: Problems of Legitimacy and Accountability*, Background Study on the Theme 'Shifts in Governance' as Part of the Strategic Plann 2002–2005 of the Netherlands Organization for Scientific Research (NWO), The Hague: NWO-MAGW; Social Science Research Council.

Kersbergen, Kees van and Frans van Waarden (2004), '"Governance" as a bridge between disciplines: Cross-disciplinary inspiration regarding shifts in governance and problems of governability, accountability and legitimacy', *European Journal of Political Research*, 43, 143–171.

Mair, Peter (2005), 'Popular Democracy and the European Union Polity', *European Governance Papers (EUROGOV)*, No. C-05-03.

March James G. and Herbert A. Simon (1993), *Organizations*, Cambridge, MA: Blackwell.

Marks, Gary (1996a), *Governance in the European Union*, London: Thousand Oaks, CA: Sage Publications Ltd.

Marks, Gary (1996b), 'An actor-centred approach to multilevel governance', *Regional and federal studies*, **6** (2), 20–40.

Marks, Gary and Liesbeth Hooghe (2006), 'Europe's blues: Theoretical soul-searching after the rejection of the European constitution', *Political science & politics*, **39** (2), 247–250.

Marks, Gary and Marco R. Steenbergen (eds) (2004), *European Integration and Political Conflict*, Cambridge: Cambridge University Press.

Mayntz Renate (2005), 'Embedded Theorizing – Perspectives on Globalization and Global Governance', *MPIfG Discussion paper* 05.

Nollkaemper, André and Erika de Wet (2004), 'The application of customary international law by national courts: Introduction', *Non-State Actors and International Law*, **4**, 1–2.

Olsen, Johan P., Ulf Sverdrup and Frode Veggeland (1997), 'A Survey of Norwegian Political Science Research on European Integration and Co-operation: 1994–1997', *Rep. Working paper No 12/1997.* [A shorter version was published in G. Ciavarini Azzi (ed.), *Survey of Current Political Science Research on European Integration Worldwide: 1994–97*, published by International Political Science Association., Oslo: ARENA].

Olsen, Johan P. (2002a), 'The Many Faces of Europeanization', *Journal of Common Market Studies*, **40**, 921–952.

Olsen, Johan P. (2002b), 'Towards a European Administrative Space?', *Journal of European Public Policy*, **10**, 506–531.

Olsen, Johan P. (2007), *Europe in Search of Political Order*, Oxford: Oxford University Press.

Rieker Pernille (2006), *Europeanization of national security identity: The EU and the changing security identities of the Nordic states*, London: Routledge.

Schendelen, Rinus Van (2002), *Machiavelli in Brussels: the art of lobbying the EU*, Amsterdam: Amsterdam University Press.

Schmitt, Hermann and Jacques Thomassen (eds) (1999), *Political Representation and Legitimacy in the European Union*, Oxford: Oxford University Press.

Schmitt, Hermann and Jacques Thomassen (2000), 'Dynamic Representation: the Case of European Integration', *European Union Politics*, **1** (3), 318–339.

Schmitter, Philippe C. (1999), 'Reflections on the Impact of the European Union upon "Domestic" Democracy in its Member States', in Morten Egeberg and Per Lægreid (eds), *Organizing Political Institutions – Essays for Johan P. Olsen*, Oslo: Scandinavian University Press, pp. 289–298.

Semetko, Holli A., Claes H. de Vreese and Jochen Peter (2000), 'Europeanised politics – Europeanised media? European integration and political communication', *West European Politics*, **23** (4), 121–141.

Sjursen Helene (ed.) (2006), *Questioning EU Enlargement: Europe in Search of Identity.* London: Routledge.

Steunenberg, Bernard (ed.) (2002), *Widening the European Union: The politics of institutional change and reform*, London: Routledge.

Steunenberg, Bernard (2003), 'Deciding among equals: The sectoral Councils of the European Union and their reform', in M.J. Holler, H. Kliemt, D. Schmidtchen and M. E. Streit (eds), *European Governance*, Tübingen: Mohr Siebeck.

Steunenberg, Bernard, Christian Koboldt and Dieter Schmidtchen (2000), 'Beyond comitology: A comparative analysis of implementation procedures with parliamentary involvement', in Peter Moser, Gerald Schneider and Gebhard Kirchgässner (eds), *Decision rules in the European Union: A rational choice prespective*, Houndsmills, Basingstoke: Palgrave Macmillan.

Stokman, Frans and Robert Thomson (2004), 'Winners and Losers in the European Union', *European Union Politics*, **5** (1), 5–23.

Stokman, Frans, Robert Thompson, Cristopher H. Achen and Thomas Koenig (eds) (2006), *The European Union decides*, Cambridge: Cambridge University Press.

Sverdrup, Ulf (2003), 'Compliance and Conflict Management in the European Union: Nordic Exceptionalism', *Scandinavian Political Studies*, **27**, 23–43.

Thomassen, Jacques J.A., Abdul G. Noury and Erik Voeten (2004), 'Political Competition in the European Parliament: Evidence from Roll Call and Survey Analysis', in Gary Marks and Marco R. Steenbergen (eds), *European Integration and Political Conflict*, Cambridge: Cambridge University Press.

Thomson, Robert, Jovanka Boerefijn and Frans Stokman (2004), 'Actor alignments in European Union decision-making', *European Journal of Political Research*, **43** (2), 273–261.

Trondal, Jarle (2001), *Administrative integration across levels of governance: integration through participation in EU committees*, Oslo: ARENA report.

Trondal, Jarle (2004), 'Re-socializing Civil Servants. The Transformative Powers of EU Institutions', *Acta Politica*, **39**, 4–30.

Trondal, Jarle and Frode Veggeland (2003), 'Access, Voice and Loyalty. The Representation of Domestic Civil Servants in EU Committees', *Journal of European Public Policy*, **10**, 65–83.

Ugland, Trygve (2003), 'Adaptation and Integration through Policy Re-categorization', *Journal of Public Policy*, **23**, 157–70.

Vanhoonacker, Sophie and Simon Duke (2006), 'Administrative governance in CFSP: development and practice', *European foreign affairs review*, **11** (2), 163–182.

Verbeek, Bertjan and Kees van Kersbergen (2004), 'Subsidiarity as a principle of governance in the European Union', *Comparative European Politics*, **2** (2), 142–162.

Vreese, Claes H. de, Susan A. Banducci, Holli A. Semetko and Hajo G. Boomgaarden (2006), 'The news coverage of the 2004 European Parliamentary election campaign in 25 countries', *European Union Politics*, **7** (4), 477–504.

Wessel, Ramses, Andreas Follesdal and Jan Wouters (eds.) (2007), *Multilevel Regulation and the EU: The Interplay between Global, European and National Normative Processes*, Leiden: Martinus Nijhoff Publishers.

Wet, Erika de (2006), 'The International Constitutional Order', *International and Comparative Law Quarterly*, **55** (1), 51–76.

6. Small Countries with Vivid Social Science Traditions: Austria, Belgium, Denmark, Finland, Sweden and Switzerland

Stefanie Edler-Wollstein and Gerda Falkner

INTRODUCTION

When compared to other small countries in Europe, the array of countries covered in this chapter stand out for their solid and long-term tradition in academic research, not least in the social sciences (OECD; Klingemann).[1] Over the last decade, teaching and research in the social sciences in general and EU studies in particular have been significantly expanded and these small countries have contributed substantially to the literature on the EU (Azzi; Wessels).

Research in many countries of this group is mainly carried out at universities, where it tends to be incorporated in the traditions of faculties and departments. In addition, non-university research centres (especially in Austria and Belgium) and private institutes (notably in Denmark) have recently gained importance and contributed to the broad field of EU matters. In regard to infrastructure and financial resources, the context conditions for social science research are very similar. Due to the size of these countries, the number of universities is limited and academic communities are small, but the standard of information facilities is rather high in comparison. Well-equipped university library systems as well as specialized European Documentation Centres offer a broad range of international literature and access to databases on EU related topics. Regarding project funding, compared to the level of financial resources of South and Eastern European countries, support from regional and national research funds is higher in this group of countries and access to international funding programs is more widely used.[2]

Another common structural feature is a distinct international orientation. In the last decade the small domestic academic markets have become more open, and overall political scientists from these small countries are well-integrated into the international scientific community. This is reflected, for instance, in their representation in the editorial advisory boards of relevant international journals.[3] Likewise, the number of participating scholars from this group of countries in international conferences such as ECPR, epsNET, IPSA, EUSA or APSA is growing throughout, which represents a further active contribution to the international debate and the production of knowledge. However, although an increasing number of national scholars are enrolled in international PhD programmes or pursue their careers in other countries, the universities and research institutes in these small countries are only just beginning to attract more researchers from abroad, with Austria and Switzerland cutting-edge in this regard.

Against this general background of similar features, it is the chapter's ambition to account for both similarities and differences in EU-related governance research executed in the six countries. It seems plausible to assume that the comparatively good general conditions for social science research had a similar positive effect on research in the field of EU governance and that differences should be attributed to other factors. Comparing governance research in Belgium and Denmark, which have been EU members since 1957 and 1973 respectively, to research in Austria, Finland and Sweden, which accessed the EU in 1995, or in Switzerland as a non-member, will provide evidence on the impact of the length of membership. Additionally, it is conceivable that national political preoccupations and the importance attached to the EU in each country will add a particular perspective. From this point of view, we will discuss if EU governance research in these small countries is biased towards projects illuminating issues of particular domestic interest, or if they are rather absorbed by the international research agenda for various reasons.

Since the chapter is largely based on the national reports and the research projects assembled in the data base, it does not present a full picture of EU-related research in the six countries but is focused on the attention given to the topic of EU multilevel governance.

COMPARISON OF RESEARCH IN AUSTRIA, BELGIUM, DENMARK, FINLAND, SWEDEN AND SWITZERLAND

It is crucial to underline at this stage that we do not know how complete the database really is and how big the difference in coverage between the countries is. Although overly deterministic conclusions should not be drawn from the findings presented in the following, the data provide a broad overview and telling indicators, from which general tendencies of the development of EU governance research in these countries become apparent and can be compared.

Number of Projects

A total number of 1 646 projects have been covered in the CONNEX database, from 29 countries covered and there are only a few countries responsible for more than 100 projects each (that is the UK, Germany, Spain and Poland). Taking a look at these numbers gives a first general impression of the scope of the research carried out. The group of countries studied in this chapter all together collected 225 research projects on recent and ongoing research on EU multi-level governance. Among the six countries, Austria reported 76 projects, which is 4.6 per cent of all the projects and thus ranks sixth place overall together with the Netherlands.[4] Belgium follows on place 13 (2.7 per cent), Denmark on place 15 (2.4 per cent), Switzerland on place 18 (1.6 per cent), Sweden on place 20 (1.6 per cent), and Finland on place 23 (0.9 per cent) of 30 places overall.

Compared to the number of inhabitants[5], it is again the Austrian part of the database that shows most projects (8.7 per 1 million inhabitants). Second comes Denmark (6.8) followed by Belgium (4.1), Switzerland (3.5), Sweden (2.7), and Finland (2.6). Were the UK and Germany among the group studied here, they would actually not be in the lead if the number of projects were weighed, to pay attention to the number of inhabitants, for they only have 3.1 (UK) and 1.8 (D) per 1 million in the database.

Change over time

Paying attention to the changing patterns of research activity over time provides an indication of the factors fostering or restraining the development of governance research.

When looking at the years when the individual research projects started, it is noticeable that only Denmark has a significant proportion of projects starting before 1994 (13.5 per cent or five projects), followed by Switzerland and Belgium with about 7 per cent each. Sweden has one project out of 25 in total, Austria and Finland have no such projects entered in the database.

Considering that Denmark is an old EU member state, the comparatively early interest in governance research might have been boosted by a 'new approach to studying European governance' (Bogason and Thomsen 2006, p. 2) at the early 1990s. On the other hand, the Danish report emphasizes that for structural reasons, that is, a research structure according to university disciplines, the subject most often has been merely a by-product from 'ordinary EU research, which then happens to include a multilevel perspective [or] from governance research, which happens to include the EU' (Bogason and Thomsen 2006, p. 3).

Switzerland and Belgium also list a comparatively higher number of old projects. In the Swiss case this seems noteworthy, since Switzerland is not an EU member. In both countries, however, their federal structure might have been a driving force, accounting for a higher interest in questions of regional representation. This can be acknowledged, for example, in the Belgian project 'Regions in the European Union' (10.1994–09.1998) which examined sub-national influences on the European decision–making process. In addition, Belgium's detailed country report concludes that in the decade studied, Belgian research on European multilevel governance 'not only *widened* but also *deepened*. A growing group of researchers borrowed these concepts and insights and the initial focus on *multilevel* was broadened to include *governance* [and] research has been conducted in a more systematic and analytical way' (Kerremans et al. 2006).

If one were to view the overall development of projects over time, one could divide the time into two intervals of five years: 1996–2000 (Phase I) and 2001–2005 (Phase II).[6] The bird's-eye view shows that the number of research projects grows over the time: 42.5 per cent (85 projects) started in the first period and 57.5 per cent (115) in the second period. Two countries, however, do not share this development in the number of started projects. Austria had more projects starting from 1996 to 2000 (38) than from 2001 to 2005 (33), and Finland had a decrease from 8 (Phase I) to 6 projects (Phase II).

Austria's report presents multi-level governance as becoming 'an established subject of research especially in political science' (Falkner, Michalowitz and Tajalli 2006, 25). The database shows that 71 per cent of the projects from Austria took place within the political science discipline; this is despite the fact that political science was only institutionalized in the 1960's. Another point is that although in Austria an expert in European integration became the first Austrian chair in political science, EU studies still only became a popular topic in the 1990s. This aspect has more than likely got a strong connection with Austria's accession to the EU. However, it seems that the boom of EU-related projects right after membership in 1995 could not be matched later even considering the Ministry's specific call for projects.[7] It seems that the special program actually produced a shift in projects towards a fresh source of money rather than strictly additional research, or that other sources of research funding gave less for topics covered within this database.

One might assume that in Finland, the tendency that there was an initial boost in EU studies directly after its accession was similar. A further explanation might be that Finnish political science as a discipline went through a period of overall restructuring, which started in 1995 and is still on-going (Berndtson 2007). Within this process the discipline was not only under increasing financial pressure, but met with an increased internal and external fragmentation, there was 'a lack of consensus on methodology and theory' and 'a tendency of the discipline's sub-fields to attempt to create new disciplines with their own identities' (ibid. 104) which might have contributed to the decrease of projects. However, researchers will have to wait some years to see if this will be a continuous decreasing trend.

Thematic orientation

Since EU research in these small countries is concentrated geographically to the limited number of universities and carried out by a small number of researchers, there is only a limited capacity to cover multi-level governance studies as a research interest in its own right, which suggests that the thematic orientation will often depend on the research focus of individual scholars. Assessing the thematic agenda in each country allows for a comparison of further influencing factors on governance research.

Generally speaking, the long tradition of theory-driven empirical research in the social sciences in most of the countries under consideration is reflected in the strong empirical focus of the EU research. The international literature and the main paradigms of the field are known, used and continually added to. In spite of the empirical emphasis, the majority of projects lean towards knowledge oriented basic research rather than applied research.

Despite these general similarities, the keywords given to research projects (multiple entries possible) show quite differential foci among the six countries (see also the country-specific sections) although 'policy' is the most commonly used keyword. This is not however any different to all the other countries in the database, where the overall top keyword was also 'policy'. The most frequently studied dimension across the six countries is 'governance and decision making' (43.5 per cent of all projects). When taking a closer look at the reported projects which specifically refer to 'EU multi-level governance' in the project title or abstract, we find that in Denmark, Finland and Switzerland approximately half of all projects use the term in the title or abstract; in Belgium it is one third and in Austria and Sweden approximately one fifth of all projects. As far as thematic dimensions are concerned, this could be read as a first indication of the differing permeation of the concept. The national reports, however, present a more differentiated picture for each country as follows.

The Swedish country report underlines 'an overall reasonably good balance between theoretical awareness and empirical research' (Gustavsson 2006, p. 6). With regard to thematic orientation, Sweden is 'well integrated in the European and American discussion on federalism, neo-functionalism and intergovernmentalism' (Gustavsson 2006, p. 5). Yet, the author of the national report sees a blank spot in the field of research following a broader paradigm of comparative federalism, rather than pointing to the notion of *sui generis* in the context of European integration (Gustavsson 2006, p. 9). Historical factors (for example, Sweden did not take part in World War II) reportedly explain why the debate within the country during 40 years 'focussed so much upon the meaning, explanation and justification of multilevel governance. In that way our foreign policy history played a role in defining the problem so important in the present debate on the legitimacy of the suprastate' (Gustavsson 2006, p. 2). The national experience of local government inside a unitary state and of a strong role for the social partners in labour market regulation 'is giving a special touch to Swedish research on the substantive aspects of EU multilevel governance' (Gustavsson 2006, p. 5). The projects listed in the database confirm this assessment regarding the thematic orientation. For example, eight out of 23 projects include the keyword 'legitimacy'.

The Belgian country report emphasizes the great 'almost natural' (Kerremans et al. 2006) interest in multi-level governance and in issues of regional actor involvement: 'Research paid attention to the representation and participation of regional actors in EU decision- and policy-making, especially to the involvement of these actors in the determination of the Belgian position in the Council of Ministers. Here, an important research focus has been the practice of coordination, especially the domestic coordination mechanisms in policy domains like environment, agriculture and social policy' (Kerremans et al. 2006). These were among the fields that were transferred from national to regional level when Belgium became a federal state in 1993. Therefore, the thematic orientation of research 'focusing on the *institutional architecture* of governance' (Kerremans et al. 2006) might be explained in part by Belgium's political development.

Austria's report highlights 'a wide variety of thematic approaches to the topic of multilevel governance in Europe' (Falkner, Michalowitz and Tajalli 2006, p. 25). Among the focal points are the influence of the regions on the European level, the enlargement process (see the projects 'Between Deepening and Enlargement: how the process of eastern enlargement is influencing the process of constitutionalisation of the European Union – a Polish view' (10.2002–09.2006) and 'Dead Letter or Living Rights? The Practice of EU Social Law in Central and Eastern Europe' (04.2005–11.2006)) and the question of democratic accountability (see the projects 'Democratizing the European Union' (02.2003–02.2006) and 'Constitutionalism and Democratic Representation in the European Union' (04.2001–04.2003)). This is seen to relate to the special conditions of Austria, that is its recent membership, the proximity to even newer member states, and Austria being a federal republic. These issues, which are widely discussed in the public, are hence unsurprisingly also subject to scientific scrutiny.

Finland's specific research interests are shaped in part by its history, political culture and geographic position between Sweden and Russia, which might have fostered the emphasis on questions of European integration (Berndtson 2007, 105). The project 'Migrants, Minorities, Belonging and

Citizenship: Globalization and Participation Dilemmas in the EU and Small States' (01.2003–12.2006), for instance, focuses on small states at the fringes of the EU in regard to the citizenship dimension of the relations between the European Union and its member states and associated countries. Many projects deal with European integration from a Finnish perspective, as for example, 'Europeanization in Finnish Politics and Administration' (dates of project not available) or 'Legislative scrutiny of the EU matters in Finland' (07.1997–01.1999). Normative issues such as topics of EU governance research are not discussed in the country report. Legitimacy and democracy were in fact hardly mentioned in the list of the projects' thematic dimensions, as the figures in the database show. The increasing frequency of cooperation with researchers from abroad, most importantly in EU projects, seems however to promote an increasingly pan-European perspective. The Finnish research policy is said to generally encourage internationalization and particularly EU participation (Kemilä 2006, p. 6).

The Danish country report underlines the relevance of the perspective of the EU as a 'multilevel governance system' and a 'networked polity' (Bogason and Thomsen 2006, p. 10). The nature of the impact of the EU upon national political structures is still a much debated subject in Denmark, recently amplified by the latest enlargement rounds. The ubiquity of the topic seems to have spurred a deeper interest that is followed up by a few individual researchers (Bogason and Thomsen 2006, p. 3). Europeanization and intra-EU diversity are on the Danish agenda; two out of 39 Danish projects in the database touch issues of integration and identity. Normative questions about legitimacy are at the core of nine projects.

In Switzerland, two of the most important university institutes – the European Institute of the University of Geneva and the Europainstitut of the University of Basel – focus on the process of European Integration, but overall, they 'have remained generalist in their coverage' (Freymond, Platel and Voutat 2007, p. 372). With Switzerland not being an EU member, the Swiss report concludes that 'interest in the EU and multilevel governance is limited but present' (Braun 2006, p. 6). However, despite the (small) national scientific community not being very interested in EU research, the topic of multilevel governance is 'well presented in Switzerland, above all because of interest into the federal structure' (Braun 2006). This already hints at the main thematic orientation. However, similar to the Finnish case, Switzerland's historical development and political culture might have spurred the Swiss interest in multi-level governance in the EU's external relations. For example, the project 'Inside-Out – New Modes of Governance in EU-Relations with Non-Member States' (10.2004–08.2008) provides an external view to the integration project.

Research by discipline

Looking at the projects in the database by discipline will shed light on the question of whether academic traditions in terms of disciplinary or interdisciplinary orientation have an impact in directing the research.

In each of the six cases under review, political science is by far the strongest discipline within the database. The relatively lowest ratio is in Switzerland, which however still shows 61.5 per cent of political science hits (Austria: 73.5 per cent; Finland: 85.7 per cent; Denmark: 94.6 per cent). Law, in turn, is relatively strongest in Switzerland (46.2 per cent), Austria (29.2 per cent) and Belgium (27.9 per cent) while all other countries show less than 10 per cent of their entries with a law specialization. Sociology is again relatively strongest in Switzerland (26.9 per cent) followed by Finland (21.4 per cent), Austria (18.1 per cent), Belgium (16.3 per cent) and Denmark with 8.1 per cent. The share of economics is more than 10 per cent of the entries in the database (Denmark with 18.9 per cent, Austria with 12.5 per cent and Switzerland with 11.5 per cent), but history doesn't pass the 10 per cent threshold and philosophy doesn't even pass the 5 per cent mark.

These results show Switzerland to be quite different to the other five countries in terms of disciplines. On the one hand, this reflects the historical tradition within the social sciences in Switzerland, where at the end of the 19th century the insights from public law, history, economics and philosophy have been synthesized into the research on governance (Freymond, Platel and Voutat 2007, 361). From a more recent perspective, the higher proportion of contributions from other disciplines can also be read to show that studies on the legal consequences of (further) integration steps are much more prominent in this country, which remains outside of both the EU and the EEA and relies solely on bilateral treaties (see also Braun 2006, p. 6). As indicated in the report, almost all of the Swiss universities have institutes or Chairs dealing with European law and it seems to be an area which is widely discussed in general in Switzerland. Although it is difficult to pin this down as a definite difference because so few projects were gathered on the whole, it was also mentioned that there is, in particular, one law researcher in Switzerland who is responsible for four of the seven projects in the law discipline. This could suggest that the high percentage of projects in the law discipline is purely due to a singular interest by one person.

It should be stated here that it seems wholly possible that the relative stronghold of political scientists within those collecting the data may have led to a certain bias. At the same time, we should keep in mind that the CONNEX definition of recent and ongoing research on EU multi-level governance might exclude some specific disciplinary work, for example, legal, if the latter does not tackle issues within the thematic structure of CONNEX which focuses on the institutional architecture of European multi-level governance, on enhancing democracy in European governance, on new governance instruments, and on civil society involvement in European multi-level governance. This may exclude, inter alia, work that rather narrowly looks at how certain fields of domestic law (for example, foodstuff regulation) might be affected by EU regulation. But in any case, governance issues (and particularly in the definition of our database) certainly are above all political science concerns, so that our results are hardly surprising.

Publication output

All six countries looked at in this chapter are smaller countries and for this reason one might expect that all the publications would show a tendency towards publishing in English. However, in that regard there are also differences amongst these countries.

The three northern European countries, Denmark, Finland and Sweden appear to concentrate on publishing in English. Both the Swedish and the Danish reports noted that 80 per cent of projects were published in English and also the Finnish report – though not giving any numbers – confirms that the emphasis is on English.

The three other countries, Austria, Belgium and Switzerland, seem to be less dependent on English as a publishing language. The Swiss report indicates that English publishing took place in 50 per cent of the cases. The Belgian report states that younger researchers and Flemish researchers are now concentrating increasingly on English but that the relation of English to French publications is still about even. 'Although English has also be winning ground in the French community, here, a better balance has been kept between foreign (English) and native (French) language publications' (Kerremans et al. 2006). In Austria, more than half the publications were written in German, although there are indications that English is also gaining ground there.

The cause of the disparity in publishing language between these small countries is an interesting point. The reports and data would suggest that across the board there is an increasing tendency towards publishing in English, as stated in the Belgium report, 'writing in English increases the accessibility of work pieces and publications, including those presented at international conferences' (Kerremans et al. 2006, p. 9). However it would seem that the countries that belong, at least partially, to a larger language family, that is, French or German, still opt to use their national language in many publications since there exists a considerable amount of political science literature in these two languages. This may encourage researchers to keep with their own language as they know that their publications will still be read internationally. There are also several journals which publish solely, or at least largely, in French or German. The main political science journal in Switzerland even accepts articles in four languages. In contrast, the three northern countries are not only smaller; there languages are also not particularly wide-spread. It is clear that a researcher in one of these countries must publish in a more widely spoken language if they wish to have their work discussed or to communicate on their subject beyond their own borders. The national reports also further strengthened this point by indicating that these three countries mainly published in international journals.

As far as the number of projects is concerned, the database shows Austria to be the leader of the six countries mentioned here. It is impossible to establish, however, if this outstanding number (which is also confirmed on the level of projects per 1 million inhabitants: 8.7) results from relatively more relevant research indeed executed in this country, or from particularly severe efforts of the Austrian CONNEX team to include many if not all existing projects (for example, by contacting relevant institutes and researchers several times). Also, when looking at the actual level of publication output, arising from this large number of projects it is disappointing to see that more than half of the Austrian projects in multi-level governance go unpublished. It is also striking that very few authors account for almost all publications, particularly those in international journals. One reason could be that until recently, Austrian political science research generally tended to be rather introverted and almost exclusively published using the German language (Falkner, Michalowitz and Tajalli 2006). Looking at the (mostly very recent) publications entered in the database, no clear patterns can be seen where and how the publications are placed. An interesting feature is the distribution of languages used for publishing: 15 articles were published in German, 14 in English, and one publication (per language) is found to be published in Hungarian, Slovenian, and Bulgarian. The publications in Eastern European languages are linked to relevant thematic projects but may also show that this part of Europe is of special importance for Austrian researchers (Falkner, Michalowitz and Tajalli 2006, 21).

The Belgian report indicates 46 projects and 87 per cent of these projects are reported to have publications. The publication output in Belgium is influenced by reasons related to employment and promotions, and hence ensues mostly in peer reviewed international journals or edited books. There is no Belgian publisher specializing in political science publications solely, but the universities publish a number of social science periodicals in Dutch, French and some in English (De Winter, Frognier, Dezeure, Berck, and Brans 2007, p. 68).

Denmark is shown to be the country among the six with the highest percentage of actual publications from the projects entered in the database (37 out of 39). This is despite the fact that there is 'a research structure based on university disciplines which does not promote multilevel governance research' (Bogason and Thomsen 2006, p. 3).

Switzerland and Sweden show very similar figures as far as project and publication output is concerned, with about 60 per cent of projects being published. The author of the Swedish report considers this a 'comparatively small output' to be explained by the relatively small size and hence also a small scientific community (Gustavsson 2006, p. 6). In comparison to other countries, however, the same situation applies and their publication output is still higher. It might be added, that due to the Swedish universities' response to a growing demand, Swedish university lecturers have the highest teaching load in Scandinavia and, thus, less time for research (Berglund and Ekman 2007, 345).

Theoretical and methodological issues

Although the subject of theoretical and methodological issues is not intensely discussed in the national reports, it seems logical to assume that they play a considerable role in the research agenda of countries that are generally expected to have rather strong social science traditions.

This hypothesis appears confirmed by the three Nordic countries of our sample. Undergraduate and post-graduate education in Denmark, Sweden and Finland traditionally puts a very strong emphasis on research methodology and theory. Supposedly, the Nordic research community is channelled from the beginning into a way of thinking which proves fruitful for the international theoretical debate on European integration theory (Miles and Mörth 2002). Taking a look at the projects in the database, in Denmark theoretical and methodological issues seem to be an integral part of most projects (64 per cent). Eleven per cent of the projects entered in the database is purely theoretical, for example 'Is economic analysis of any help in studies of legitimacy in the EU?' (12.1999–06.2004), which looks at institutional perspectives on how democratic legitimacy is built, or 'The Centre of democratic Network Governance' (01.2003–12.2007), which analyzes the uses of concepts and typologies linked to governance networks.

The Belgian national report also suggests that theoretical and methodological issues play an increasing role. It is said that research developed from rather descriptive projects towards theory-driven analysis, now often from a comparative perspective (Kerremans et al. 2006, p. 10–11). 'The European Union as external environmental actor: an analysis of the internal policy-making process' (10.2003–09.2008), is a project which fits that description as it combines principal-agent theory with sociological institutionalist insights in order to examine and compare a sample of EU policy-making processes.

CONCLUSION

All countries studied in this chapter are very similar in regard to the overall level of social science research they carry out and they benefit from advantageous general conditions for research. Yet, as has been shown by illuminating the subject from various angles, *contrasting images* of European governance research are clearly discernable.

Our final reflection is concerned with the question whether EU governance research in these small countries is absorbed by the international research agenda or if these countries are rather leaning towards projects of particular domestic interest. Based on our comparison it can be stated that all countries studied show specific interest in a number of issues that are closely related to internal affairs. This is true for the role of regions in multilevel governance in Belgium, Denmark and Austria, for issues of selective policy adaptation in Switzerland, and for local government and social partnership in Sweden.

At the same time, however, a number of country reports highlight an increasing emersion of the domestic scientific communities into the international one. In the longer run, this could well bring about more absorption by the 'supranational' research agenda. In actual fact, a few country reports already point to such phenomena (for example, Belgium and Austria). In that sense, the internationalization of the scientific community, for instance via 'must go' conferences worldwide, EU research programs, the incoming European Science Foundation, and so on could induce a reorientation in the interests of the researchers – something quite similar to the neo-functionalist spill-over logic expected in early integration theory.

It remains to be seen if there are also countervailing factors, and what their relative strength can be. To some extent, in any case, national funding (at least from governmental sources) will probably always stay geared towards studies researching specific domestic facets and problems. Some EU governance research could therefore still continue to work outside the new mainstream of the international agenda, at least in the more applied research areas.

NOTES

1.   Another chapter is dedicated to Norway and the Netherlands, two countries that also would fit very well in the above-mentioned category but stand out in terms of having provided special input to EU governance research.
2.   According to the Govdata database, the proportion of research projects which receive external funding from public authorities at regional, national or European level, foundations, etc, is 42 per cent in Austria, 84 per cent in Belgium, 66 per cent in Denmark, 78 per cent in Finland, 87 per cent in Sweden and 80 per cent in Switzerland. This compares to, for example, 35 per cent in Portugal, 39 per cent in Spain, 37 per cent in Russia or 8 per cent in Poland.

3. In the editorial advisory boards of four of the most prominent English language journals focusing on 'EU politics' (*European Foreign Affairs Review, European Union Politics, Journal of European Integration, Journal of European Public Policy*), 5 members are from Belgium, 3 from Switzerland, 2 from Sweden, 1 from Denmark and 1 from Austria. In addition, European Integration online Papers is published by ECSA-Austria.
4. While the European University Institute is covered as a separate unit in the database we exclude it from the country ranking.
5. Source: Eurostat (http://epp.eurostat.ec.europa.eu), Data for 2005. Last view: 2006-12-14.
6. Note that the sum will not add up to 100 per cent for some projects from 1994 and before are part of the database, and for Belgium some projects are included which started as late as 2005.
7. The research programme >node< (New Orientations for Democracy in Europe; 2002–2006) of the Austrian Federal Ministry for Science and Research (http://www.node-research.at) revolved around the possibilities and options for the realisation of modern democracy in the EU.

REFERENCES

Berglund, Sten and Joakim Ekman (2007), 'The Current State of Political Science in Sweden', in Hans-Dieter Klingemann (ed.), *The State of Political Science in Western Europe*, Opladen: Barbara Budrich Publishers, pp. 341–360.

Berndtson, Erkki (2007), 'The Current State of Political Science in Finland', in Hans-Dieter Klingemann (ed.), *The State of Political Science in Western Europe*, Opladen: Barbara Budrich Publishers, pp. 103–136.

Bogason, Peter and Jannie Thomsen (2006), *Research on EU multilevel governance in Denmark: A state of research*, Mannheim. http://www.connex-network.org/govdata/reports/Report-Denmark.pdf.

Braun, Dietmar (2006), *Research on EU multilevel governance in Switzerland: A state of research*, Mannheim. http://www.connex-network.org/govdata/reports/Report-Switzerland.pdf.

De Winter, Lieven, André-Paul Frognier, Karolien Dezeure, Anee-Sylvie Berck, and Marleen Brans (2007), 'Belgium: From One to Two Political Sciences?', in Hans-Dieter Klingemann (ed.), *The State of Political Science in Western Europe*, Opladen: Barbara Budrich Publishers, pp. 57–71.

Falkner, Gerda, Irina Michalowitz and Eric Tajalli (2006), *Research on EU multilevel governance in Austria: A state of research*, Mannheim. http://www.connex-network.org/govdata/reports/Report-Austria.pdf.

Freymond, Nicolas, Christophe Platel, and Bernard Voutat (2007), 'The State of Political Science in Switzerland in Teaching and Research', in Hans-Dieter Klingemann (ed.), *The State of Political Science in Western Europe*, Opladen: Barbara Budrich Publishers, pp. 359–379.

Gustavsson, Sverker (2006), *Research on EU multilevel governance in Sweden: A state of research*, Mannheim. http://www.connex-network.org/govdata/reports/Report-Sweden.pdf.

Kemilä, Sampo (2006), *Research on EU multilevel governance in Finland: A state of research*, Mannheim. http://www.connex-network.org/govdata/reports/Report-Finland.pdf.

Kerremans, Bart, Edith Drieskens, Karoline Van den Brande and Tom Delreux (2006), *Research on EU multilevel governance in Belgium : A state of research*, Mannheim. http://www.connex-network.org/govdata/reports/Report-Belgium.pdf

Miles, Lee and Ulrika Mörth (2002), 'Nordic Political Science and the Study of European Integration', *Journal of European Public Policy*, **9** (3), 488–495.

7.   Europe's South:
Similarities and Differences in
Governance Research

Fabrice Larat

Country-clustering is a hazardous undertaking. Due to the fact that everything is relative, even the use of geographical terms or cardinal points can be misleading. The countries analysed in this chapter, France, Italy, Spain, Portugal and Greece reveal a number of common features in regard to the level and thematic orientation of their research activities on EU governance. Obviously, they are located in the Southern part of Europe, however, Europe's South does not mean a specific sub-region or a well delimited and homogenous area *per se*. It is, therefore, important to find the cluster's appropriate denomination before discussing similarities and differences between these countries. To complicate matters, they cannot be qualified as the group of romance language countries (since Greek is not a romance language); neither can we define them as Mediterranean bordering states (since this is not true for Portugal). Hence, the concept of 'Europe's South' will be used here as a relative denomination for a composite group of five countries that share many cultural and structural similarities, even if a number of variations and some major differences can be noticed.[1] Due to its size, to its level of economic development and to its weight in the European research area, France has a particular status in this group, as will be illustrated while looking at the parallels in the profiles of these five countries.

CHAPTER OUTLINE AND FIRST IMPRESSIONS

Academic research does not 'float freely', but is always rooted in specific contexts and structures. Consequently, in order to give an appropriate general assessment, that might explain the state of research on EU multilevel governance in a particular country and its contribution to the academic debate; first of all it is important to know more about the infrastructural and scientific background of this country. In particular, it is helpful to reflect on the sources of knowledge available, as well as to consider the traditions and conditions of social science research in the group of countries to be analysed. An outline of first impressions emerging from the picture given by Southern European research on EU governance activities will be followed by a presentation of the general conditions in those countries. Against this background, we will highlight the general stand of EU studies in the respective countries, including references to available research facilities in the field.

The first impression gained when looking at the GOVDATA results is the relative disregard for EU governance research that characterises Europe's South in comparison to the other Western European countries that are at the root of the European integration process. To put it in a nutshell, the governance turn in EU studies, as identified in international academic research (Kohler-Koch and Rittberger 2006), seems not to have reached Europe's South to the same degree as it has in their neighbouring countries of 'old' Europe. The discrepancy particularly comes to light when comparing, on the one hand, the thematic priorities and research approaches followed in these countries and, on the other hand, the questions addressed in the international academic debate, as reflected in leading journals and publications in the last decade.

Research projects conducted in Europe's South account for 21 per cent of all single projects listed in the CONNEX database. A superficial look at the geographical distribution gives a contrasted, if not contra-intuitive, picture of the situation: Spain has listed 129 projects, there are 89 projects in France, 43 in Italy, 51 in Portugal and 26 in Greece. At this point, reference needs to be made to the technical difficulties faced in the stock-taking exercise while trying to retrieve information on relevant projects for a country (see Chapter 10). Furthermore, it has to be mentioned that the high number of projects entered is not automatically a proof of vivid research activities dedicated to EU governance. It is quite possible, as in the case of Spain, that the selection criteria could not be applied as restrictively as in other countries because governance issues are anything but central in research conducted on EU affairs.

It is remarkable that only 20 projects, out of 339 entered in the database for this group of countries, use the word 'governance' in their title (half of which are French projects). For the whole database, the relationship is twice as high.[2] This does not mean that the governance approach is totally neglected or even ignored by South European scholars working on EU questions. We will show that, in their way, academics of Europe's South do actively contribute to enhancing our understanding of the workings of EU-multilevel governance. However, it is significant that even for topics that can be considered as belonging to the core thematic complex of governance, most of the scholars do not refer explicitly to this analytical approach, that is their research is not embedded in the broader theoretical frameworks known as 'Multi-Level Governance' or 'new modes of governance'. As a matter of fact, there is a need to find explanations for an apparent paradox ('Are South European scholars doing governance research without knowing it?'), and for some real differences when compared to the level, intensity and thematic focus of EU governance research in EU member states with a strong academic input like the UK, Germany, the Netherlands or even in many small countries located in the Northern or Western part of Europe.

SCIENTIFIC TRADITIONS AND STRUCTURE OF SOCIAL SCIENCES IN EUROPE'S SOUTH

A common feature regarding the aforementioned structural background is the weak status of social sciences and especially of political science in these countries. Since the governance approach is strongly embedded in political science, it is worthwhile paying attention to the status and level of development of this discipline. In these countries, political science only became properly institutionalised and consolidated comparably late. Political science as an autonomous discipline was first established in the early 1980s (in Italy a bit earlier, in Spain even later in the early 1990s). In Greece, like in the Iberian Peninsula, the transition to democracy has constituted a turning point in the development of political studies in particular and for the social sciences as a whole. Before the end of the dictatorships in the 1970s there were hardly any political science departments in these countries. Apart from the political reasons, the late development of modern political science also ensues from specific academic traditions, that is the strong position of humanities and legal studies in these countries. In Italy, political science is fairly weak and considered less important than other social sciences, such as history of law (Graziano 2006). As for the Spanish case, the splitting of political science and public administration from constitutional law finally gave political science its autonomy (Clifton 2006).

In this respect, France, as is often the case in this group, occupies a special position. The creation of institutes for political studies directly after World War II played a major role in the expansion of political science as a discipline. The institutional recognition of political science in the law faculties came about later, from the 1950s onward, when the discipline received an independent status (Blondiaux and Déloye 2007, 138). Hence, in comparison to its Romance neighbours, political science in France undeniably can look back to a long tradition. Nevertheless, outside the Instituts d'Etudes Politiques, political science is still the *parent pauvre* in French universities, where this discipline is subordinated to the faculties of law.

The strong weight of legal studies in academia in general, and in EU studies in particular, is the main common feature shared by this group of countries. In many cases, political science research remains in the shadow of constitutional law, state theory and political philosophy. This epistemological background explains to a great extent the predominance of hermeneutical approaches over empirical social research, which can be often observed not only with regard to EU governance research. Similarly, theory-driven research is rare. Generally speaking and despite some notable exceptions (France and to some extend Italy) and variations within the countries, political science research in Europe's South tends to be primarily descriptive and to follow a historical approach.[3]

Further similarities can be found regarding the financial background of research in this part of Europe. Unlike Germany, with the *Deutsche Forschungsgemeinschaft* or the *Economic and Social Research Council* in the UK, which allocate resources through a system of application and strict selection, the countries of Europe's South do not have specific funding organisations that provide financial support for research projects carried out in universities and other publicly financed research institutions. Institutions, such as *Centre National de la Recherche Scientifique* (France), *National Hellenic Research Foundation* (Greece*)*, *Consiglio Nazionale delle Ricerche* (Italy), and *Consejo Superior de Investigaciones Científicas* (Spain), aim to carry out, promote, spread, transfer and improve research activities directly and merely through funding research institutes and equipment. In this regard, the set-up of the *Agence Nationale de la Recherche* as a funding organisation, in 2006, represents a major turning point in the way of financing research in France.

With the notable exception of France (2.13 per cent of GDP in 2005), research and development (R&D) expenditures are below the EU average of R&D investment (1.84 per cent of GDP). External funding is rare, either because there is no need for it (like in France), or because it is not offered (as in Spain, Italy or Greece). In Spain, aside from regional governments and the universities, the main source of financing is the Ministry of Education and Science, 'the most helpful institution in providing systematic support for research projects and funding for PhD theses' (Morata and Etherington 2007, 334).

EU STUDIES IN SOUTHERN EUROPEAN COUNTRIES

Research on EU governance is by nature primarily routed in the broad academic field of EU studies. Even if governance research also emerges outside the community of researchers dedicated to EU issues, we can still assume that the degree of development and advancement of EU studies in a country is an important factor for determinating the research capacity and interest in EU governance research.[4] In general, EU affairs are a widely taught subject in these countries. When it comes to research on EU matters, however, the situation is much more contrasted, revealing different levels of development.

According to the CONNEX national reports, the progress of research on the EU in the Southern European countries is, nevertheless, to a great extent related to the course and position of each individual country towards European integration and the institutional and political development involved. The accession of Greece to the EEC, for instance, together with its institutional obligation to adapt to community law in a number of policy areas, have instantly rendered the development EC legal studies in this country an essential requirement, which in conjunction with the underdevelopment of political science, favoured and reinforced the legalistic approach to European studies, or to be more precise, to European legal studies in this new member state (Pagoulatos 2006). It was only in the early 1990s that research centres in the field of European studies were founded in Greece, following increased pressure for adjustment and deepening of the integration process. This assessment could be extended to the situation in Spain and Portugal.

In France, in contrast to legal studies on EU integration, political science research devoted to European politics is rather new, yet significant (Belot, Magnette Saurugger 2008). It corresponds to the publication of a specialised periodical (the peer review journal *Politique européenne*, established in 2000) and the formation of a professional association (the *Société d'Etudes Européennes*, established 2005 as a section of the French association of political scientists). For the time being, the number of teachers and specialised researchers in this field remains small compared, for instance, to the number of experts in political sociology (Blondiaux and Déloye 2007, 147).

Generally speaking, until recently, scholars working on questions of European integration in these countries (mainly from a legal or historical perspective) were neither particularly interested in social science methods and questions, nor in the theoretical conceptualisation of the European Communities. This is due to the traditional diplomatic history approach combined with legal traditions that have dominated academia in this region to this point. For instance, a consequence of the enduring influence of the tradition of legal positivism in Italy is that only recently legal and political science agendas have begun to converge and merge (Cassese 2006). Basically, the legalistic and constitutionalist approach to political phenomena and the political realm that has dominated Southern European political science for a long time, strongly influences the methodological approach towards the phenomenon of European integration in these countries.

The strong bias of legal sciences in EU studies is well-reflected in the thematic and disciplinary orientation of the main academic journals devoted to EU issues. There are no less than four journals dedicated to EU law in Italy. Similarly, the main journal dedicated to EU issues in Spain is the

Revista de derecho Comunitario Europeo (before *Revista de institution europeas* 1974–1996). In Greece, papers and studies featured in the *Review of the European Communities* (established 1980) are known more for their legalistic and institutional orientation (it includes extensive references to community law and the case-law of the Court of the European Communities) and less for their theoretical treatment of the phenomenon of European integration. Again, the French case is somewhat different. Most contributors of the venerable *Revue du marché commun et de l'Union européenne* (established 1958) are in fact lawyers and high civil servants. Yet, the recent development of political science research devoted to European politics has brought about the creation of the abovementioned periodical *Politique européenne*, which in its contents and ambitions is close to the leading journals in the field, the *Journal of Common Market Studies* and *Journal of European Public Policy*.

A close look at the instruments of communication and cooperation that support the dissemination of and discussion on the research carried out on EU issues in these countries, can also help to better understand the situation. There is a well-developed network of Jean Monnet Chairs and Centres of Excellence in these countries (maybe with the exception of Portugal). Yet we know that this kind of infrastructure of higher education does not always matter regarding the level – not to say the quality – of research on EU affairs. The same applies to the available sources of information (European documentation centres), even though libraries and facilities in most of the Spanish, Portuguese and Greek universities cannot be compared to the infrastructure of large universities in wealthier countries of Northern Europe.

As to the means and places of socialisation that are important to foster the emergence of a research community, all five countries are members of the European Community Studies Association. Here again, there are some important differences that well reflect the national specificities of the five countries, but also reveal their commonality as a group. The French *Commission pour l'Etude des Communautés Européennes* was set up in 1965. With 400 members, it is a strong association dedicated to the study of 'the European communities'. Despite its objective to be a multi-disciplinary platform, it is strongly dominated by lawyers (70 per cent of the members). It should, however, be mentioned that partly in reaction to this, a *Section d'Etudes Européenne* was established in 2005 as a section of the French Association of Political Scientists, in order to serve as a platform for all political scientists working on the EU.

In Spain, the *Associacion Universitaria de Estudios Comunitarios* with around 150 members is also strongly dominated by lawyers; there are some economists, but almost no political scientists. The *Hellenic University Association for European Studies* focuses on economics and law, but is weak in political science, and the Portuguese *Associação Interuniversitaria Portuguesa de Estudos Europeos* has a similar profile with strong participation from economists and lawyers but very few political scientists. By contrast, the *Associazione Universitaria di Studi Europei* gathers around 300 Italian scholars on EU studies in four different areas (economics, political science, law and history) and membership is well-balanced between these disciplines. All in all, the countries of Europe's South show a very different profile compared to the two largest ECSA national associations, the EUSA and British UACES, in which a majority of members are political scientists (Rosamond 2007, 10).

RESEARCH ON EU AFFAIRS IN FRANCE: A PARADIGMATIC CASE?

Research on European integration has a long tradition in France. At the same time, as Andy Smith pointed out, the relationship between French political science and European integration is, to say the least, paradoxical (Smith 2000, 663). Therefore, it is worthwhile to have a close look at the way EU affairs are studied by French researchers, for the existing particularities may help us to better understand why research on EU governance remains underdeveloped in comparison to countries such as the UK and Germany, although they have comparable resources and research infrastructures. France is still a key actor and driving force of EU politics and possesses a well-developed research community in this field. At the same time, a large number of renowned scholars discovered the importance of European integration fairly late, many of them due to the ideological bias of Marxist influence.[5] Another particularity is that for a long time the process of integration and the emergence of a European polity were merely comprehended as a 'construction', rather than a process of integration. Last but not least, from the very beginning, the study of the EU and its preceding organisations was mainly captured by experts in constitutional or administrative law, some of them personally dedicated to the cause of European integration, such as the pioneers Paul Reuter or Louis Cartou.[6] Indeed, a short review of bibliographical references from major text books of the 1970s and 1980s shows that most references came from legal studies. Because of their key academic functions, legal scholars such as Joel Rideau, Maurice Croisat and Jean-Paul Jacqué had a durable impact on the field of EU studies. Significantly, not only institutional issues but also the Community's policies seem to have belonged to the legal sphere of influence in France.

Having said that, one should add that what makes French research on EU affairs stand out is its broad multidisciplinary scope that not only includes sociologists or philosophers, but also anthropologists (see the research conducted by Marc Abélès and Irène Bellier). However, intellectual exchange between disciplines is anything but smooth. A strong stance of historical research (B. Voyenne, P. Gerbet, R. Poidevin, G. Bossuat, R. Frank, most of them coming from international relations) went parallel to the research in political science, but without developing durable interrelations.[7] Although political science research on the EU is rather new, following the steps of pioneer scholars, such as Jean-Louis Quermonne, a new generation of political science researchers increasingly chose EU topics for systematic investigations. Typical for this type of approach is the focus on ideas, trans-national actors and movements, and the role of individuals and law mechanisms.

In view of the minor importance of the governance approach in French EU studies, it is noteworthy that structural reasons, in terms of deficient infrastructure or lack of resources, do not play a role in explaining the French situation, except maybe if one considers foreign language skills and international openness as resources. Until recently, research on European integration, just as French political science, was very self-centred and maintained only a few connections to the international academic community. Much more, it seems to be a mix of academic traditions and political priorities that explains the relative disregard of French political scientists for the governance concept. Here, there is an important difference between the situation in France and some comparable countries, such as Germany or Great Britain. When these countries launched ambitious national research programmes dealing with EU integration in general (UK) and with governance issues in particular (Germany), the *Centre National de la Recherche Scientifique* initiated a three year funding scheme in 1998, 'L'identité européenne en question', which was aimed at achieving a better structuring of comparative research on Europe and the EU in France.[8] Yet, due to its short term span and because of the great disparity of topics covered, the impact of the programme remained limited. The topic of EU governance was not a priority and the issue was only addressed in one of the three thematic foci.[9]

MAIN STRANDS OF EU GOVERNANCE RESEARCH IN EUROPE'S SOUTH

As already indicated, only a limited number of the identified projects actually address *stricto-sensu* questions that belong to the governance problematic. A brief overview on the main tendencies should help us to better understand this common feature, before having a closer look at the national specificities. According to the GOVDATA records, law is by far the leading discipline in Italy and Spain, whereas a majority of projects derive from political science in France and Greece. In Portugal, the distribution between political science, sociology, economics and law is about equal. Except for Italy, and to a lesser degree Greece, the number of research projects has remained fairly constant over the years, without any significant increase in recent years. In Spain (94 PhD thesis out of 129 projects) and Portugal (31 out of 51) a large portion of the projects are actually PhD-theses, most of them conducted without external funding.[10] Likewise, in Greece, even though doctoral dissertations constitute more than half of the recorded research projects, only three of them have secured some form of funding. It should be noticed, that except for France, all research projects entered in the database are individual projects; none of them establish networks of research.

Information gathered on the geographical space that has been covered by the research projects under scrutiny provides evidence for another common denominator. In this respect, one can speak of nationally introspective research since most of the projects in Italy, Spain, Portugal and Greece primarily deal with their own country, even if they address issues of EU-multilevel governance.[11] A comparative perspective is rare, except for a few projects in France. When it comes to the methodology used, it can be noted that most of the projects in Spain, Portugal and Greece have a strong descriptive character. Similarly, a significant number of Italian political scientists do not have much in common with what we call empirical social sciences because their paradigms are those of normative philosophy, legal doctrine and history (Freddi and Giannetti 2007, 272). But this is evidence that is rather traditional.

National variations in the thematic focus often depend on the perception of a problem at national level and the respective understanding of politics: what is a legitimate political system, and what should be the political priorities. As to the research agenda in the countries of Europe's South, common patterns can be identified as well. Mostly, governance is associated with a sub-national dimension (urban governance, regional governance). Yet, apart from the traditional institutional, legalistic and constitutionalist approaches from the year 2000 onwards a tendency is discernible towards topics which do not exclusively touch on 'circumstantial' institutional EU issues that make the headlines, but also on basic and more fundamental questions. These include the relationship between democracy and European integration, the links of European integration with particular streams or schools of political theory, the comparative study of cases of Europeanisation of public policy, as well as issues of identity. This trend clearly favours the emergence of new issues, such as a more dynamic approach to integration, as well as more attention to the multidimensional character of EU governance. In the following, we will now portray national specificities, while introducing the main strands of research on EU governance in theses countries and providing some examples for the kind of projects conducted.

National specificities: EU governance research in Greece

Recorded research projects in the field of EU governance in Greece are relatively limited (26 projects), due to the dominance of classical research questions in domestic political science and the limited participation of domestic researchers in European research projects. Only recently have research efforts developed in the field of European governance in departments of European studies and political science. Traditionally, dissertations in political science usually refer to classical research areas, such as the party system, political history and interest groups in the national political system. As to the thematic focus of Greek research projects, from 1980 onwards basic institutional developments within the European Union (enlargement, revision procedures, EMU, Convention) these constitute a steady source for research topics and publications. Among the questions addressed by Greek projects, Europeanisation and the challenge of adjustment for public administration within the new European institutional and economic environment is a major one. Projects carried out between 1994 and 2006 highlight issues within the Greek political and scientific agenda, such as the boundaries between state and society, participation in the shaping of policy, and the strengthening of tendencies towards decentralisation (see for instance *'EU enlargement and multilevel governance in European regional and environmental policies'* 2001–2003). The need for effective management of development and structural programmes within the scope of European structural and regional policy necessitated the study of adjustment problems in the planning and implementation of the overall development strategy (*'The adjustment of public administration to the EU's regional policy management'* 2001–2007). In general, there is a tendency towards dealing with issues that demand theoretical treatment, such as the relationship between democracy and European integration (*'Democratising the Political Constitution of Europe'* 1999–2001; *'The role of individual and social responsibility in building a democratic framework of social policy'*, 2003–2005), the links of European integration with particular streams or schools of political theory (*'Theories of European Integration and the Case of Greece'* 2002–2006), the comparative study of cases of Europeanization of public policy (*'Decentralisation in the most unitary EU-15 member states: A comparative study of the implementation of the partnership principle in Ireland and Greece'*, 2004–2007), as well as issues of identity and public support (*'European integration and public support'*, 2004–2008). In recent years, this trend has contributed to the transgression of formalistic-legalistic approaches to the phenomenon of European integration (Pagoulatos 2006, 18).[12]

EU governance research in Portugal

Portuguese research on EU governance in the stricter sense of the word is almost non-existent. The research projects identified during the stock-taking exercise deal only marginally with governance issues. Furthermore, the data collected for this purpose often turned out to be incomplete (for instance regarding the project duration), because of difficulties in retrieving information. Governing in the EU is still understood in a narrow, not to say traditional way. Favourite topics for Portuguese researchers are European policies (in particular, cooperation and development policies, and monetary policies), the history of the integration process, migration, enlargement, legal development, or the social dimension of European integration.[13] Regional and development policy are other areas of interest, most of the time with a narrow focus (*'European Integration Impact on the development of Portuguese region – Minho'*, 1992–1994; *'The impact of the 1992 reform of the common agricultural policy on soil erosion in the Alentejo region'*, 1998). Two strands of research set apart: investigations related to the democratic quality of the EU (*'Deliberative democracy in the EU and multilingualism's challenge*, 2004–2005; *'People, Parliament and the Constitution: the future of democratic representation in the new political construction of the EU'* 2003–2004); and research on issues related to the constitutionalisation process (*'Constitutional Paradigms in a Changing Order: Europe and Constitutionalism'*, 2000; *'The European Communities law – route to an eventual constitutionalization'*, 2001–2003).

EU governance research in Spain

A core feature of Spanish research is that a large majority of the projects are carried out individually rather than in collaboration with other Spanish researchers, not to say with colleagues from abroad. Less than one third of the projects lead to publications, but interestingly, most of them in the discipline of political science, albeit law accounts for more than 46 per cent of all research projects included in the database. Having said that, and given the previously mentioned bias of juridical sciences, it is not surprising that about one third of the Spanish projects identified, mainly focus on the EU's legal framework. Typical for Spanish projects with this kind of focus is the study of legal mechanisms (*'Regulation and Fundamental Law in the European Integration'*, 2004–2006) or of constitutional issues. Further, there is a great interest in institutional questions (*'The Presidency of the EU Council from the perspective of Historical Institutionalism: a positive-sum exercise'*, 2003–2005).

Many projects address questions that are of direct interest to Spain, such as specific European policies (*'Foundations, Evolution and Configuration of the European Social Fund: application in Galicia'*, 1998–2002; *'The politicization of immigration: the relationship between the political and the social discourse in Spain and the EU immigration politics'*, 2004–2007), the sub national level (*'The participation of the regions in the European Union decision making process. Possible ways for the Spanish Autonomous Communities'*, 2002–2004; *'Adjusting Multi-level Governance in the UE: Sub-national participation between Maastricht and the European Constitution'*, 2002–2006), whereas issues of transformation seem to draw less attention (*'On economic convergence. Theoretical and empirical aspects for European and Spanish regions'*, 1995–2002).

The shift from a classical understanding of the EU to the study of multi-level governance and the process of Europeanisation is primarily made by junior scholars with a strong international orientation, who are ready to adopt new theoretical approaches, as for instance reflected in the project *'Reviewing theories of European Integration'*, 2003–2004, which closely examines recent international literature on European integration.

EU governance research in Italy

Similar to the countries already mentioned, in the Italian case few research projects refer explicitly to the concept of governance. As already pointed out, the thematic focus of the Italian projects is mainly on legal aspects. From this perspective, the general theoretical assumption is the emergence of a unitary European legal order or public sphere, which includes the national legal orders and modifies their characters, varying according to the different aspects considered (Cassese 2006, 6).[14] There are two main streams of legal approaches to EU governance in Italy, both of which can be ascribed to the public law sphere: the first is the constitutional stream; the second is the administrative one. Within the constitutional stream, the most controversial issues are the nature of the European Constitution, its 'material' existence apart from the entering into force of the new draft treaty, the identification of a democratic deficit at the supranational level, the alternative between shared powers and divided powers in the EU institutional architecture, the principle of subsidiarity (and its enforceability), the existence of a European demos, the protection of fundamental rights, the possible outcomes of the ongoing process of ratification, and so on. The consistent and still growing body of European administrative research has produced very significant theoretical developments. Organisational models, such as co-administration, models of decentralised integration and common organisation of regulators, or concepts like mixed (administrative) procedures, composite legal order, procedural supranationalism and European polysinody (in relation to the EU committees and comitology) have been fully elaborated and discussed in the Italian debate (*'The execution of European administrative decisions at a national level'*, 2000–2001; *'The evolution of a polycentric administrative space'*, 2004–2005; *'The European judicial space in penal law field'*, 2003–2004;

'*The evolution of the judicial cooperation in the civil field in EU: uniformity and contradictions*', 2004–2005).

Besides the legal approach, Italian research projects on EU governance also explore the ways in which the process of change of the governing processes was received by the member states and the institutions of the European Union. The chosen approaches here favour a wide conception of institutional change, intended to be a learning process. Based on the experiences, made on the availability of new information and on mutual observations and interactions actors may redefine their preferences in terms of conceptions and values (*'Governance intended as learning. New governance methods in the European Union'*, 2004–2005). Other relevant projects focus on how social movement-related organisations and their sympathisers can provide useful new ideas to the policy process (*'Organized Civil Society and European Governance'*, 2003–2006). Some researchers aim to better understand the position of Italy in the system of European governance through analysing elite participation in the decision-making process towards the constitution of the European Union during the last 20 years, or the constitution and the operation methods of the European policy networks in diachronic perspective (*'Italy in European Governance system inner elites, networks of decision and policy choices'*, 2002–2003). Others study the concrete changes generated inside the Italian political and social systems by the progressive European integration and the overlaps between the national level and European governance (*'Supranational governance and Italian politics: the impact of the first one on the second one considered as a whole'*, 2000–2001). Noticeably, many of the projects have a political sociology background and are located in Trento, a strongly internationalised university.[15]

EU governance research in France

As to the particular situation in France, one should first remark that the very idea of governance seems politically suspicious to many French opinion makers since it is equated with the ideological shift from politics toward the market. Against this background, it is not a surprise that many scholars in France (with notable exceptions such as Patrick Le Galès or Andy Smith) still feel uncomfortable with the concept of governance. The problem is not the move from an ordered hierarchy of authority and from a more concentrated focus of politics towards new forms of regulation and of public action beyond the state, but rather the question of what politics will mean in this new context. Representative for this kind of question is the title of an overall reflection on the essence of being 'governed': 'Qui gouverne quand personne ne gouverne?' (Favre 2003), a question that gains particular significance in the European multilevel system of governance, with the EU as a polity but not a state, and a wide range of actors involved in the decision-making and implementation process of European policies. All this might explain why the reception of the Commission's White Paper of European Governance in France was very limited, so that some observers even speak of a 'non-reception' (De Lassalle 2007, 230), and why French political elites show very little permeability for the governance concept.[16] In this context, when it comes to the particular case of EU governance, it is not by chance that the bibliographic references given in the article devoted to the term 'governance' in the reference dictionary *Les mots de l'Europe* (Grossman, Irondelle, Saurugger, Quermonne 2001) are all by foreign scholars.

Concerning the thematic orientation of EU governance research in France, a glance at the main journals suffices to demonstrate the strong focus on issues of public policies. Significantly, the first article published by the newly established journal *Politique européenne* dealt with the question whether EU policies are public policies like others (Hassenteufel and Surel, 2000). This focus on sectoral approaches reflects a general tendency in French political science, where the study of public policies or public action, both in terms of teaching and research, tends to constitute an almost independent subfield at the heart of the discipline (Blondiaux and Déloye, 2007).[17] The same applies to analysis from the perspective of political sociology, an emphasis that corresponds with the traditional importance of this kind of work devoted to France and its institutions in French political science research. Typical for this strand of research is the project '*Sociography of European elites*', 2001–2004. Another expanding, yet second-rank stand of research are interest groups. Astoundingly, one of the very first academic research projects conducted on interest representation in the then EEC came from French speaking scholars.[18] For decades, this topic had been neglected until in the 1990s a new generation of young scholars well-connected to the international debate started to conduct research on interest groups ('*The banking groups of interest in front of the European integration*', 1998–2002; '*Towards a European Pattern of Interest Representation? French and German Interest Groups in the Ostpolitik of the European Union*', 1997–2001; '*Representation modes in the EU*', 1999–2003). New avenues of research are opened now, ('*Choice and Combination of Policy Instruments*', 2004–2008; '*Rules and delegation in Europe*'; 2004–2005; '*Governing by committees. Political sociology of European experts groups*', 2004–2007), frequently in connection with the involvement of scholars from these countries in international collaborative research projects. As a matter of fact, one can say that in France, there are some governance elements in EU studies, as well as research on governance with reference to the EU, but no EU governance school of thought exists as yet.[19]

General remarks

The achievement of the Common Market in 1993 and, more generally, the strengthening of the European integration process during the 1990s have induced relevant effects on the national levels: the legal, social, economic and political autonomy of each member state has been undermined. Consequently, as Sabino Cassese put it when regarding Italy, the academic research and debate in all these fields has progressively shifted its focus to the European level (Cassese 2006). The constitutional debate had noticeable impact on the number and the nature of research on EU topics; the process which started in 2001 with the Laeken Declaration and culminated in 2003 in the Draft Treaty establishing a Constitution for Europe, has attracted great attention, as is demonstrated by the increased amount of research on European constitutional issues.

Against this background we can assume first, that the level of EU governance research depends on the attention paid and the significance given to the EU level in politics. It is decisive whether EU-affairs are considered to belong to the international realm, that is the national system is considered independent from the EU, or if the European Union is seen as system of different levels of governance, interacting with each other. A core reason for the underdevelopment, or late start of governance research in comparison to the countries of Northern Europe, is that the countries under scrutiny still experience forms of statism in which network governance is less developed. Indeed, the general understanding of the state and of its role turns out to be essential in order to explain the success (or the failure) of research on EU governance, that is the question whether there is a dominant state centric approach focusing on the steering capacity of the state, or if there is a society centred point of departure (Pierre 2000, quoted in Kohler-Koch and Rittberger 2006, 28–29). One can thus assume that many legal scholars, as well as historians find it difficult to connect with the understanding of EU politics as multilevel governance because their analysis departs from a state- and nation-centred approach.[20]

In this sense, regarding the French specificity one could make a similar assessment as in the UK case: it is an old polity with particular traditions and experiences, as well as significantly different operating norms and practices in comparison to those of the current EU (Wallace 2003, 6). The French model serves as a frame of reference for most French scholars and the consequence of this conceptual lens is the special attention paid to issues such as power, the role of the state, or notions such as the common good (*bien commun*) and common interest (*intérêt général*), that are all derived from the French traditional representation of legitimate political order.

CONCLUSION AND TRENDS FOR THE FUTURE

To take up Helen Wallace's meaningful metaphor (2003), contrasting images of European governance can be found in the countries of Europe's South, although the national scientific cultures feature many similarities. This is why clusters built on the map of EU governance research (see page 175) are larger than national boundaries. As to the research activities in the countries studied in this chapter, a first common denominator is their point of reference. In contrast to the works emerging from the UK programme 'One Europe or several' that followed a pan-European approach of European Governance, existing studies on governance in Europe's South are very much concentrated on the EU. Except in the case of some Italian projects dealing with administrative law from an international perspective, the European Union seems to be the central frame for examining trans-national and multilateral governance, a perspective shared by most of the continental Western European countries. Another common and maybe even more significant denominator is the legalistic and constitutionalist approach to EU studies. The focus on constitutional law, on state sovereignty, on the struggle for acquisition, holding and exercising of power, does not predestine for exploring new avenues of research, such as policy networks, the role of civil society, or non-formal mechanisms of regulation. This may be a reason why such topics are scarcely addressed by Greek scholars or by their colleagues from the Iberian Peninsula.

In other words, one can say that the governance turn in EU studies observed in some European countries has not really taken place in the Southern part of the continent until now, for the reason that the steering approach that focuses on actors is still very strong in comparison to the analysis dealing with structures and institutions. In any case, because of the strong legal tradition in EU studies, much more attention is paid to formal arrangements and to the central position of the state. An exception to this is the French focus on policy analysis, although even this analysis is rarely encapsulated in a general approach that explicitly considers the EU as a system of governance. In this regard, there is a correlation between, on the one hand, the tradition of prioritising the theories of the state and denying autonomy to political science through the sustained comprehensiveness of constitutional law, as stressed by Adriano Moreira regarding the situation in Portugal (2007, 315), and on the other hand, the reluctance and delay (compared to other countries) of Southern European social science research in conceiving governance beyond and besides government.

Nonetheless, in the near future, the consequences of the process of European integration for domestic political institutions and policy processes well captured in the concept of Europeanisation, will certainly induce some change of direction and focus regarding the analyses of the political systems of the member states as members of the broader European multilevel system of governance. As Sabino Cassese pointed it out, the Italian debate on the EU twenty years ago was very poor and isolated, and now it is not only becoming more vivid, but also closer to the European debate. Still, this two-way process – a richer Italian debate on EU issues leading to a richer European debate and vice versa – is, so far, only partially satisfactory due to the persistent language problem and to weak interdisciplinary integration and cooperation among different disciplines at the national level (Cassese 2006). To summarise, the lack of visibility of the existing EU governance research conducted in these countries is based as much on structural factors (limited resources, language barriers, lesser mobility) as on their intellectual particularities (specific traditions, topics of study, methods and approaches) which do not tie in with the leading international academic discourse.

Language barriers, in fact, greatly account for the weak integration of South Europe's national scientific communities in the international academic debate that is mainly English speaking and framed by means of communication (journals, publishers, conferences, networks) with a strong anglo-US-american bias.[21] In the five countries investigated, publications resulting from national research projects are mainly in national languages, and therefore are accessible only to those international scholars having the necessary language skills, which, ultimately, limits their diffusion in a considerable way. Besides the specific thematic and epistemological orientations highlighted by this chapter, this cultural particularity explains why also the resonance of research conducted in these countries is rather weak, for it will not be noticed if it is not published in English and in the leading journals. In this sense, the following diagnosis that can be made regarding France, also applies to a large extend to the others countries of Europe's South: despite high-level expertise and interesting projects, French research mostly remains invisible at the international level for it is not well connected to the fora that contribute to the leading academic debate.[22]

This problem, however, is to a great degree a question of generation. In comparison to their more senior fellow researchers, young Southern European scholars seem to attend more and more international conferences.[23] Further, trans-national cooperation projects open new windows of opportunity by getting connected with and confronting new approaches and broadening perspectives.[24] As a matter of fact, it remains to be seen whether international ties such as large collaborative research projects funded within the EU framework programmes will bring about a kind of Europeanisation of EU governance research in Europe's Southern academic periphery, both in form of a stronger connection to international leading concepts and questions, but also of a better reception of their contribution into the scientific debate of reference.

NOTES

1. The significance of cultural factors can be seen in the strong links between French Belgium and Switzerland. EU-member states that are also located in the geographical South, such as Slovenia or Romania, have been deliberately excluded from this group because their structural and cultural backgrounds make them belong to the group of Central and Eastern European countries.
2. The same applies for projects using the word 'governance' in the title and/or in the project abstract: This concerns only 12 per cent of the South European research projects while the share is 21 per cent for all countries together.
3. Interestingly, in France, case studies and research on the ground are much more widely used than survey questionnaires or comparative analysis (Blondiaux and Déloye 2007).
4. Regarding the debate about the nature and range of EU studies, see Rosamond 2007 and Cini and Bourne 2006.
5. Characteristic for this attitude is Edgar Morin's acknowledgement in his book, published in 1987, *Penser l'Europe*, or Michel Foucher in *La république Européenne*, 1998.
6. The first edition of Cartou's reference text book on European integration was published in 1965 under the title *Organisations européennes*. The last one was published in 2000.
7. Few historians have related to theoretical and even less so empirical research in the social sciences in a systematic way (Kaiser 2006, 197).
8. The network of research activities, as well as single conferences and workshops, were eligible for funding by the CNRS programme.
9. The list of selected projects which can be related to the concept of governance is a good representation of the thematic priorities and favoured approaches in France: 'Institutionnalisation de l'espace européen et recomposition de l'Etat' / 'Espace public, citoyenneté européenne et identité postnationale' / 'Les commissaires européens et la représentation politique de l'Europe' / 'L'Union européenne, une démocratie diffuse ? L'émergence de modes alternatifs de contrôle' / 'Bringing the top civil servants back in: Quelle place pour les hauts fonctionnaires dans les procès de gouvernement des sociétés européennes'.
10. For technical reasons, it was not possible to retrieve information on PhD-theses dealing with EU-governance issues in Italy.
11. For the ethnocentric character of mainstream political science in these countries see Clifton 2006, 238) and Contogeorgis (2007, 222–223).
12. See for instance the special issue Nr 10, Spring 2003, by the journal 'Episteme kai koinonia' ('Science and society') on governance ('Diakyvernisi').
13. Having said that, one should add that Portuguese scholars are nevertheless well-integrated in research projects which are part of large international comparative networks (Euromanifesto, European Social Survey).
14. A relevant part of the Italian research projects – ongoing and completed in the last decade – deals with the emergence of a European administration and the impact of the EU on the activities and functions of the national administrative bodies.
15. Next to the university of Trento, EU governance research in Italy is mainly located in Rome and Florence. One should also mention the Research Unit on European Governance (URGE), a research centre set up in December 2003 at the Collegio Carlo Alberto of Moncalieri in Turin.
16. In French social sciences, the main uses of the concept of governance are concentrated in the fields of economic governance, metropolitan governance or international relations.
17. For some emblematic projects see: '*Governance of salt-water fishing in Europe*', 1998–2000; '*The European identity between the market and the solidarity: the case of the transformation of the European health protection systems*', 2000–2001; '*The Europeanization of immigration policy*' 2001–2006; '*The institutionalization of the European space and the recomposition of the Nation State*', 1998–2001.

18. Dusan Sidjanski and Jean Meynaud's pioneer book *L'Europe des affaires* was first published 1967.
19. Unlike in Great Britain or in Germany, governance did not become the scientific leading paradigm for studying local public action in France (De Lassalle 2007).
20. Even when the term *governance* is used in a book title, as for instance in the volume 'Gouvernance et identités en Europe' edited by Robert Frank 2005, the analytical approach remains traditional.
21. On the predominance of English speaking academic actors and communication instruments in EU studies, see Popa 2007. Popa's empirical analysis of the geographical provenience of all articles published in three of the leading journals in the field of EU studies (JCMS, JEPP, JESP) demonstrates that whereas articles from French authors account for between 1 and 2 per cent of the total, UK scholars account for 44.7 per cent, Germans for 6.9 per cent and Dutch for 4.5 per cent. Articles from authors affiliated to Italian, Spanish, Portuguese or Greek institutions are all less than 1 per cent.
22. That said, it is worth recalling that strong cooperation ties connect scholars from French Universities and research institutions with their colleagues from the French speaking part of Belgium and from Switzerland.
23. The geographical repartition of attendees to the *Third ECPR Pan-European Conference on EU Politics* held in Istanbul on 21–23 September 2006 gives a good picture of the unbalance in terms of regional provenience: 40 participants from Europe's South (among them 11 from Italy and 11 from Greece) compared to 42 from the British Islands, 45 from the Benelux, 62 from German speaking countries, 30 Scandinavian participants and 13 from the European University Institute in Florence.
24. The Italian academic debate on EU governance, for instance, seems less self-referential today than a few years ago. It is possible to notice a trend towards a more intense engrossment of the Italian scholars in relations to the European academic debate, in particular in the legal and political science fields (Cassese 2006, 5).

REFERENCES

Belot, Céline, Magnette, Paul and Saurugger Sabine (eds) (2008), 'Science politique de l'union européenne', Paris : Economica.

Blondiaux, Loic and Yves Déloye (2007), 'The current State of Political Science: Report on the Situation in France', in Hans-Dieter Klingemann (ed.), *The State of Political Science in Western Europe*, Opladen/Farmington Hills: Leske+Budrich, pp. 137–162.

Cassese, Sabino (2006), *Research on EU multilevel governance in Italy: A state of research*, Mannheim: CONNEX [http://www.connex-network.org/govdata/reports/Report-Italy.pdf].

Cini, Michelle and Angel Bourne (eds) (2006), *Palgrave advances in European Studies*, Basingstoke: Palgrave MacMillan.

Clifton, Judith (2006), 'Political Science in Spain: What hope for young professionals?', *European Political Science*, 5 (3), 235–244.

De Lassalle, Marine (2007), 'Parlez vous gouvernance? Champs des pouvoirs et réception de la gouvernance en France', in Didier Georgakakis and Marine de Lassalle, *La 'nouvelle gouvernance européenne'. Genèses et usages politiques d'un livre blanc*, Strasbourg: Presse Universitaires de Strasbourg, pp. 230–260.

Favre, Pierre (2003) 'Qui gouverne quand personne ne gouverne ?', in Favre, P. ; Hayward, J., Être gouverné – Études en l'honneur de Jean Leca. Paris: presses de Science Po, pp. 259–271.

Freddi, Giorgio and Daniela Giannetti (2007), 'The current state of political science in Italy', in Hans-Dieter Klingemann (ed.), *The State of Political Science in Western Europe*, Opladen/Farmington Hills: Leske+Budrich, pp. 255–274.

Graziano, Paolo (2006), 'Entering Italian Academia in Political Science: Can the "Sacred Fire" Keep Burning?', *European Political Science*, **5** (3), 264–270.

Grossmann, Emiliano, Bastien Irondelle, Sabine Saurugger and Jean-Louis Quermonne (2001), *Les Mots de l'Europe : lexique de l'intégration européenne*, Paris: Presses de Sciences Po.

Hassenteufel, Patrick and Yves Surel (2000), 'Des politiques publiques commes les autres? Construction de l'objet et outils d'analyse des politiques européennes', *Politique européenne*, **1** (April 2000), 8–23.

Kaiser, Wolfram (2006), 'From state to society? The historiography of European integration', in Michelle Cini and Angela K. Bourne (eds), *Palgrave advances in European Union studies*, Basingstoke: Palgrave MacMillan, 190-208.

Kohler-Koch, Beate; Rittberger, Berthold (2006), Review article 'The governance turn in EU studies', *Journal of Common Market Studies*, **44**, 2006, 27–49.

Moreira, Adriano (2007), 'Political science in Portugal', in Hans-Dieter Klingemann (ed.), *The State of Political Science in Western Europe*, Opladen/Farmington Hills: Leske+Budrich, pp. 311–324.

Morata, Francesc and John Etherington (2007), 'The Current State of Political Science in Spain', in Hans-Dieter Klingemann (ed.), *The State of Political Science in Western Europe*, Opladen/Farmington Hills: Leske+Budrich, pp. 326–339.

Pagoulatos, George (2006), *Research on EU multilevel governance in Greece: A state of research*, Mannheim: CONNEX [http://www.connex-network.org/govdata/reports/Report-Greece.pdf].

Rosamond, Ben (2007), 'The Political Sciences of European Integration: Disciplinary History and EU Studies', in Knud Erik Jørgensen, Mark A. Pollack and Ben Rosamond, *Handbook of European Union Politics*, London and Thousand Oaks: Sage Publications Ltd, pp. 7–30.

Smith, Andy (2000), 'French Political Science and European Integration', *Journal of European Public Policy*, **7** (4), 663–669.

Wallace, Helen (2003), 'Contrasting Images of European Governance', in Beate Kohler-Koch (ed.), *Linking EU and National Governance*, Oxford: Oxford University Press, pp. 1–10.

8. Research on EU Governance in Central and Eastern Europe: National Specificities and a Common Legacy

Josef Niżnik and Krzysztof Iszkowski

Central and Eastern European countries (CEE) used to be perceived mainly in opposition to the countries of Western Europe. For a long time, this geographical characterization (West *versus* East) was used as a synonym for Europe's separation into two antagonist blocs. Also, it has been quite common to assume that their communist past brought about so much similarity, that any possible differences among the CEE countries have become irrelevant. Indeed, the traces of communist experience appear to be common in the region, marking practically all areas of life including academics, and in particular social science research. The studies of governance and more specifically multi-level governance in the EU are no exception. Compared to the major countries of Western and Northern Europe, the level of research on EU governance in the new member states that joined the EU in 2005 and 2007 is rather low, not to mention the countries of Eastern Europe in which this kind of research is almost non-existent. On the other hand, apart from structural similarities due to the past, the results of the stock-taking exercise carried out by CONNEX demonstrate substantial differences in the general settings and in the scope of research. We will show that factors such as the size of the country, its past relation to the Soviet Union, the degree of ideological control under the previous regime and local traditions of social science are mainly responsible for the variations.

Therefore, we will discuss both similarities and differences, focusing first on the enduring structural impact of communist political and economic systems, before turning to the growing differences between the countries of the region with regard to their respective contribution to EU governance research. We will attempt to analyse the impact of the Eastern enlargement on research in EU governance and finally, we will discuss the consequences of the relative unpopularity of the governance approach in Central and Eastern Europe for the future development of political sciences in the region, as well as for the current and future attitudes of its politicians and civil servants towards the EU decision-making process.

All authors of the CONNEX reports on CEE countries stress the fact that the last decade has been a time of political and social transformation.[1] However, this process differed significantly in the countries under scrutiny in this chapter. The same applies to the development of political studies. Consequently, we start with focusing on what we perceive as the commonalities of the countries in this area; the preference given to applied research, the very cautious use of more refined and innovative research tools and, as a result thereof, limited contribution of CEE scholars and scientific institutions to European studies in general and EU governance in particular. We begin with taking a closer look at the impact of two structural factors, human resources and financing.

STRUCTURAL FACTORS (1): HUMAN RESOURCES

The detrimental influence of communism on political sciences varied across the CEE countries, but even in the places where it was weakest (Poland, Slovenia and Hungary), the majority of senior scholars currently in the discipline were educated under Marxist orthodoxy. Interestingly, this issue has been addressed only in two country reports (Latvia, Poland). In other reports there is only a candid reference to this problem, stating that the European studies were launched after the fall of communism. The question of 'who launched them?' usually remains unaddressed, but it is legitimate to suppose that many former Marxist ideologists took their chance to pass over as experts of European integration, especially as the possibilities of verifying their competences have been very limited. On the other hand, the relatively fast reorientation of political scientists in the region, who managed effectively to turn their attentions to European issues, seems to show the superficiality of their attachment to the previous, ideologically loaded, context. It should be also noted that after 1989 some scholars, who earlier represented other disciplines (like sociology or philosophy) entered the European studies area. The ensuing weakness of the theoretical background of some of them, combined with the fact that under the previous system innovation and critical assessment were not considered to be assets of political scientists, resulted in uninspired and descriptive ways of performing research. As Marina Strezneva observes, in the research descriptions gathered in Russia '...there are few theoretical reflections ... When you do find any hints of theory at all, it is sure to be "imported" from the West, more or less uncritically' (Strezneva and Voitolovsky 2006).

Drawing on both, on the CONNEX reports and on earlier studies prepared under the framework of Knowledge Base 'Social Sciences in Eastern Europe' (www.cee-socialscience.net), it can be inferred that at least in some countries under scrutiny, the previous communist structures of academic life persisted after the transformation, which resulted in fierce criticism of new liberal economic practices. Nonetheless, new, non-Marxist institutions emerged. This led to a coexistence of two parallel political science communities – post-communist and post-dissident (Barbu 2002, Iszkowski 2006). In Slovakia, a similar situation arose during the political developments of the 1990s: 'the political polarization of the whole society ... led to the existence of two sets of universities and political science departments – those that claimed to be politically independent (mostly in opposition to the former government of Prime Minister Mečiar – for example, Comenius University, University of Trnava) and those that were established directly by and were therefore loyal to the former government' (Malová and Mihálviková 2002).

However, even those senior researchers who had not been subject to Marxist indoctrination, had been isolated from Western intellectual life for decades, which led to a certain methodological and organizational conservatism, that is less interactive relations with students, and a more or less open reluctance towards interdisciplinary tools and new approaches, such as multi-level governance. It should also be stressed that until the late 1980s, European integration in general received very little attention in the region, both in politics and in academia.

The impact of Marxism and communism-induced isolation on the Central European political science might have been even more subtle and vicious. As András Körösényi claims, the political science that grew from Western Marxism and oppositional discourses has led to a 'society versus the state' paradigm, with a latent – or manifest – plea for the self-governing civil society (Körösényi 1999).[2] If this assessment is correct, it might help to explain the weak interest in EU governance issues in the region, since this approach, which is also seen in the network analysis assumes an organizational and axiological continuity between citizens, civic organizations and governing institutions.

Today, the problems described regarding human resources are of decreasing importance. Almost 20 years after the fall of communism, a significant number of young scholars have emerged in the region, the majority of whom have had at least short-term experience of studying abroad, mostly in Western Europe (for example under the Erasmus scheme), but also in the United States, thanks to Fullbright Scholarships or the programs sponsored by the Open Society Institute. The Central European University in Budapest, founded and generously sponsored by George Soros, has also been crucial for the dissemination of Western science and educational practices in the region – it hosted 13 of the 62 research projects on EU governance conducted in Hungary and listed in the CONNEX database. By 2006, the number of PhDs or PhD candidates who had been educated under the conditions of political and academic freedom was large enough to make a difference. Their impact is particularly strong in fields such as European studies, which were created only after the fall of communism.

As for the gender distribution among the EU researchers, it can be noticed that men seem to be much more active in this field than women. The most equal country in this respect is Poland with 48 percent of female researchers.

STRUCTURAL FACTORS (2): FINANCIAL ISSUES

Except for Slovenia and Hungary, all countries of the region spent in 2003 less than the EU-25 average (1.15 percent of GDP)[3] on higher education. The proportions of spending on R&D are similar, with none of the CEE countries reaching the EU-25 average (1.92 percent of GDP), and the great majority spending less than half of this figure. With the GDP per capita in the region ranging from 32 percent (Bulgaria) to 80 percent (Slovenia) of the EU-25 average, the spending per researcher is markedly lower than in the Western part of the continent. This fact is reflected in many country reports mentioning insufficient financing as one of the key problems.

In some cases, the problem is not as much the scarcity of funds as the structure of funding. Some areas of research, among them European studies, are better funded than others, which induces many researchers – both senior and junior – to 'bend' their projects so that they fit into more generous funding schemes. This accounts for a considerable number of nominally EU-related research projects conducted by scholars from disciplines other than European studies or political sciences, who do not have the relevant background and expertise. In other cases, the connection to the EU as identified by the database seems to be confined to their keywords. Projects such as: 'The Improvement of the International Relations of Croatia: European Integration Aspects'; 'Position of the head of state in parliamentary and semi-presidential systems: the Czech Republic in a comparative perspective'; 'Influence of foreign trade development on regional specialization and industrial location in Estonia in the context of economic integration into the EU'; and 'Problems of perfecting the legal regulation and protection of economic mechanism' (a study on gambling) – all included in the GOVDATA database – seem to provide appropriate examples of this category. It was decided to include these projects in the database despite their marginal thematic relevance because these kinds of projects are rather typical for the way EU issues are addressed in CEE countries. Indeed, the number of projects with a genuine EU dimension and whose thematic focus is directly related to European governance *stricto sensu* is marginal. Moreover, since the grants from various sources are not coordinated, the more competent researchers are involved in many projects at the same time, which can potentially compromise the quality of their contributions. To put it in a nutshell, there is a limited number of EU experts in the region and the most capable are, thus, often overcommitted in national as well as in international projects.

Another result of 'bending' research projects to existing financial schemes has been the focus on applied research, quite often very general, usually focused on the conditions and predicted effects of accession of a particular country. These kinds of projects, motivated by political needs, have been conducted with the aim of explaining the EU institutions and processes to local authorities and to other national actors, rather than contributing an original insight into the development of European studies. As the Lithuanian CONNEX stock-taking team observed, 'the urgent problems and need for economic reforms and integration into the European economic space and the adoption of *acquis communautaire* have dominated research, which has meant that deeper issues have been neglected' (Augustinaitis et al. 2006b). In Slovenia, 5 out of 6 of the identified projects dealt with the challenges and opportunities the membership posed for this country (Bahovec 2006). The percentages for other countries of the region are comparable.

Similar attitudes, based on the widely spread belief that knowledge about the EU can pay off by providing relatively easy access to 'Brussels money', has induced many undergraduate students to seek training in European integration, and a considerable number of higher education institutions to offer seemingly relevant programs. Institutes of Veterinary Medicine and Animal Sciences, as well as those for Forestry and Rural Engineering at the Estonian Agricultural University are among them. Even where those new programs have managed to hire specialists in European studies as lecturers (not a very common profession in this part of Europe), the overall impact of the growing demand for knowledge in the field could have ambivalent effects, because the academics are overloaded with teaching and, in consequence, are likely to treat research as a lower priority activity.

The problem of funding also affects the younger generation's career decisions. The stipends for younger researchers (including PhD students) are usually too low to cover the costs of living at a level they aspire to, which induces them to accept positions in the private sector, not connected to their area of scientific interest and distracting them from research. The other consequence is the emigration of many talented young political scientists, mainly to Western Europe, but also to the United States. On the other hand, there is a significant mobility of students and researchers within the region, with the Central European University in Budapest and HESP-supported Graduate School for Social Research in Warsaw having the highest shares of foreign students. Such institutions may play a positive role as 'regional platforms' for the development of advanced research, especially when they are well-connected to international networks.

The percentage of PhD works and postdoctoral theses in the overall number of the research projects in a country could possibly indicate the prospects for the future expertise in the given area of studies for that country.

From this point of view, Poland clearly leads the field with over 90 percent of research projects being PhD theses or postdoctoral dissertations. The second country on this scale is Spain, where the percentage of such works exceeds 70 percent of all projects and from the newly accessed states it is Slovenia with over 30 percent of PhD and postdoctoral thesis among all research projects collected. The rest of the CEE countries have less than 20 percent. What is especially interesting is that Poland is in the lowest position on the scale of external funding. It may explain the lowest number of research projects other than theses worked out for degrees and consequently the highest percent of the latter.[4]

INTERNAL DIVERSITY

Among the factors that produced the differences between CEE countries in the field of European studies, the degree of ideological control under the previous systems seems to have the greatest importance. The ideological control should not be mistaken with the dependence from the Soviet Union; two countries where ideological control was stronger than elsewhere in the region, Albania and Romania, were also among the most independent from the Kremlin. On the other hand, two countries in which the communist ideology had the least impact on social and political science – Hungary and Poland – 'hosted' Soviet troops and, respectively experienced or feared their military intervention. In former Yugoslavia (present Slovenia, Croatia, Bosnia-Herzegovina, Serbia, Montenegro and Macedonia), there was no Soviet control at all and the ideological checks were relatively moderate.

The degree of ideological control was reversely correlated with the openness of national academia to contacts and influence from the West. In Poland, political studies had been relatively well-developed before 1989, and although ideological restrictions were still present, international cooperation with the European and American political scientists was quite intensive. This is probably one of the reasons why the Polish research projects on EU governance – although as in most other countries, the majority of them originated in political science – demonstrated a more interdisciplinary character. Among the CEE countries, Poland shows the largest variety of backgrounds in EU governance studies, covering a broad range of disciplines, as indicated in the stock-taking statistics (political science, sociology, economics, law, history, philosophy, and other disciplines). Hungary under communism was another relatively open country with access to foreign literature and with Western ideas being discussed. When talking about differences among CEE countries, one should also note that in some of the countries it was not political science, but economics that created the framework for most of the projects on EU governance (Estonia, Lithuania, Bulgaria) and in one country (Romania) it was law.

The second factor impacting the development of research on EU governance is, in our opinion, the size of the country. In Poland, a country as populous as the other seven CEE new member states combined and to a significant degree decentralized in the late 1990s, the research on regional and local politics – relevant to multilevel governance investigations – is very well developed. About 20 percent of the Polish projects included in the database are defined as dealing with sub-national level, and this amounts to two thirds of all CEE GOVDATA projects focused on sub-national issues.

On the other hand, one could expect that the idea of multi-level governance in a complex, multinational political system would be especially attractive for those scholars who experienced some kind of political coexistence of different nations in a single state and who would, thus, be in an advantageous position to conduct comparative analysis. The countries that come to mind are the Soviet Union, Yugoslavia and Czechoslovakia. It seems that the problems of governance in those, (at the time non-democratic) federal states could make a spectacular reference to the governance problems in the EU that are being tackled with the help of a multi-level governance idea. The same applies to the case of contemporary Russia. However, there are no indications of any attempts to compare the EU and the Russian Federation from the perspective of a multilevel system analysis.

We would also like to point out that a few countries in the region, most of them proclaiming an interest in European integration and accession to the EU, were not covered by the stock-taking action. In addition to the fact that this absence was caused by the inability to find partner institutions in those countries to conduct the survey, one can legitimately assume that the European studies and EU governance research in Albania, Belarus, Macedonia, Moldavia, Montenegro and Ukraine is poorly developed. However, this assessment is not based on any empirical findings.

THE IMPACT OF EASTERN ENLARGEMENT ON EU-GOVERNANCE RESEARCH

Eastern and Central Europe changed profoundly during the 1990s. These changes are deep and long-lasting as they represent a leap forward in the belated modernization of the region. Evidently, all the changes, tensions and open conflicts have been reflected in the thematic orientation, institutional framework, cognitive results and practical relevance of social sciences in the region (Genov and Becker 2001, 8). As a matter of fact, one could expect that the recent waves of accession to the EU would boost research on governance issues in CEE, because this research is necessary, at least in order to better understand the specificity of the European Union and how it works. Yet, research on EU-related issues in these countries suffers from what could be called a 'passivity complex', that is, the perception that the CEE countries are merely decision-takers and that, therefore, they do not have any significant prospect of influencing or shaping EU policies and programs. Hence, most of the research is dedicated to issues such as adaptation and Europeanisation processes in those countries.

The political situation in the region during the 1990s created strong incentives to focus on practical aspects of European integration, such as conditions, procedures and consequences of accession of particular countries to the Union. A rapid increase of new research projects started in the years between 1999 and 2001, when the prospect for the accession of a number of CEE countries seemed to be close. In Hungary and the Czech Republic, however, this movement has been delayed, due to the accession year being 2004.

Interestingly, European studies have also been highly politically-sensitive in those countries which did not undertake any significant efforts to become integrated in the EU. Reporting on the state of research on EU multilevel governance in Russia, Marina Strezneva writes: 'European research was very important in the national academic debate during the perestroika years. At present, this is no longer the case. Practical problems of Russian-European rapprochement have proved detrimental to the pro-European idealism prevalent in Russia during its previous stage of development.' (Strezneva and Voitolovsky 2006). In fact, Russia is the only country where 'integration' does not appear amongst the keywords of the collected projects. The most frequent keywords of the Russian sample were 'social space' and 'transformation'. In the other countries under discussion, it is 'integration'. Further top concepts are changing from 'policy' to 'transformation' or 'social space'.

Generally speaking, the concept of governance – so broadly used now in the European academic debate – has, until recently, been perceived as a new category in political science. Moreover, national (or perhaps regional) specificity (hypothesized in Beate Kohler-Koch's introduction) has clearly had an impact on the understanding of governance. In the Lithuanian report it is even suggested that this specificity demands 'new research models'. Despite this assumed specificity, the general meaning of governance – as reconstructed from the reports – seems to cover the substance quite well. Governance has been understood as the interacting of people and institutions, according to specific norms, in order to maintain political or economic entity and to achieve its aims. The concept of political power has been somehow put aside in this discourse. However, at the same time, the notions of network governance seem to be still unpopular. This could be attributed to the prevalence of the traditional paradigm of the nation state, which is visible both, in academia and in the political debate. For example, the sitting Polish and Czech presidents Lech Kaczynski and Václav Klaus, as well as the right-wing politicians in Hungary and Romania, said at various occasions that the 'national interests' of their countries needed to be 'defended' against the EU and other member states. The Union is more often perceived as an 'international organization' than as an 'emerging federation' or even a 'polity *sui generis*'. Such ambivalent attitudes toward the EU and its specific form of polity stem from the attachment to the traditional understanding of a nation state. It reflects a kind of cognitive dissonance in a situation, when stressing recently regained national sovereignty and, as a consequence of the integration process, giving up part of it in the form of competence transfer takes place simultaneously. Having said that, we should recall that the most obvious feature of a democratically oriented multi-national system such as the EU is the fact that governance takes place on different levels. In a sense, the concept of multi-level governance is relevant for any complex political system aspiring to democracy (the state, the region and so on). Against this background, post-communist countries, with the experience of centrally planned economies and totalitarian or authoritarian political regimes, could still be expected to embrace the concept of multi-level governance with more enthusiasm than other EU member states. In fact, among the research projects collected in the database, very few directly address this issue although all of them are somehow related to this approach. In effect, the contribution of CEE research to the general debate was not significant enough to reflect on this specific perspective. However, one can expect that in a relatively short time new innovative ideas and important theories may emerge out of those numerous, very promising dissertations that are being written at present.

POSSIBLE CONSEQUENCES

If political science is meant to be meaningful and relevant, it not only reacts to the developments in the world of politics, but also has a feedback function, helping political actors to organize their perception of reality and, thus, shape their attitudes and actions. Therefore, the relative underdevelopment of research on the EU in Central and Eastern Europe, as well as the reluctance to perceive politics through the new governance approach may have an unfortunate impact on the future actions of the CEE's politicians, social and academic actors in the European political system.

The most frequent and potentially confusing consequence of underestimating the meaning and the scope of the governance turn is the tendency to perceive the European Union as a classic international organisation, with the bulk of decision making left to the national level. This explains the attention paid by national politicians to such issues as the number of votes in the Council, as well as the habit of postponing the negotiations until the moment when an issue reaches the level of ministers or, even worse, heads of governments (which might be explained also by the shortage of competent officials at the lower levels of national administrations). Since it considerably compromises the speed of the common decision-making process, such approaches are non-instrumental for the Union as a whole.

More generally, the reluctance to perceive EU governance as a multi-level trans-national phenomenon is coupled with the 19th-century idea of a hierarchical nation state. This idea influences the attitudes of Central and Eastern European politicians both, to the EU (the Czech and Polish presidents perceive it as a threat to their nations' sovereignties), and to the other states (the poor shape of bilateral Polish–German and Czech–German relations resulting from the reaction of Polish and Czech governments to some initiatives and actions of German non-governmental actors).

The EU enlargement in 2004 has accelerated the speed of societal changes in Central and Eastern Europe. Among other phenomena, various, frequently trans-national networks have been developed (Stark, Vedres and Bruszt 2005), and there are increasing numbers of public-private partnerships (NEWGOV 2005) as well as of civil society involvement in EU policy (Zimmer and Priller 2004). Regardless of whether national political elites like it or not, this is a strong stimulus for a bottom-up development of multi-level governance practices. Unlike the situation in most of the Western countries, where the concept of governance has emerged as a result of structural changes in politics and policies, in the CEE countries the shift from 'government to governance' first became apparent with the consequences of Europeanization. For this reason, up until now academic research using a governance approach remained very limited in this part of Europe. In conclusion, the EU governance studies in the region need to be intensified in order to facilitate the understanding, not only of the EU governance practices, but also of the social and political processes in the CEE countries themselves.

NOTES

*   This chapter deals with EU governance research in the following countries: Bulgaria, Bosnia and Herzegovina, Croatia, Czech Republic, Estonia, Hungary, Latvia, Lithuania, Former Yugoslav Republic of Macedonia, Montenegro, Poland, Romania, Russian Federation, Serbia, Slovakia and Slovenia.
1.   See the list of national reports in the Annex.
2.   The anticommunist opposition in the region was to a great extent formed by revisionist scholars who pointed to the divergences between original Marxist theory and its practical application aimed at legitimation of oppressive regimes. While revisionists, sometimes at the cost of imprisonment, alienation and emigration, pursued intellectually independent research programmes that corresponded and were often inspired by the free development of Marxism in the West, the majority of political scientists focused on providing ideological excuses for increasingly corrupt regimes and thus contributed to a growing discrepancies bewteen 'western' and 'eastern' strains of Marxism.
3.   Data from Eurostat: Expenditure on education as percentage of GDP or public expenditure http://epp.eurostat.ec.europa.eu.
4.   Another explanation of a large number of PhD theses among the listed research projects is that Poland has a central register for PhD theses (including the majority, but not all

dissertations), so it was easier to find relevant PhD theses – which was not the case in most of the other countries covered by the survey. On the other hand, those countries are smaller and access to such information is generally easier.

REFERENCES

Augustinaitis, Arunas, Saulius Spurga, Saule Maciukaite-Zviniene, Jolanta Grigaliunaite, Laura Stracinskiene (2006b), *Research on EU multilevel governance in Lithuania: A state of research*. [http://www.connex-network.org/govdata/reports/Report-Lithuania.pdf].

Bahovec, Igor (2006), *Research on EU multilevel governance in Slovenia: A state of research*. [http://www.connex-network.org/govdata/reports/Report-Slovenia.pdf].

Barbu, Daniel (2002), *Political Science – Romania*. [http://www.cee-socialscience.net/archive/politicalscience/romania/report1.html].

Genov, Nikolai and Ulricke Becker (Eds) (2001), *Social Sciences in Southeastern Europe*, Paris/Berlin: CISS/IZ.

Iszkowski, Krzysztof (2006), *Research on EU multilevel governance in Poland: A state of research*. [http://www.connex-network.org/govdata/reports/Report-Poland.pdf].

Körösényi, András (1999), *The Hungarian Political System*, Budapest: Central European University Press.

Malová, Darina, Silvia Mihálíková (2002), *Political Science – Slovakia* [http://www.cee-socialscience.net/archive/politicalscience/slovakia/report1.html].

NEWGOV (2005), *Evolving Regional Governance Regimes: Challenges for Institution Building in the CEE Countries* [http://www.eu-newgov.org/datalists/deliverables_detail.asp?Project_ID=15].

Stark, David, Vedres Balazs and Laszlo Bruszt (2005), 'Global Links, Local Roots? Varieties of Transnationalization and Forms of Civic Integration', *Theory and Society* (forthcoming); also: ISERP working paper 05-0, Columbia University [http://www.iserp.columbia.edu/research/working_papers/downloads/2005_08.pdf].

Strezneva, Marina and Fiodor Voitolovsky (2006), *Research on EU multilevel governance in Russia: A state of research*. [http://www.connex-network.org/govdata/reports/Report-Russia.pdf].

Zimmer, Annette and Eckhard Priller (eds) (2004), *Future of Civil Society. Making Central-European Non-Profit Organisations Work*. Wiesbaden: VS Verlag für Sozialwissenschaften.

9. Researching Governance in a Multinational Environment: The European University Institute

Sandra Eckert*

INTRODUCTION

This contribution to the stock-taking exercise is peculiar in nature and limited in scope. Unlike the regional or country lens through which research is apprehended in the other chapters, the focus here is on research activities within one single academic institution, the European University Institute in Florence (EUI) that, moreover, is not routed in a national context but was designed as a multinational place for teaching and doing research on Europe. It was established in 1972 by the Member States of the European Communities with the objective to provide advanced academic training to PhD students and to promote interdisciplinary research on European integration. The EUI and, more specifically, its Robert Schuman Centre for Advanced Studies (RSCAS) have built up a reputation as a privileged place for post-doctoral research and for EU-wide research networks and projects. Compared to the founding period however, the EUI today has to compete with an increasing variety of EU-centred research institutions and an increasing number of structured PhD programmes offered elsewhere. Given this altered landscape, the CONNEX stock-taking exercise comes as a timely opportunity to reconsider the relative strengths of the EUI's research profile.

The choice to create a single database for the EUI and to analyse the entries separately is based on the assumptions that, firstly, governance research at the EUI is too important to be omitted – which would have been the natural consequence if only 'national' traditions of research were considered; and, secondly, that governance research at the EUI is, to some extent, specific and forms its own category. These two assumptions are questioned in this paper. What has been the EUI's role for the last decade of research on EU multilevel governance? Has the institution functioned as a thematic trend-setter or has it rather been following tendencies in different European countries? What is the impact of the multi-disciplinary and the multinational set-up on the substance of governance research?

Looking for answers to these questions based on empirical evidence raises some methodological problems. Because of the strong mobility and the high turn-over of research staff, one may ask which kind of projects can be considered genuine products of EUI research. Many projects that 'officially' start once funding has been granted are de facto an extension of previous research or at least have been prepared well in advance. Furthermore, during the relatively short period of their stay, researchers often maintain their strong links with their previous or home institutions, that is, in the framework of projects which are coordinated and managed elsewhere. This issue particularly pertains for projects that 'move' with their coordinators entering or leaving the EUI. For this reason, the list of projects entered into the GOVDATA database under the label EUI has been closely screened in order to avoid duplications and make sure they can all be related correctly to the specific environment that is the European University Institute.[1]

EUI entries constitute the largest sample in the database with 146 data entries in total. Single research projects amount to 137 entries, out of which 97 projects are PhD theses (completed or under preparation). Given the impossibility of being exhaustive, broader thematic tendencies will be identified and discussed by making reference to individual research projects for illustrative purposes. In conceptual terms, 'governance' will be apprehended from a pragmatic angle since the EUI's specific character makes it difficult to identify a dominant research paradigm. The chapter will start out presenting the EUI's peculiarities as a research environment, and in the ensuing sections the major themes of EUI governance research are being presented. A final section will assess the EUI's overall contribution to the state of the art.

THE RESEARCH ENVIRONMENT AT THE EUI

Since its foundation, the European University Institute (EUI) has become a well-established institution welcoming doctoral and post-doctoral researchers from a variety of countries. Whilst the training of PhD students constitutes the core activity of the four departments, the majority of the fellowships and externally funded research projects is located within the Robert Schuman Centre for Advanced Studies (RSCAS). The RSCAS brings together the Robert Schuman Centre and the European Forum, both established in 1992 as complementary initiatives to develop inter-disciplinary and comparative research. The major asset of a research institution is its capacity to attract excellent academics at all levels. Beyond the beautiful surroundings of Florence which provide for an appealing environment, it is above all the professors holding chairs at the four departments or joint chairs at the RSCAS who function as multipliers by attracting promising doctoral and post-doctoral students. Former doctoral students from the EUI have been highly successful in taking up posts in academia across Europe, with many of them holding professorships at an early stage of their academic career.[2] Similarly, the Institute and the RSCAS are an interesting place for post-doctoral research. For many former fellows the year spent at the EUI has turned out to be a stepping stone.

A specific feature of the EUI is that it cultivates close contacts and personal exchange with the European institutions: many EUI PhD students participate in the EU *stage* programmes, and EU officials hold 'practitioners' fellowships. There is also a considerable number of former EUI students who take up posts as civil servants at the European level. This proximity facilitates exchange and cooperation, which can take the form of direct intellectual input into ongoing reforms – the 'Basic Treaty for the European Union' that EUI scholars have prepared at the request of the European Parliament can be referred to as an example in this context (rf. 'Reorganisation of the European Treaties' 1996–2003 Renaud Dehousse et al.).

The Institute profits from a comparative advantage in building up and sustaining transnational networks among academics, and in managing their cooperation. Alongside a few other institutions across Europe, the EUI disposes of the administrative capacity to coordinate big, transnational research networks. In addition to academic excellence this explains the EUI's and the RSCAS's relative success in obtaining considerable amounts of external funding. The big majority of research networks coordinated at the EUI has been financed under the 5th and 6th European Union Framework Programme. Under the 5th Framework Programme, examples one can refer to are IDNET ('Europeanization, Collective Identities, and Public Discourses' 2000–2002 Thomas Risse) and EURONAT ('Representations of Europe and the Nation in Current and Prospective Member-States: Media, Elites and Civil Society' 2001–2004 Bo Stråth), both coordinated at the RSCAS. Under the Sixth Framework Programme DEMOS ('Democracy in Europe and the Mobilization of Society' 2004–2007 Donatella della Porta) has been coordinated at the department of Political and Social Sciences (SPS), and NEWGOV ('New Modes of Governance' 2004–2008 Martin Rhodes and Adrienne Héritier) at the RSCAS. Similarly, a considerable share of single research projects in which the EUI was one of the partner institutions, has been financed by EU funds,[3] followed by funding from national institutions.

In terms of substance, cross-border contacts and fluctuation cause a certain degree of dis-embeddedness from national and disciplinary research paradigms and traditions. On the other hand, it facilitates the transfer of knowledge and ideas beyond national borders: young researchers will develop and sharpen their profile when studying at the EUI, whilst more senior academics will bring with them or 'import' their research agendas. During their stay in Florence, scholars will necessarily take on board new ideas and 'export' and diffuse these insights afterwards. It can be observed that EUI alumni frequently continue cooperating with EUI-based scholars. NEWGOV is an excellent example in order to illustrate this dynamic of self-reinforcing networks; looking at the composition of the partners in the project, it appears that roughly 70 per cent of the participants have an 'EUI history'.

A DECADE OF EU GOVERNANCE RESEARCH AT THE EUI

Data entries confirm that governance is most frequently addressed by political scientists and lawyers, and only in rare cases by economists and historians. When it comes to specific national research traditions which have played a major role, the most obvious pattern is the difference between a rather complex discussion in German speaking academia and a more pragmatic approach in the Anglo-Saxon and Scandinavian world. EUI scholars from other countries – for example from France and Southern Europe – have not been equally active in engaging in the governance debate. Overall, four core themes of research will be identified: a) the European polity between governance and constitutionalism; b) the quest for legitimacy in a transnational regime; c) policy-making in a multi-level context; and d) the European political economy and regulatory governance.

The European Polity between Governance and Constitutionalism

For the sake of convenience we will distinguish between two routes of research on the European polity, which are connected, however. A first route looks at the evolution and reforms of both, the European institutions and the treaties. A second route focuses on governance at the supranational level in a more narrow sense, that is specifically on what has been called 'new modes of governance'.

Institutional change and treaty reforms can either be more incremental and piecemeal, or more radical and path-breaking. Incremental change has been investigated in projects such as 'The European Council' (2001–2002 Helen Wallace) looking at the historical context in which the European Council has gradually developed and the remedies which could be applied to its identified weaknesses (Wallace and de Schoutheete 2002). This project has built on a long-enduring cooperation with Fiona Hayes-Renshaw (Hayes-Renshaw and Wallace 1997; Hayes-Renshaw and Wallace 2006). Another example would be the project 'Competing Competencies – Institutional Conflict and Interstitial Change in the European Union' (2002–2006 Adrienne Héritier) which examined the changing relationship between the Council, the European Parliament and the European Commission, analysing why, how and to what extent shifts of competences have occurred between formal treaty revisions (Héritier 2007; Héritier and Farell 2007; Héritier and Farell 2003). Subsequent treaty reforms and the discussion about a European constitution have been extensively researched at the EUI. Between 1996 and 2003 research activities at the RSCAS have been dedicated to the 'Reorganisation of the European Treaties' (Giuliano Amato and other researchers). In the first instance, a multi-disciplinary team codified and simplified the treaties, producing a single document at the request of the European Parliament. A second project aimed at progressively converting the treaties into a European Constitution. In addition, for such as the 'Symposium. Responses to Joschka Fischer' (Christian Joerges, Yves Mény, Joseph Weiler 2000) provided timely academic input to topical discussions.

Another line of research has been dedicated to the 'governance turn' at the European level. Although it is difficult to reconstruct the genealogy of EUI research on governance, it can certainly be stated that political developments triggered a re-consideration of long-standing research paradigms. This being said, the use of the term 'governance' was quite innovative from a legal point of view, whilst the political science literature (notably in Germany) had addressed issues related to steering and governance some decades ago. Anticipating the publication of the Commission's famous 'White Paper on Governance', a community of high-level researchers had rapidly been brought together during the summer of 2000 in order to publish academic input timely. With the resulting publication of 'Mountain or Molehill. A Critical Appraisal of the Commission White Paper on Governance' (2000–2001 Christian Joerges, Yves Mény and Joseph Weiler), the EUI positioned itself early on as an academic focal point in the governance debate.

Hence, it does not come as a surprise that the biggest and most prominent research network so far, which examines what has been called 'new modes of governance' (NEWGOV) is based in Florence. Its 24 projects and two transversal task forces examine the emergence, execution, evaluation and evolution of new modes in different policy fields. The majority of participants are political scientists, yet new governance is also being analysed from a legal perspective (de Burca and Scott 2006). EUI PhD theses have been dedicated to a variety of new modes, such as, for example, the Open Method of Coordination ('Soft Harmonisation: Labour Law, Economic Theory and the European Employment' 1998–2002 Diamond Ashiagbor, 'The Evolution and Influence of the Open Method of Coordination: The Cases of Employment And Social Inclusion' 2002–2007 Caroline de la Porte, 'The Choice for the Open Method of Coordination 2003–2007 Rik de Ruiter).

The Quest for Legitimacy in a Transnational Regime

A second, broad field of research interest dealt with the legitimacy of the European polity. Three sub-themes have been particularly present at the EUI: identity, citizenship and participation. Several EUI research networks have been dedicated to identity research, such as IDNET ('Europeanization, Collective Identities and Public Discourses' 2000–2002 Thomas Risse) or EURONAT ('Representations of Europe and the Nation in Current and Prospective Member-States: Media, Elites and Civil Society' 2001–2004 Bo Stråth). A similar thematic cluster at the RSCAS has dealt with issues related to 'citizenship'. The Institute has been involved as a partner institution in the FP 5 funded research network CIDEL ('Citizenship and Democratic Legitimacy in Europe' 2002–2005 Christian Joerges), imagining Europe as a rights-based post-national union (Eriksen et al. 2003; Eriksen et al. forthcoming). A historical approach has complemented this line of research more recently, looking at 'A European Social Citizenship? Preconditions for Future Policies in Historical Light' (2002–2004 Bo Stråth). Closely related to citizenship, the potential for a 'European public sphere' has been analysed in PhD research ('Europolis. Constitutional Patriotism beyond the Nation State' 1997-2001 Patrizia Nanz) or in the framework of research networks, such as the FP 6 funded project EMEDIATE ('Media and Ethics of a European Public Sphere from the Treaty of Rome to the War on Terror' 2004–2007 Bo Stråth).

The third area of research under the legitimacy headline has been dedicated to participatory governance. The research project 'Achieving Sustainable and Innovative Policies through Participatory Governance in a Multi-Level Context' (2000–2002 Philippe Schmitter) analysed old and new forms of governance in order to identify elements which foster participation (Schmitter 2002). A different perspective, putting the emphasis on the role of the media, has been adopted by the project 'Democratic Participation and Political Communication in Systems of Multi-level Governance' (2000–2003 Jean Blondel). In a similar vein, the RSCAS has been a partner institution in the research network CIVICACTIVE ('The Determinants of Active Civic Participation of European and National Level and the Impact of Political Parties. The Media and the Socio-Political Context' 2004–2007 Jean Blondel), which examines the determinants for participation. Finally, 'DEMOS. Democracy in Europe and the Mobilization of Society' (2004–2007 Donatella della Porta) focuses on forms of participatory democracy as they are elaborated from below and implemented within the internal organisation of social movements (della Porta et al. 2006). A number of PhD researchers have investigated issues related to participation from different angles and in different contexts ('Functional Participation in European Health and Safety Policy: Democratic Nightmare or Additional Source of

Legitimacy?' 1996–2002 Stijn Smismans), but also Jean Monnet Fellows have examined participatory governance (Nickel 2006).

Policy-Making in a Multi-Level Context

Policy-making in a multi-level context is another theme where it becomes evident how the EUI is reinforcing agendas and fuelling thematic clusters. Two major lines of analysis can be distinguished: whereas more classical European integration studies privilege the 'top down' or 'downloading' perspective by looking at the compliance with, the implementation and the enforcement of European law, 'Europeanisation' (Börzel and Risse 2000) studies put more emphasis on processes at the domestic level, notably by looking at how national institutional settings influence adaptation and how they feed back into EU-level policy-making through processes of 'uploading'.

From a 'top-down' perspective, compliance with and enforcement of European law are issues which have traditionally been addressed by legal scholars. A number of doctoral theses at the EUI law department have been dedicated to compliance and enforcement issues (for example, 'Optimizing the Commission's Role in Ensuring Member State Compliance with Community Law – New mechanisms against Infringements' 2003–2007 Stine Andersen). However, political scientists in recent years have increasingly become interested in studying compliance. In doing so, they may cooperate with legal scholars, for instance within the project 'Compliance in Modern Political Systems. Characterising the European Union by Comparison with National and International Regulations' (1996–2002 Christian Joerges and Michael Zürn). The 'Database on EU Member State Compliance with Community Law' (1999–2001 Tanja Börzel) needs to be mentioned as an ambitious attempt to improve available data on compliance. The researchers developed a sophisticated coding procedure of the official data provided by the European Commission. Based on this evidence, they drew innovative conclusions about non-compliance (Börzel 2001; Börzel 2000). Finally, implementation has been examined for a variety of policy areas, for example, for the area of immigration strategies ('Does Implementation Matter? Informal Administrative Practices and Shifting Immigrant Strategies in Four Member States' 2000–2003 Bo Stråth). The implementation of other EU policies or specific directives (for example, 'Developing Capacity Against Tradition: The Implementation of the EU Environmental Information Directive in Germany, Great Britain and Ireland' 1996–2001 Sonia Budgahn) has been analysed in PhD theses.

Putting into perspective the contribution of EUI scholars to the emerging and developing concept of Europeanisation, there is again a dynamic of reinforcing agendas. Europeanisation research at the EUI reached its peak between the mid-1990s and the beginning of the new millennium. At the outset, empirical research very much focused on processes at the domestic level in different policy fields. Taking the example of transport policy, the project 'Differential Europe' (1995–1998 Adrienne Héritier) brought forward that an identical European policy has remarkably diverse impacts within individual member states (Héritier et al. 2001). A number of political science PhD theses analysed the Europeanisation of domestic policies in different policy areas (The Domestic Impact of Europe. Institutional Adaptation in Germany and Spain 1995–1999 Tanja Börzel, The Europeanization of Refugee Policies: Between Human Rights and Internal Security 1995–1999 Sandra Lavenex). An encompassing viewpoint was adopted by a team of European and American scholars cooperating in the project 'Transforming Europe. Europeanisation and Domestic Change' (1997–2001 Thomas Risse). Again, the RSCAS functioned as an opportunity structure even for sustained collaboration across the Atlantic. Based on empirical studies on a number of issues related to the transformation of the nation-state, the team suggested an elaborate theoretic framework for studying 'Europeanisation' (Risse et al. 2001). Claudio Radealli is another scholar who has contributed eminently to the Europeanisation debate. He spent time at the EUI as a Jean Monnet Fellow (1997–1998) and co-directed a European Forum (2002–2003). Other EUI scholars sought to analyse the relationship between Europeanisation and globalisation, notably by looking at politics that seek to set off negative consequences of economic internationalisation (Verdier and Breen 2001). In conclusion, it can be stated that the EUI was one of the focal points of the academic debate on Europeanisation.

The European Political Economy and Regulatory Governance

Research on the European political economy and regulatory governance are treated separately in this article, not only because they constitute a core element of EUI scholarly work but also because they incorporate the essential tension between what Fritz Scharpf has called 'negative' and 'positive' integration, that is, market-creating versus market-correcting policies (Scharpf 1999). Research at the EUI has tackled different elements of economic and social governance early on, and the RSCAS has built up a reputation in regulation studies.

Considering political economy research at the EUI stipulates mentioning of the path-breaking contribution of Gösta Esping Andersen. When being a professor at the SPS department between 1986 and 1994, he set the scene with his 'Three Worlds of Capitalism' (Esping Andersen 1990). Ever since, there has been a continuity of political economy research at the EUI with relevant appointments (for example, Colin Crouch, Martin Rhodes, Philippe Schmitter, Sven Steinmo). A number of PhD theses addressed related questions, comparing specific welfare state reforms across countries or examining the potential for a 'Social Europe (for example, 'The redefinition of the contemporary welfare state: the reform of pensions in France and Italy' 1998–2002 David Natali). At the law department, a continuity of expertise on social aspects and especially labour law (Moreau 2006; Sciarra 2001) can be observed. A number of PhD theses are being prepared or have been completed on related issues, such as the social dialogue, labour protection or social exclusion (for example, 'The Future Function of the Social Dialogue' 2005–2009 Ann-Christine Hartzen).

Another eminent scholar needs to be named when reporting on the EUI's record in researching regulation: Giandomenico Majone. He left the Institute in 1995, at the beginning of the stock-taking period. But the impact of his innovative work on the 'regulatory state' (Majone 1994) goes beyond that time and since then the RSCAS is a prominent address for students of regulation. A number of research projects have been accomplished in the field of regulatory governance, for example on 'Regulatory Regimes in Europe' (2003–2005 Adrienne Héritier). Conducted in cooperation with the University College London, this project investigated the process of market opening in the network utilities at the European and national levels (Héritier and Coen 2005). At the departments, a number of PhD thesis have been dedicated to regulatory governance at a more transversal, cross-sector level ('The Constitution of Private Governance. Product Standards in the Regulation of Integrating Markets' 1993–2003 Harm Schepel, 'Institutional Frameworks of Community Health and Safety Regulation - Committees, Agencies and Private Bodies' 1990–1997 Ellen Vos) or with a focus on specific policy fields, such as GMOs or financial markets ('Hybrid solution for Hybrid Products? EU Governance of GMOs' 2002–2006 Patrycja Dabrowska; 'Law and Governance in the Institutional Organisation of EU financial services – The Single Supervisor Revisited' 2003–2007 Despina Chatzimanoli).

THE EUI's CONTRIBUTION TO THE STATE OF THE ART

The so-called 'governance turn', which has guided academic research about the EU throughout the last decade, is well-documented for the EUI; the data base entries illustrate that the concept has been rapidly picked up and further developed by EUI scholars. Taking the year 2000 as a 'cut-off' date for the governance debate, we find that 36 per cent or 23 out of the total of 64 projects where the term 'governance' forms part of the abstract have been launched in or after 2000. This pattern is even more striking when we look at projects where the paradigm features more prominently in the title; 73 per cent of those projects have been conducted in the new millennium. The prominent place given to the governance issue at the EUI certainly lies with its specificity as a transnational institution. It seems obvious that this new term is more useful than older categories, such as the 'state', in a context where none of the national traditions are conceptually dominant and could guide state-centred analysis. Unlike research at the national level, where the 'state' and its current transformation is often located at the core of analysis,[4] 'governance' shifts the interest to a polity 'sui generis' and allows to account for new methods of governing. Speaking about 'European governance' more specifically, the concept has not lost any of its validity, but rather has regained momentum with the failure of the Constitutional Treaty. Taking stock of research on EU governance at the EUI illustrates the Institute's specific focus on European studies. Multi-level governance is predominantly being approached in a European perspective, putting considerable emphasis on the relationship between national and supranational governance. The internationalisation of governance, that is, 'global governance', has been less of an issue although Europeanisation and globalisation can be considered as complementary, mutually reinforcing, but also as competing processes (Snyder 2000).

If one was to highlight the comparative advantage of the EUI and in particular of the RSCAS, it is certainly the institution's capacity to function as a platform and as a multiplier for individual researchers seeking to build up transnational contacts and networks in their field of interest. The particularly high degree of fluctuation at all levels – professors, fellows and researchers – and a considerable number of visiting scholars further sustain this feature. The flipside of fluctuation is, of course, a certain discontinuity which is characteristic for the EUI. Unlike other research institutions that enjoy a high standing in their country-specific or European context solely, the EUI has in addition built up a reputation across the Atlantic. Returning to the questions asked initially, it appears that the EUI has not been so much of a trend-setter for governance research, but has rather functioned as a platform for a variety of research themes. At times, EUI scholars have set the agenda and introduced new, innovative concepts such as the 'regulatory state'. Yet, such moments are linked with contingencies rather than with the structural features of the institution. More frequently, research interests have been reinforced due to the opportunity structure that the EUI and its RSCAS provide for scholars at the doctoral and postdoctoral level and beyond. In addition, the EUI functions as a multiplier in the sense that the dissemination of ideas and knowledge is guaranteed through fluctuation, that is, ideas travel with people. EUI people also frequently travel back to the EUI once they have left the institution, which leads to a remarkable dynamic of self-reinforcing networks. Taking all these characteristic elements together, the EUI's contribution to the state of the art has been substantial.

NOTES

* I am greatly indebted to Christian Joerges who substantially contributed to this article. Helpful comments from Tanja Börzel, Ingo Linsenmann and Thomas Risse are gratefully acknowledged.
1. However, some border cases may remain. With respect to the EUI database entries, it must be emphasised at this point that there will necessarily be duplications with national entries.
2. A non-exhaustive list of former PhD students whose work is included in the database and who are now holding professorships: Tanja Börzel [defense 1999, professorship 2003], Simon Hix [defense 1995, professorship 2004], Charalampos Koutalakis [defense 2001, professorship 2006], Sandra Lavenex [defense 1999, professorship 2006], Dirk Lehmkuhl [defense 1998, professorship 2007], Amy Verdun [defense 1995, assistant professor 1997-2000, professorship 2005].
3. Sustainable and Innovative Policies through Participatory Governance in a Multi-Level Context 2000–2002, E-Democracy 2002–2003, CIDEL (Citizenship and Democratic Legitimacy in Europe) 2002–2005; CIVICACTIVE (Democratic Participation and Political Communication in Systems of Multi-level Governance) , EUROREG (Changing Interests and Identities in European Border Regions) 2004–2007, POLITIS (Building Europe with New Citizens? An Inquiry on the Civic Participation of Naturalized Citizens in 25 Countries) 2004–2007.
4. For example the Collaborative Research Center in Bremen 'Transformations of the State', at http://www.sfb597.uni-bremen.de/700.

REFERENCES

Börzel, Tanja A. (2000), 'Why there is no Southern Problem. On Environmental Leader and Laggards in the EU', *Journal of European Public Policy*, **7** (1), 141–62.

Börzel, Tanja A. (2001), 'Non-Compliance in the European Union. Pathology or Statistical Artifact?', *Journal of European Public Policy*, **8** (5), 803–824.

Börzel, Tanja A. and Thomas Risse (2000), 'When Europe Hits Home: Europeanization and Domestic Change', *European Integration Online Papers (EIoP)*, **4** (15).

de Burca, Gráinne and Joanne Scott (2006), *New Governance and Constitutionalism in Europe and the U.S.*, Oxford: Hart Publishing.

della Porta, Donatella, Massimiliano Andretta, Lorenzo Mosca and Herbert Reiter (2006), *Globalization from Below*, Minneapolis: The University of Minnesota Press.

Eriksen, Erik O., Christian Joerges and Jürgen Neyer (2003), *European Governance, Deliberation and the Quest for Democratisation*, Oslo and Florence: ARENA Report 2/03.

Eriksen, Erik O., Christian Joerges and Florian Rödl (forthcoming), *Law, Democracy, and Solidarity in Europe's Post-National Constellation*, London: Routledge.

Esping Andersen, Gösta (1990), *Three Worlds of Welfare Capitalism*, Princeton/ Cambridge: Princeton University Press and Polity Press.

Hayes-Renshaw, Fiona and Helen Wallace (1997), *The Council of Ministers*, New York: St. Martin's Press.

Hayes-Renshaw, Fiona and Helen Wallace (2006), *The Council of Ministers*, New York and Houndmills: Palgrave Macmillan.

Héritier, Adrienne (2007), *Explaining institutional change in Europe*, Oxford: Oxford University Press.

Héritier, Adrienne and David Coen (2005), *Refining Regulatory Regimes. Utilities in Europe*, Cheltenham: Edward Elgar.

Héritier, Adrienne and Henry Farell (2007), 'Contested Competences in Europe: Incomplete Contracts and Interstitial Institutional Change. Special Issue', *West European Politics*, 30 (2).

Héritier, Adrienne and Henry Farell (2003), 'Formal and Informal Institutions under Codecision: Continuous Constitution Building in Europe', *Governance*, 16 (4), 577–600.

Héritier, Adrienne, Dieter Kerwer, Christoph Knill, Dirk Lehmkuhl, Michael Teutsch and Anne-Cécile Douillet (2001), *Differential Europe. The European Union Impact on National Policymaking*, Lanham: Rowman & Littlefield.

Majone, Giandomenico (1994), 'The Rise of the Regulatory State in Europe', *West European Politics*, 17, 77–101.

Moreau, Marie-Ange (2006), *Normes sociales, droit du travail et Mondialisation*, Paris: Dalloz.

Nickel, Rainer (2006), 'Participatory Transnational Governance', in Christian Joerges and Ernst-Ulrich Petersmann (eds), *Constitutionalism, Multilevel Trade Governance, and Social Regulation*, Oxford: Hart Publishing, pp. 157–196.

Risse, Thomas, Maria Green Cowles, and A. James Caporaso (2001), *Transforming Europe. Europeanisation and Domestic Change*, Ithaca, NY: Cornell University Press.

Scharpf, Fritz W. (1999), *Governing in Europe. Effective and Democratic*, Oxford: Oxford University Press.

Schmitter, Philippe (2002), 'Participation in Governance Arrangements: Is there any Reason to Expect it will Achieve "Sustainable and Innovative Policies in a Multilevel Context?"', in Jürgen Grote and Bernard Gbikpi (eds), *Participatory Governance. Political and Social Implications*, Opladen: Leske+Budrich, pp. 51–70.

Sciarra, Silvana (2001), *Labour law in the courts: national judges and the European Court of Justice*, Oxford: Hart Publishing.

Snyder, Francis (2000), 'Europeanisation and Globalisation as Friends and Rivals: European Union Law in Global Economic Networks', in Francis Snyder (ed.), *The Europeanisation of Law: The Legal Effects of European Integration*, Oxford: Hart Publishing.

Verdier, Daniel and Richard Breen (2001), 'Europeanization and Globalization: Politics against Markets in the European Union', *Comparative Political Studies*, 34 (3), 227–62.

Wallace, Helen and Philippe de Schoutheete (2002), *The European Council*. Paris: Notre Europe.

PART III

TRENDS AND PATTERNS IN RESEARCH

10. Trends and Patterns in Governance Research: What Do the GovData Tell Us?

Fabrice Larat and Thomas Schneider

BACKGROUND

From the outset of designing the programme of activities for the CONNEX network, emphasis was laid on two main aspects of scientific integration: first, to bring researchers of EU-governance together and second, to link issues in order to develop a multi-disciplinary perspective and a more open thematic approach on the subject of 'European multilevel governance, democracy and new modes of governance'. The assumption was that the project of integrating the topics and people required extensive prior knowledge of the copious research conducted in the field hitherto. This kind of information, however, was not readily available at the time.

The CONNEX objective to carry out a survey on EU governance research began with two observations: the first one is related to the extensive wealth of knowledge, research results and studies on the subject that are produced in Europe every year. When the subject of EU governance is taken to encompass the ways and means of governing the European Union universe and its member states, many indices show that great progress has been made. One of these indicators is, of course, the large number of EU specialists in Europe. Yet, for scholars, and even those who are internationally very well connected, it turns out to be very difficult to keep track of the diversity and richness of this existing research, let alone to have access to it. Knowledge and expertise on EU matters are widely fragmented and scattered due to language and issue boundaries, disciplinary self-sufficiency, and geographical disparities in Europe. Many research results, especially of empirical studies, are published only in the scholar's native languages, which restricts their dissemination to a smaller audience.

Based on this awareness of an already existing, yet fragmented wealth of knowledge on EU governance issues in Europe, it was decided that the project had to start with gathering information on relevant research.

Accordingly, our second observation regarded the pressing need to take stock of the bulk of accumulated research. Thus, CONNEX set out to conduct a stock-taking survey of relevant research in different disciplines in the EU member states and the countries of 'wider Europe'. The survey was conducted in 2005 and completed in the beginning of 2006. It includes ongoing or already concluded single research projects and research networks which started between 1994 (the start of the 4th Framework Programme of the EU) and 2006. The results of this survey were collected and made accessible in GOVDATA, an online database of research projects dedicated to the topic of EU Governance. Since April 2006, the database has been giving free access to all prospective users. Academics from all around the world, who are interested in governance issues, can search for information regarding research institutions and find scholars relevant to the field, as well as to obtain detailed information on research projects of the period of reference and take note of findings and results when referring to the resulting literature.[1]

Preparatory work

Several stock-taking conferences on selected issues of EU governance were organised prior to the start of CONNEX in order to get an overview of the diversity and complexity of the research areas such as 'Debating the democratic legitimacy of the EU', 'Interest representation in European Politics' or 'The Europeanisation of national parliamentary democracies'. During the first working period of CONNEX a stock-taking conference took place on 'Multi-level governance in Europe. Linking European, national and sub-national levels of governance: Drawing lessons from structural funds, regional and environmental policy' since this policy field was considered to be already well-researched and central to the issue of governance in the EU multilevel system. The conference revealed not only the plurality of research, trends and patterns in theoretical and methodological approaches in different parts of Europe and showed the structural differences of the linkage to European research in old and new member states, but it also highlighted the communication deficits between scholars coming from different disciplines and language backgrounds, and the difficulties of arriving at general conclusions.

A Europe-wide network of scholars was established to organise the stock-taking research. Twenty two 'national correspondents' were appointed because insight knowledge is needed to conduct such a survey. Apart from data gathering they provided 'national reports' (see list in Annex 1 at the end of the volume), that present background information on the particular features of EU governance research in each of the countries under scrutiny.[2]

METHOD AND APPROACH

The survey focused only on project-based research, defined as the systematic exploration of parts of social reality (mostly a 'puzzle' that needs explanation), drawing on existing or developing new theoretical knowledge in order to describe and explain real phenomena. Because of the differences in scope and structure, a distinction was made between so called 'single research projects', on the one hand, and 'research networks', on the other. Single projects are research projects (including PhD or Post PhD theses) with one or several researchers involved at one institution. Research networks are structures of collaborative research, involving several scholars from different institutions. According to the GOVDATA definition, a research project should run at least for one year and result in publications or reports. Publications that are not related to a research project have not been included in the database.[3] The survey covers academic research conducted within all kinds of public and private organisations, such as universities, research centres and institutes.[4] In order to facilitate the identification of the projects' thematic foci and to ensure their relevance for GOVDATA users, a detailed thesaurus was developed.[5] Depending on the projects' topic and content, between one and four keywords were assigned to the respective projects.

As was to be expected, the selected data was rather heterogeneous and partly incomplete. Three types of difficulties emerged. The first obstacle was the lack of official data (or public databases) in most of the countries under scrutiny for social sciences in general and research on EU topics in particular. In some cases (for example, France, Spain, Portugal, Greece, Poland), it was possible to use online PhD registers, which proved to be useful sources of information, even if they were not always complete and up-to-date. For most countries, it was difficult to retrieve the necessary information due to the fact that national contact points for collecting and storing data on research activities are rather the exception than the norm. Furthermore, only a few universities, research institutions or even individual scholars maintain a list of research projects that is available online.[6] Thus, the survey mostly reverted to systematic investigations of websites of relevant researchers and research institutions (university departments, faculties, research centres, organisations) in combination with individual contacts and interviews with those responsible at universities and research centres, carried out by the national correspondents.

The second type of difficulty concerns the lack of information regarding the outcome of the completed research. Publications (such as books, articles, or other), resulting from the research projects were often not listed. In some cases, only a few projects could be identified altogether, but this does not mean that no academic discussion on EU governance took place in this country, nor that this topic is not present in publications. Publications that address EU governance often were quite obviously based on insight gained from scientific endeavours but could not be traced back to specific research projects.

Last but not least, cultural and academic traditions account for a differentiated approach to research. At the first meeting of the national correspondents, it resulted that we did not have a uniform understanding of what constitutes a research project. Countries with a long social science research tradition and a well-established system of research funding find it easy to agree on formal criteria to define research and to equate it with a project.

In other words, in its attempt to take stock and evaluate the existing wealth of research on governance in the EU multilevel system, CONNEX faced the dilemma of whether to stick to a narrow definition of what research projects are, a solution that would guarantee a high homogeneity of the dataset while in some cases considerably restricting the quantity of available information; or, what has been done, to select some forms of 'research outcomes' that might allow for certain deviations from the common definition, but this way the plurality of situations would be reflected. The main challenge was, therefore, to ensure comparability across different national settings while being open to a range of national or academic variations and conceptualisation of what had been jointly identified as being suitable for the database.

MAPPING EU GOVERNANCE RESEARCH

GOVDATA contains around 1 600 research projects.[7] The database does not pretend to be fully exhaustive and for different reasons, some relevant projects might be missing. Since at the time of our inquiry governance had not yet been established as an approach in all disciplines and countries alike, it was often difficult to identify relevant projects. Many research projects dealing with constitutional or policy issues dealt with core aspects of governance. Retrieving information was not always easy; therefore, some relevant projects could have been overseen. On the other hand, because CONNEX had decided against a narrow understanding, some projects might be included that touch governance questions only on the margin.

With this caveat in mind, the data should be interpreted with some caution. Nevertheless, they provide striking evidence with regard to the attention paid by scholars to the issues related to EU governance. In the following, we will take a closer look at the spatial distribution and the evolution of research over time, as well as at the variations in the thematic orientation.

Figure 10.1 Spatial distribution of research on governance in Europe

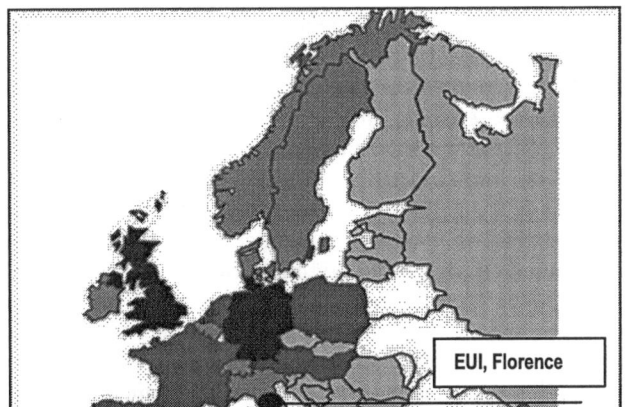

Note: Black: >= 8.5 % of the total number of single projects listed in GOVDATA; Grey: 4%
          - 8.5%; Light grey: 1.5% - 4 %; Very light grey: <= 1.5%; White: Country not covered
          by the survey;
          N = 1572 single research projects entered.

The data provide a rather clear picture of the 'strength' of governance
research in terms of projects listed. The number of identified projects can be
considered an indicator for the salience of this issue in the different national
academic communities in Europe. As depicted on the map (figure 10.1), the
research communities can be clustered: four big clusters of countries appear
in relation to the number of research projects dedicated to EU governance
issues. During the survey period (1994–2006), more than 30 per cent of all
projects were located in only three places: the United Kingdom (187),
Germany (155) and the European University Institute (EUI)[8] in Florence
(137).[9] Further places where intensive research in terms of quantity of
projects has been carried out are France (89), the Netherlands, and Austria
(each with 72 projects identified).

Compared to our expectations based on the size of the respective national
research communities, some results might appear rather surprising. Italy, a
founding member with a large and well-established university system, for
example, has entered a comparatively small number of projects (43). This
may be partly due to difficulties in retrieving information, but can also be
explained by more structural reasons.[10] The high number of identified
projects for Spain (129) stems from the fact that many PhD theses have been
included, for retrieving information on PhD research was easier than in most
other countries surveyed where no national register has been available.

Nonetheless, the projects' expressed references to 'governance' are rather weak.[11] The same applies to the figures for Poland.[12] Whereas small EU member states like Belgium, Ireland, or the Scandinavian countries have registered a significant number of relevant projects (between 20 and 50), only a few projects have been listed by the smaller countries at the southern periphery (Portugal, Greece) and, not surprisingly, in the non-EU member states. Within the countries of Central and Eastern Europe, that joined the EU in 2005 and 2007, there are also quite obvious variations, with more projects in countries like Lithuania and Hungary and less in Bulgaria or Romania.[13]

The geographical embeddedness of governance research

EU governance as a concept and an object of research has emerged in a particular environment. The geographical concentration of research projects and the strong bias on North-West Europe is so far not really surprising. The centre-periphery image in the geographical distribution of governance research reflects, on the one hand, differences of scientific interest and, on the other hand, differences in resources. As research is always embedded in a specific material and intellectual environment, however, this includes not only material capabilities but also other forms of resources, such as academic traditions. Especially research in Central and Eastern European countries suffers from a lack of public funding and is hampered by a lack of appropriate research traditions, albeit to different degrees, since there was no room for autonomous social sciences under Communist rule.[14] In other countries the respective weight and influence of disciplines might be a source of variation.

However, the concentration of research in particular countries and the geographical divide between countries are not the only features of the spatial repartition of governance research. At the sub-national level huge variations can be observed as well. In some cases a large number of projects is concentrated in a limited number of research institutions. In this regard, the size and level of resources available at a research institution are significant, when going together with academic excellence.[15] In addition, according to our records, the role of individuals should not be underestimated. Often, the wealth of research accumulated in a research institution or even in a country depends on few individuals. This is not altogether astonishing given the fact that EU governance is a rather new and specific research topic.[16]

As is generally known, academics are subject to strong inter-institutional and transnational mobility. Many names of key individuals in the field of EU-governance research (both in terms of number of projects and publications) appear in the database in different institutional contexts. This holds especially true for scholars who are at an early stage of their career (PhD or Post Doc level), for career patterns are determined according to supply (opportunities offered; for example Marie Curie Fellowships, bi- or international programmes) and demand (necessary mobility to make a career). With regard to research conducted (mostly PhD theses) by scholars working abroad, following academic research hubs can be identified: the European University Institute in Florence, the Central European University in Budapest and several British universities with a high percentage of foreign doctoral students (above all the London School of Economics and the University of Sussex).

From an epistemological point of view, the main finding of this survey is certainly that in many countries, governance is not a research interest of its own, but merely a by-product of ordinary research activities on the EU. In few places, like the EUI, the United Kingdom, Germany, Denmark and the Netherlands (and to a lesser extend in Switzerland and Belgium), a large share of the identified projects directly refer to the concept of governance, either in the project title or in the abstract describing the research objectives. In other places, many researchers apparently do not see the advantage of linking the particular topics of their research to a more general framework of analysis. Conceivable reasons for this might be an avoidance of abstract concepts or the unfamiliarity with the ongoing theoretical debate.

EVOLUTION OF, AND TRENDS IN GOVERNANCE RESEARCH

A close look at the development of research on EU governance over time shall help us to better understand how and under which conditions this topic has been established on the research agenda of EU affairs. The data collected by CONNEX indeed documents an exponential growth rate from the early 1990s and another remarkable jump in 1999. If we consider not only the number of projects starting every year, but the cumulated number of projects conducted at a certain time, it appears that after the considerable leap at the very end of the 1990s, almost 500 research projects were running simultaneously between January 2000 and January 2002.

From a theoretical perspective, it is plausible to assume that external factors also play a role in this development. The constitutional development of the EU, the accelerated pace of institutional reforms and transfers of political competences (Treaties of Maastricht and Amsterdam), as well as growing public scepticism about the governability of an ever larger Union might have provoked a shift in academic attention. However, interest in governance issues might also be driven by questions raised by sub-disciplines such as research on public policies, public administration and comparative government. When closely scrutinised, the data reveal another story: that is, research is not immediately driven by events, but responds to intellectual input and the availability of material and non-material resources. Whenever academic entrepreneurs translate political concerns and scientific interests into a focused (national) research programme and succeed in obtaining substantial funding, a window of opportunity opens. In the years 1996, 1998, and especially 1999, the huge increase from one year to the next has been supported by the launch of national research programmes in a small, yet important number of countries.

Figure 10.2 Cumulated number of single research projects per year

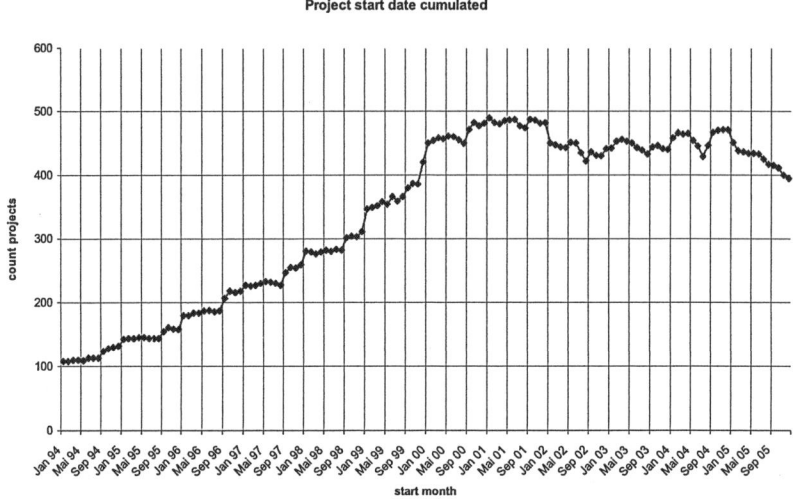

Obviously, the 'research policy' factor in the form of nation- and European-wide framework programmes seems to account for a great part of the general trend towards more EU governance research. The decision to set up a first research programme focusing on European integration and European governance in Norway in 1994 is paradigmatic for the impact of such national initiatives (see Chapter 5). In the following years, similar research schemes focusing on European issues have been established independently by the German Research Foundation and by the British Economic and Social Research Council. These large-scale programmes eased the communication and exchanges between scholars of EU studies working on different questions.

Table 10.1 National research programmes dedicated to the study of EU affairs

Country	Name of the national programmes	Duration	Funding Organisation
Norway	'Advanced Research on the Europeanisation of the Nation-State'[17] (ARENA)	1994–2003 2004–open.[18]	Norwegian Research Council
Germany	'Governing in the EU'[19] 'Institutional design of federal system'	1996–2005 2002–2008	German Science Foundation
France	'Les identités européennes en question'[20]	1998–2002	Centre National de la Recherche Scientifique
Great Britain	'One Europe or several'[21]	1998–2003	British Economic and Social Research Council
Sweden	'Swedish Network for European Studies'[22]	1998–open ended	Swedish Parliament
Netherlands	'From Government to Governance'[23] 'Shifts in Governance' 'Governance in the European Union'	2001–2005 2002–2006 2006–2010	Netherlands Institute of Government; Netherlands Organisation for Scientific Research
Austria	'New Perspectives on Democracy in Europe' (NODE)	2003–2006	Federal Ministry for Education, Research and Culture

By virtue of the financial resources made available, of the number of scholars mobilised and of the thematic priorities they set, such national research programmes have a restructuring effect on the research communities dedicated to EU affairs. As can be observed in the Netherlands, they provide the organisational framework for the emergence of numerous PhD theses and also facilitate the gathering of scholars from various backgrounds around related topics.[24] Furthermore, they provide the conditions for developing synergies and for achieving the critical mass that is needed for large comparative studies and for in-depth empirical research on the different aspects of EU governance. Last but not least, such programmes establish continuity by building schools of thought between scholars sharing similar theoretical or methodological approaches and epistemic communities. On this basis, a national academic community dedicated to EU governance can emerge (see Chapters 3 and 4).

Yet, despite a common focus on Europe and similar research interests, these national networks operate in quite an isolated way and most of the time very differently from each other. They strongly reflect national intellectual traditions, structures and priorities.[25] Apart from meeting at international conferences, there are few contacts between the networks (mostly limited to the invitation of 'keynote speakers' at conferences) and no institutionalised cross-cutting connections.[26]

The transnational dimension of EU governance research

During the period of reference, large research schemes were launched well beyond the national level networks, that is, projects involving scholars from two or more research institutions could be identified, either at the national level or with a transnational dimension.[27] Indeed, in this respect it is worth mentioning that besides being the object of study, the European Union is also an actor in the development of research in and on the EU. The figures presented in the following table highlight the influence of the European Framework Programmes on the evolution of EU governance research.

Table 10.2 Impact of the EU funding on the development of EU governance research[28]

Framework Programme	Number of relevant projects funded	Number of partner organisations involved	Funding
FP4 (1994–1998)	4	82	-[29]
FP5 (1998–2002)	29	178	18 436 300 €
FP6 (2002–2006)	40	491	44 518 700 €
Total	**73**	**751**	**62 955 000 €**

Whereas in the year 2000, EU-funded projects accounted 'only' for four out of seven research projects involving more than one research institution (so called 'research networks' in the GOVDATA terminology), the relationship totally changed one year later with 14 EU funded projects out of 16 in 2001, and 11 out of 15 in 2002. The huge number of partner institutions (either universities or research centres) involved in the research projects funded under FP5 and especially FP6, in combination with the considerable amount of funding available, had a strong effect on the development of EU governance research, both in countries where it had been already well-established, and in countries where it had hardly existed so far. Besides encouraging the integration of the different stances of EU governance research and boosting the confrontation of approaches between different disciplines and academic traditions, the main advantage of the large projects funded by the EU is that they institutionalise cross-country communication and provide an appropriate frame to Europeanise the expertise accumulated at national level, either in individual projects or in national networks.

THEMATIC VARIATIONS

A key question concerning the development of EU governance research is whether there is an interplay between the development of the political agenda, on the one hand, and of the academic research agenda, on the other. Thematic variations over time and across countries provide some evidence on this matter.

Time variations of thematic priorities

Since the beginning of the 1990s, many projects have focused on traditional aspects of EU studies, most notably on the Union's public policies. Similarly important has been the research on the EU institutions and on the different aspects of its legal framework (EU treaties and constitution, *Acquis communautaire*, EU regulations and process of standardisation). Yet, as shown by the following figure, during the last two years of the survey (2004 and 2005), the share of projects related to the decision-making process in the EU (agenda-setting, policy formulation, implementation and evaluation) and dealing with governance issues *stricto-sensus* (multi-level governance, policy networks, public-private partnership, soft policy instruments, Open Method of Coordination, comitology) has considerably increased.

When we follow the proposition that 'external' (Rosamond 2006) or 'pull' factors (Wessels 2006) affect the thematic orientation of EU studies, we should expect that each national research community has the propensity to take up issues directly related to the specific national situation, above all how EU governance affects its national polity. Variations among EU member states would then been generated from a) differences in the significance of governance questions in different policy domains; b) as far as institutional questions are concerned (for example, the role of sub-national level, which would be more important for federal countries); and c) the types of 'modes of governance' some countries are more interested in, because of their own socio-political structure (for instance, interest in issues related to the involvement of civil society organisations or stakeholders *versus* horizontal administrative forms of adjustment and coordination).

Trends and Patterns in Research

Figure 10.3 Evolution of the projects' thematic dimensions of research over time

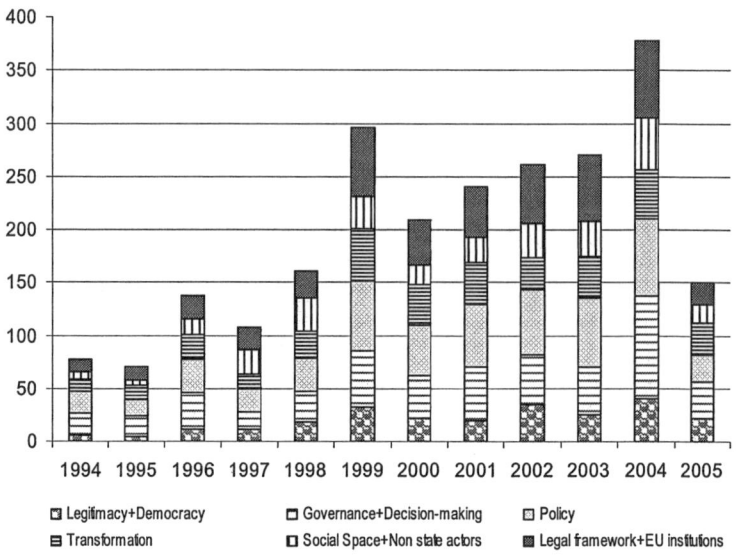

The picture revealed by GOVDATA, however, shows that epistemological factors are relevant, too. Whenever thematic preoccupations and priorities follow political changes at EU or national level, the way issues are tackled remains a matter of the respective research communities' perception and awareness of the significance, scope and range of these changes. Scholars tend to deal with the changing nature of the EU, that is, the relative significance of political change in the real world for their respective country, through the prism of their accustomed academic traditions, for instance in terms of disciplines and schools of thought. This tension makes clear why some major variations in the geographical distribution of thematic priorities can be also observed between countries that are in similar situations in terms of political setting or length of EU membership.

Geographical variations of thematic priorities

It is notable that in Eastern and Central European countries European integration has a broader meaning than in Western Europe; that is why numerous projects cover not just the EU, but also NATO or the Council of Europe. In this context, it appears that governance research in the new member states and in the neighbouring countries is linked to their integration in the European regional organisations in general and to the transformations in the course of accession.[30] A look at the projects from these countries reveals that often the research is focused either on the adaptation of the domestic administrative system or policies of specific national interest, above all regional and structural policy.[31] Furthermore, it is worth mentioning that many projects conducted in the countries of Eastern Europe apply a 'down to earth' approach to Europeanisation and its effects, that is, one can observe that in countries that are newcomers to the EU, the few EU specialists often work as policy advisers and thus do not engage as much in fundamental as in applied research. This circumstance accounts for the strong focus on practical aspects, and by the same token the relative disregard for explicit reference to theories or advanced conceptual tools, such as governance.

For reasons developed in the previous chapters, huge variations also exist between the countries of Western Europe. EU policies are a favourite field of governance research in the old member states.[32] This concentration on policies reflects both the country-specific interests and the traditional focus of the disciplines in governance research. Policy studies rank very high in countries like Switzerland (61.5 per cent of all single projects identified for this country), Greece (50 per cent), UK (47.6 per cent) and Belgium (39.5 per cent). Although, here again, interests and priorities diverge. Along with Norway, most of the Swiss projects are related to the impact of EU policies on their country. In Greece, more than 40 per cent of these projects deal with regional policy or environmental issues, whereas in the UK, research covers a wide range of public policies, which also may be due to the large number of existing projects. Social policy is an important issue among governance projects in Greece, Austria, Hungary and Germany; as are trade issues in the United Kingdom and at the EUI, or the monetary union in Germany, Benelux and Poland. Great attention is paid to the subject of competition policy at the EUI, in the UK and in Italy. Immigration issues play a notable role in research conducted in France, Switzerland and at the EUI. Generally, first pillar issues still dominate the agenda of policy-oriented governance research. Only very recently several research projects have been dedicated to exploring the governance of common foreign policy, security and defence policy, as well as policing.

Equally important are questions of transformation, covering issues such as adaptation, modernisation, institutional change and Europeanisation, which do not have the same relevance everywhere. Hence, it is not surprising that these topics rank high in new member states like Hungary and Slovenia (and to some extent Poland), but also in countries like Norway and Switzerland that are closely connected to the EU.

About one third of all research projects explicitly refer and contribute to the conceptualisation of European governance. Though multi-level governance has been a prominent and much debated approach since the early 1990s, only one of 12 projects follows an approach that conceptualises the EU as a multi-level polity. For obvious reasons this approach is likely to appeal to researchers in countries with a federal structure (for example, Germany, Austria and Belgium), where more than one third of the projects' research refer to this multi-level approach. However, the concept of multi-level governance is also popular in the United Kingdom and in the Netherlands. Countries at the southern and eastern periphery, in contrast, seem to make very little use of this approach, despite the fact that a large number of projects in these countries are dedicated to the sub-national level, for example in Spain or Poland.

Since the formal recommendation of the 'Open Method of Coordination' by the Lisbon strategy, agreed upon by the European Council in March 2000, research on new modes of governance has become a growing industry. In contrast to the Community method, the new modes of governance rely on arriving at mutual agreements by way of voluntary cooperation, learning from best practice and communication, and benchmarking. Coordination is achieved through non-coercive methods and through the incorporation of private actors in policy formulation. Most of the projects dedicated to this question started in 2004 and thereafter, and they are concentrated in a few places, most notably the EUI (between 2004–2008 it coordinated a large network of scholars dedicated to New Modes of Governance[33]), and Switzerland, as this country's experience with new modes of regulation provides a fruitful background for this kind of research.

As to the normative dimension of governance, issues of democracy and legitimacy have played a minor role until recently.[34] They are however more a matter of theoretical reflections than of empirical research. Significantly, there are just 28 projects referring to the concept of 'democratic deficit' in their title or abstract, and very few of them are carried out in the southern or eastern part of Europe. The concentration of such projects in some countries seems to reflect the political concerns regarding the democratic quality of the EU expressed by their political elites. In Sweden, 48 per cent of the projects deal with issues of democracy and 32 per cent with legitimacy. In Austria, we find 22 per cent, respectively 20 per cent, and in Norway 34 per cent, respectively 22 per cent. Projects focusing on legitimacy and democracy always reveal a normative orientation, which can be observed in France where both topics rank high and particular attention is paid, for example, to questions of civic participation and 'democracy from below'. In contrast, research on accountability is clearly concentrated in the Netherlands and in the United Kingdom, and to a lesser extent in Germany.[35]

Given the strong dominance of political science in governance research, it is not surprising that a large number of projects are dedicated to traditional aspects of the EU polity, such as the role of individual EU institutions, their interaction with member states, as well as the role of and impact on member state institutions. Interestingly, the share of projects dedicated to studying the role of national governments, parliaments, courts or administrations in the European multi-level system of governance is much higher in the new member states and in the United Kingdom, whereas these topics play a quite subsidiary role in old core countries such as France, the Netherlands and Germany.

Research on political participation, including issues like the European party system and European elections, is not very well-spread, except in Sweden, the Czech Republic, Ireland or Hungary. In Germany, some scholars have been strong in initiating European Elections Studies and are still today very much engaged in this kind of research.

Here again, the geographical distribution is all but balanced, which shows that European countries do not have the same thematic priorities when conducting research. In many cases, the relative strength of a topic within national governance research greatly depends on the research priorities of some individual scholars. Besides the political relevance of some topics, structural factors, such as graduate schools or research centres carrying out focused research, hence play a role, for they facilitate thematic continuity over time. Although research on interest intermediation is equally weak in general (less than 5 per cent of all projects deal with issues such as lobbying or advocacy (this corresponds to the keyword 'interest intermediation'), geographical focal points can be seen in Germany, Austria and Belgium. These are countries with a long tradition of research on national interest representation.

The study of the societal basis of European democracy has developed rather late in European research. The empirical exploration of Europe's civil society and of the emergent transnational public space started with a sudden leap at the end of the 1990s. Since then, academic interest has been steady, but compared to other thematic dimensions of EU governance research, it remains at a low level, which is not unexpected since the 'social space' is a traditional domain of sociology, a discipline underrepresented in EU research in general and in governance research in particular. Sociological research in Europe is still caught in the trap of 'methodological nationalism' and takes little notice of the trans national dimension of societies.[36]

Overall, the survey reveals two common denominators of all the projects listed. First, EU governance research tends to follow a pattern of self-centred and self-referring national focuses. Although many opportunities for European-wide exchange do exist (for example, international conferences and other places for academic exchange) and research results are disseminated in internationally renowned journals and book series, the national agendas with their specific preoccupations and interests still matter. This can represent a serious obstacle for an Europeanisation of research, as desired by the EU Commission.[37] Secondly, research based on cross-national comparisons is limited and mostly restricted to a few countries, that is, the 'usual suspects' Great Britain, Germany, and France, as well as some of the new member states (in regard to research on Europeanisation).[38] Because of the high transaction costs, fragmented resources and expertise, no Europe-wide comparison on governance research had been carried out until the two EU funded large-scaled research cooperation projects that were CONNEX and NEWGOV. Here, one of the main obstacles for the study of the EU polity becomes obvious, namely that an individual researcher will hardly be capable of grasping and digging into all the different facets of EU governance which is multi-level policy specific with a great variety of actor constellations. Furthermore, research cooperation is the only guarantee that the different perspectives that individual disciplines and national experiences can add, will come to the fore.

As can be seen from the comparative evaluation, different patterns of research foci and thematic priorities of projects emerge. Despite some variations, similarities come into light between the Nordic countries, between countries from the southern part of the EU and between countries from Eastern and Central Europe. Political reasons play a role, but also the scientific background is of importance, especially the degree of development of the social sciences.

DISCIPLINARY BIAS

EU research does not exist in a vacuum, of course, but reflects prevalent theoretical and methodological priorities (Wessels 2006, 243). This applies to all disciplines involved. On this matter, the empirical evidence provided by GOVDATA confirms the general impression gained by surveying the academic literature; that is, research on EU governance is predominantly a concern of political science. More than two thirds of all projects have a political science background, whereas law and economics together give input to nearly half of the projects and sociology to 11.5 per cent.[39] Related to the total number of 2226 entries), the share of projects with a political science background still accounts for 52 per cent (see figure below). This bias becomes even more manifest when we look at the projects that deal specifically with governance issues, that is, focus on multi-level governance, network governance, private–public network/partnership, comitology, soft policy instruments, and Open Method of Coordination.[40] However, among the mono-disciplinary governance projects, the role of political science is less prominent (61.5 per cent). Projects solely following a legal approach account for 19 per cent, 13 per cent have an economic approach, 2.2 per cent a sociological approach and 4.3 per cent from other disciplines (history, philosophy, etc.).

Multi-disciplinary research is not very common since on average less than 25 per cent of the 1 572 single projects combine two or more disciplines. Political science occupies a pivotal position; most frequent combinations are political science and law, political science and economics, and political science and sociology. In fact, there are very few multi-disciplinary projects that exclude political science. The share of multi-disciplinary projects is higher in Switzerland, Hungary, Germany and France than in other countries. Yet only in few places (Switzerland, France, Germany and Poland), do all four major disciplines contribute significantly to EU governance research.[41]

Although 'interdisciplinary work' ranks very high in the self-conception of the scientific community, obviously it is still an exception in European research. There is a general lack of communication and co-operation between disciplines and sub-disciplines. Disciplinary entrenched approaches retain much of their force, which makes co-operation and cross-fertilisation in multidisciplinary projects very difficult. Furthermore, the disciplines are at different stages of development as to the significance of the EU governance issues, which represents another problem, for some disciplines are much more advanced than others.

Figure 10.4 Distribution of research projects according to the disciplinary affiliation of the researchers involved

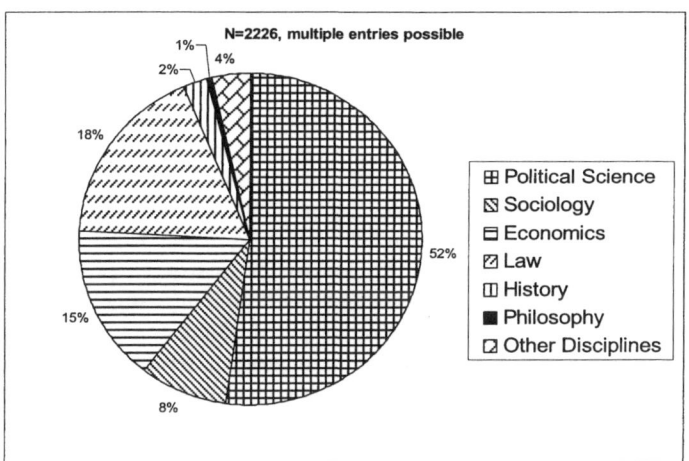

Note: For each project, depending on the disciplinary affiliation of the researcher involved, several keywords could be attributed. This distribution is based on the total number of entries (2226) and not on the number of single projects.

For structural reasons that are analysed in Part II of this book, some disciplines are more strongly represented than others in governance research, depending on where the projects are located. Research in law is particularly prevalent in Italy, at the EUI, in the Netherlands, Switzerland and in the Czech Republic. Sociology is relatively strong in France and economics in Lithuania and Poland.[42] Disciplinary specificities are coupled with thematic issues. Economists concentrate on policies and integration and to a lesser extent on transformation,[43] whilst sociologists are strongly involved in research focusing on the 'social space', integration and EU policies. Unsurprisingly, the study of the EU legal framework is a matter of law scholars: Two thirds of the projects dealing with this topic have a law background, against one third coming from political science. In contrast, research on EU institutions is clearly a matter of political science (74 per cent against 25 per cent for law). The topic of transformation is dominated by political science (73 per cent), yet, it is also addressed by a significant number of law scholars (22 per cent), of economists (18 per cent) and also by sociologists (11.5 per cent).[44]

UNEQUAL RESOURCES

It goes without saying that the level and intensity of academic research very much depends on the personal and financial resources and infrastructure available. Because of its complexity and of its broad geographical coverage, EU governance research in particular requires a critical mass of research capacities. In this sense, the huge imbalance in terms of funding available for research does have an impact on the differentiated level of research conducted so far all over Europe.

The existence of financial incentives through national research funding schemes or other external funding opportunities at national level (for example, foundations) has proved to be a positive factor in establishing environments favourable to the emergence of EU governance research. This can take many forms, such as establishing large research programmes (like in the United Kingdom and in Germany) or national research schools (Netherlands Institute of Government), not to mention long-term commitments like the ARENA Centre for European Studies in Norway. Apart from providing resources for ambitious research projects, such external factors exert a positive influence on multi-disciplinary research co-operation which is mostly strongly encouraged by public donors, like in the Netherlands, in Germany or in Switzerland.

Competition for subsidies from national or international funding authorities seems to be the best condition of developing and maintaining scientific excellence, since selection is based on a peer review evaluation. In large parts of Europe however, the research infrastructure is weak and external sources of funding are limited, in that not all countries are able to equip their universities with money for research. In some countries, scholars still receive no research funding aside from their own salary. Whereas in the Netherlands or Norway all PhD theses are funded; in Spain, Portugal, Greece, Bulgaria and Romania, only few PhD students receive grants to conduct their research.[45] This is still the case in Germany, but here rapid changes are taking place, as interdisciplinary and international graduate colleges are being established and more money is being allocated for the support of interdisciplinary research networking.

Funding provided by intergovernmental (bilateral and international) funding schemes such as the European Science Foundation, or by the supranational level (EU Framework Programmes of Research, Jean-Monnet initiative) open new windows of opportunity and have a structuring effect. They facilitate cross-national networking and strengthen research in parts of Europe that have been less privileged in terms of resources so far. In Greece, for instance, the financial opportunities provided by European projects led to the creation of European Centres and institutes within universities, thus setting-up the necessary infrastructure for EU governance research. Moreover, the involvement of scholars from the periphery in large- or medium-scale international projects enables them to become connected to mainstream research. The benefit of such a participation, however, is not limited to a one way transfer of academic excellence to the periphery but can turn to cross-fertilization and mutual benefit owing to the confrontation of different intellectual perspectives.

That said, it is worth recalling that not all research and *a fortiori* not all knowledge production results from formal research projects. A review of EU governance research should not overlook the fact that the books and articles which decisively contribute to the academic debate might not necessarily be the outcome of formal research projects, whether externally or internally funded. Here again, what emerges in the European landscape is not a unified picture, but rather contrasting views of a heterogeneous, fragmentary European research area that is characterised by varied practices, modes of funding and levels of resources. The current state of EU governance research is, therefore, a mixed result. On the one side, there are organised forms of research: research programmes or frameworks with a top-down definition of thematic priorities (EU Framework programmes) or built on bottom-up initiatives by individual researchers and then funded by national or European donors (such as the DFG or now the European Research Council). On the other side, we find the richness of varied individual initiatives that for a long time were more or less isolated from each others or, on the contrary, embedded in schools of thought and in research strands.

CONCLUSION

As brought to light by this analysis, recent years have witnessed a general increase of the number of projects dedicated to EU governance. Still, some key questions remain. The first type of question concerns the further evolution of this trend. There are some dynamic factors such as existing thematic networks, acknowledged standards for scientific research, intensified presence of broader circles of scholars at international conferences, or improved mobility of scholars, which indicate an evolution in the direction of further professionalisation of research on EU affairs. However, when it comes to the topic of EU governance, the future of research dedicated to such issues is more uncertain. Governance is not a thematic priority anymore in the 7th Framework Programme of the EU. In addition, research on some aspects of the governance *problèmatique* has already been worked through: the Open Method of Coordination was not as groundbreaking as expected and the question of what is really new in the 'new instruments' has been extensively investigated (Dehousse and Boussaguet 2008). Furthermore, if we consider that all new concepts are subject to a typical life cycle, we can also predict a decrease of interest in and resources allocated to this topic in the years to come.

Another important question relates to the coherence of the concept in future research. Since no common ground for a governance theory has been established (Kohler-Koch and Rittberger 2007; Olsen in this volume), it has to be expected that the concept will be used in an even more heterogeneous way than at present. Nevertheless, cognitive and social integration achieved in large research projects such as CONNEX contribute to a mutual understanding and a convergence of views among a large international and inter-disciplinary community of researchers.[46]

The CONNEX stock-taking exercise has displayed the great pluralism of EU governance research in Europe. In this context, there is obviously no danger of a conceptual hegemony originating from places where governance research is strong. Regarding some concerns expressed about the dominance of English speaking literature on EU affairs and its bias (Poppa 2008), it has to be kept in mind that different and partly competing conceptions co-existing in Europe about what a legitimate political order is or should be (Wiener 2007) will maintain the conceptual diversity. Therefore, for tackling the evolving and multi-faced nature of multilevel governance in an appropriate way, it is even more necessary to invest in developing common intellectual frameworks that combine different geographical and disciplinary perspectives.

NOTES

1. http://www.connex-network.org/govdata/
2. Data about research projects conducted in the following countries were compiled: Austria, Belgium, Bulgaria, Croatia, Czech Republic, Denmark, Estonia, Finland, France, Germany, Greece, Hungary, Ireland, Italy, Latvia, Lithuania, Netherlands, Norway, Poland, Portugal, Romania, Russia, Albania and other countries of former Yugoslavia: (Serbia and Monte Negro – Bosnia and Herzegovina – Macedonia), Slovakia, Slovenia, Spain, Sweden, Switzerland and the United Kingdom. Projects carried out at the European University Institute in Florence were recorded separately, since the institute attracts PhD students from all over Europe.

3. Within the framework of the stock-taking exercise, another database called GOVLIT was dedicated to register the academic literature dealing with EU governance. For an analysis of the EU governance debate in scientific literature, see also the chapter on the EU governance debate in scientific literature.

4. Not the nationality of the responsible researcher was a criteria for the geographical classification of a project but the localisation of the place (university, research centre) to which the project coordinator was affiliated to at the time when the project was going on.

5. See: http://www.connex-network.org/govdata/thesaurus.

6. More often than not online information was available only during the lifetime of a project but was not updated or even closed after funding of a project had expired.

7. Due to some adjustments and completions since the beginning of the task, the current number of projects listed in GOVDATA may not exactly correspond to the figures we refer to in this chapter. The figures used for the following map and figures relate to the advancement of GOVDATA at December 2006: 1572 'single research projects' and 70 'research networks'.

8. The EUI, of course, is not a country but an institution and as such an important place for research within and on Europe, with its own tradition of comparative and transnational research.

9. A main criterion for the national classification of a research project was the country in which it has primarily been conducted, independent from the nationality of the researchers.

10. See chapter on the particularities of Europe's South.

11. Only 5 per cent of the 129 projects selected for the database use the word 'governance' in their title or in the abstract.

12. There are 103 research projects listed for Poland, but only 8.5 per cent of them are directly related to the concept of governance.

13. Research in Hungary may be slightly overrepresented because of the input from the Central European University in Budapest. For further explanations, see the chapter 'Research on EU governance in central and eastern Europe'.

14. In many Central and East European countries some disciplines were more affected, and others were less affected by political oppression and international isolation. Hence, the contribution of economics to EU research ranks higher than in Western Europe where political science is the leading discipline in EU governance.

15. For each of the following research institutions, more than 20 single research projects could be identified during the survey period: London School of Economics, MZES University of Mannheim, Science Po Paris and its different labs, ARENA Oslo, University of Utrecht.

16. On the whole, non-academic research in this field is weak, except in some of the new EU member states, for example, Lithuania, where think-tanks and other private actors are conducting studies related to governance issues. These are mainly research contracts from Ministries or other public administrations asking for reports on salient issues.

17. http://www.arena.uio.no.

18. In 2004 the ARENA program was terminated, but at the same time ARENA – a permanent Centre for European Studies - was created at the University of Oslo. In year 2007, ARENA has been granted 26 million NOK by the Norwegian Research Council to do research on the basic foundations of the political order in Europe.

19. http://www.mzes.uni-mannheim.de/projekte/reg_europ/dfg.htm

20. http://www.msh-alpes.prd.fr/programmecnrs/europe/base.htm

21. http://www.one-europe.ac.uk/

22. http://europaperspektiv.statsvet.uu.se/index.htm

23. http://www.bsk.utwente.nl/nig/research.htm

24. See part on the Netherlands.

25. For a stimulating analysis of the differences between Germany and Great Britain, see Wallace 2003.

26. It should be remembered that in the late 1990s, the EU did not support applications for cross-national cooperations because, at that time, the Commission viewed the governance topic not as relevant.

27. Besides the EU with the different Framework Programmes of research, there are other sources of funding for international research projects, such as the European Science Foundation or consortia of national funding schemes, but they have not been engaged in large research projects on EU governance.

28. Source: CORDIS; own calculation. The number of relevant projects funded includes all forms of collaborative projects as well as Marie Curie Fellowships, but not the funding of conferences.

29. No data available.

30. Up to three keywords could be attached to each project; the keyword 'integration' was attached to 84 per cent of research projects in applicant countries, to about 60 per cent of the projects of new member states and to less than 30 per cent of projects of old member states.

31. Around one third of the Polish projects deal with (among other issues) the sub-national level.

32. In this respect, Lithuania is an exception, since it is the only new member state whose share of projects dedicated to policy research is far higher than the average number of projects in the whole sample.

33. http://www.eu-newgov.org/

34. There is a perceptible increase of the number of projects dedicated to legitimacy issues from 2001 onwards.

35. Each with between 23 per cent of all projects referring to this word in their title or abstract.

36. More than one third of sociological research listed in GOVDATA is dedicated to the 'social space'.

37. This, however, does not apply to countries like the United Kingdom and to a lesser extent to Hungary, with a high number of foreign PhD students who bring along their own thematic interests.

38. There are simple reasons for this: 1) a high percentage of research is dissertation research, which means that one person cannot manage more than three countries; 2) language barriers limit the possibilities of comparisons; and 3) even with sufficient funding, the transaction costs of research cooperation are deterring – only possible when the cooperation limits itself to pre-existing data collection (poll and opinion research).

39. Because several projects are interdisciplinary, the disciplines do not add up to 100 per cent. Other disciplines (philosophy or history) are – in quantitative terms – negligible. 385 projects out of 1 572 combine two or more disciplines.

40. 85 per cent of these projects have a political science background. Other disciplines, such as law, economics and sociology, together account for less than 50 per cent.

41. That is, each of the four disciplines accounts for at least 10 per cent of all the single projects.

42. However, some methodological bias, such as the disciplinary affiliation of the national correspondent in charge of supervising the data collection, may have lead to a statistical distortion in the sense of over-representation of his/her own discipline.

43. For instance, 66.5 per cent of the projects involving economists deal with EU policies.

44. Since up to three disciplines could be attributed, the total is more than 100 per cent.

45. At the same time, three out of four Spanish research projects are doctoral theses. There is only little research conducted by established scholars because of the limited funding that is available.

46. Social integration pertain to the interactions between, on the one hand, research actors and the object of research and, on the other hand, between the actors and the knowledge already existing or being produced and which may lead to a process of socialisation. Cognitive integration deals more with the content and conditions of knowledge production and concern interactions between knowledge and actors and knowledge and object of research, and can on its part lead to cross-fertilization and accumulation of shared knowledge (Larat and Edler 2008).

REFERENCES

Dehousse, Renaud and Laurie Boussaguet (eds) (2008), *The Transformation of EU Policies? EU Governance at Work*, Connex Report Series Vol. 8, Mannheim.
Kohler-Koch, Beate and Berthold Rittberger (2006), Review article 'The governance turn in EU studies', *Journal of Common Market Studies*, **44**, 2006.
Larat, Fabrice and Jakob Edler (2008), 'How does research integration work? Assessing the work and impact of FP6 new instruments in the field of social sciences and humanities', paper presented at the conference *How Does Research Integration Work?*, Brussels, 17 June 2008, http://www.connex-network.org/research-integration/.
Popa, Ioana (2008), 'La structuration internationale des études européennes: un espace scientifique dissymétrique', in Didier Georgakakis and Marine de Lasalle (eds), *La 'nouvelle gouvernance européenne'. Genèses et usages politiques d'un livre blanc*, Strasbourg: Presse Universitaires de Strasbourg, pp. 92–117.
Rosamond, Ben (2006), 'The political sciences of European integration: Disciplinary history and EU studies', in Knud Erik Jørgensen, Mark A. Pollack and Ben Rosamond (eds), *Handbook of European Union Politics*, London: Sage Publications Ltd, pp. 7–30.
Wallace, Helen (2003), 'Contrasting images of European governance', in Beate Kohler-Koch (ed.), *Linking EU and national governance*, Oxford: Oxford University Press, pp. 1–9.
Wessels, Wolfgang (2006), 'Cleavages, controversies and convergences in European Union studies', in Michelle Cini and Angela K. Bourne (eds), *European Union Studies*, Houndmills: Palgrave Macmillan, pp. 233–246.
Wiener, Antje (ed.) (2007), 'Contested Meanings of Principles and Procedures of Democracy: The Challenge of Democratic Governance beyond the State', Special Issue *Comparative European Politics*, **5** (1).

11. EU Governance: Where Do We Go From Here?

Johan P. Olsen

RECENT ADVANCES INTO NEW DIRECTIONS

A stock-taking exercise of research on patterns and trends in the governance of the European Union inevitably brings up questions. How can students of the EU get from describing recent advances to speculating about possible new directions and research agendas? How promising are terms such as 'governance' and 'the new governance' for improving our understanding of how the Union is governed and whether, and to what degree, there is a transformation in its system of governance?[1]

This epilogue holds that improved theoretical understanding, first requires the ability to overcome four impediments present in the literature. The challenges are to tidy up the conceptual morass, to amend the inconclusive evidence, to oust the ghost of 'the state' as a major frame of reference, and to get beyond the tyranny of dichotomies. Second, it is acknowledged that the observation of a 'governance turn' in EU studies (Kohler-Koch and Rittberger 2006) is an important one, including the assertions that the 'new governance' involves a transformation of, and a new perspective on, the European Union's system of governance (Kohler-Koch and Eising 1999), a new theoretical and normative agenda (Hix 1998), and a new form of political domination (Schmitter 1996). Nevertheless, it is far from obvious that dichotomies such as 'government' versus 'governance' and 'old' versus 'new' modes of governance are the most useful analytical tools for improving the understanding of EU developments, although they are treated as exclusive alternatives.

The main argument is that the analysis of the EU system of governance can benefit from being better-related to some enduring and recurrent themes in the theoretical study of democratic governance and thereby to the long history of ideas about how societies can and should be governed best. This implies a reappraisal of how systems of governance may be conceptualised and what are the key characteristics that differentiate among modes of governance. It also implies a reassessment of the achievements and significance of different modes of governance. To what degree, and under what conditions, are systems of governance likely to have independent and enduring implications and what kinds of political phenomena do they impact on? Furthermore, there is a need to make explicit the normative assumptions the different modes of governance are based upon, their presumed virtues and claims to legitimacy, and their alleged causal effects upon relevant values, goals, interests, norms and values. Finally, it is necessary to reappraise our understanding of the occurrence of modes of governance and the shifts within them, that is, their emergence, their ups and downs, their transformations and their disappearance.

TRANSCENDING FOUR IMPEDIMENTS

Undoubtedly, the term 'governance' as a way of describing, explaining and justifying of how the common affairs of political communities are, and should be governed, has been very popular in the last few decades. It has been used in analyses of states and New Public Management reforms, world politics, international law-making and private corporations (Rhodes 1996, 1997, Rosenau and Czempiel 1992, Boyle and Chinkin 2007). 'Governance' has even been dedicated its own encyclopaedia (Bevir 2006). Nevertheless, the popularity of the term has not led to a consensus on its precise meaning, purpose, utility, or how it can best be studied.

Tidying up the conceptual morass

'Governance' implies a process-oriented approach to influence and control. It has been argued that a new language is needed in order to capture changes in the real world, involving a transformation from an old mode of governance to a new mode (Rhodes 2003). The 'new' mode is characterised by civil society involvement in public policy-making and by an extensive use of informal networks. The Open Method of Coordination (OMC) is also often mentioned as an example of 'the new governance' in the European Union. The OMC is a 'soft' method, featuring agreed standards, goals, guidelines, benchmarks, 'best practice', indicators, monitoring arrangements, and time tables. Yet, the member states are free to choose how they meet the requirements. There is some control through the processes of blaming and shaming, but the Union has no legal means to enforce compliance.

However, 'governance' remains a contested term. While suggesting that 'governance' involves 'the continuous political process of setting explicit goals for society and engage in their implementation and enforcement', Kohler-Koch observes that 'no consensus concept has emerged' (Kohler-Koch 2008a: 104, also Rhodes 1996, 1997, Pierre and Peters 2000). The problematic conceptual ambiguity of 'governance' is also aggravated because there is a similar lack of clarity when it comes to other key concepts in the study of the EU, for example, 'integration', 'Europeanization', and 'democracy'. In none of these cases has there, over time, been a clear trend towards clarification and consensus about a single meaning, or a small set of competing meanings. As long as there are many and often ambiguous answers to what 'governance' is and what makes certain modes of governance 'new', students of EU governance are likely to address different empirical phenomena using the same term. As a result, it becomes difficult to agree upon what is actually happening in the Union.

Inconclusive evidence

In spite of a rapidly growing body of empirical studies, the evidence of key aspects of EU governance is inconclusive. Among the many contested issues are questions such as: how new is the 'new mode of governance' and how significant is this mode in the EU? How important are private actors from civil society associations, industry and private enterprises compared to governmental actors, and how important are informal networks compared to formal organisational arrangements? Have new modes of governance replaced or complemented the original mode of EU governance, the Community Method? What are the impacts upon member states (Börzel and Risse 2006, Citi and Rhodes 2007, Börzel 2008, Dehousse and Boussaguet 2008, Dehousse 2008, Kohler-Koch 2008b)?

Here the attention is primarily focused upon the inconclusive evidence when it comes to three major claims made by advocates of the 'new mode'. It is held that it is giving rise to 'good governance' by improving (a) the functional performance and problem solving capabilities of the Union; (b) the democratic quality of the Union and reducing its 'democratic deficit'; and (c) its flexibility and its ability to learn, adapt, and reorganise itself.

Explanations of the emergence and success of the 'new' modes also vary. While some see such modes as the OMC as post-modern innovations and improvements, others interpret the use of 'soft' modes as a result of weakness and conflict. That is, their use reflects the member states' unwillingness to grant European level institutions authority, power and resources in specific policy areas. It is also suggested that modes such as the OMC may represent a transitional episode in a development dominated by traditional forms of governance, as a prelude to legally binding rules (Eberlein and Kerwer 2004). One factor contributing to these different interpretations is whether 'the state' is used as the key frame of reference or not.

Ousting the ghost of 'the state'

The assumed shift in modes of governance from 'old' to 'new', like the assumed shift from 'Old Public Administration' to 'New Public Management' (Dunleavy and Hood 1994), is often interpreted within a framework in which the ghost of 'the state' plays a key role. 'The state' is portrayed as being organised on the basis of an overarching public authority and a monopoly of coercive power, hierarchy, command and enforcement of laws. This 'traditional form of government' is then contrasted with the 'new governance', including private actors ('stakeholders') and bargaining within informal, decentralised, flexible and non-hierarchical networks. No one is in command or controls all relevant resources. The central government is no longer supreme. It is 'hollowed out' and replaced by more diffuse systems of governance and control (Rhodes 1996).

This interpretation resembles an ideal model of the sovereign and autonomous territorial state that is able to make and enforce binding decisions for a territory and a population. Weber, for example, argued that 'in the end, the modern state controls the total means of political organization, which actually come together under a single head' (Weber 1970: 82). In contrast, Bendix saw 'the state' as a historically delimited term that implied 'not only a transition in the early modern period but sooner or later a transition to new and yet unrealized or unrecognized institutional patterns in the future' (Bendix 1968: 9). This interpretation of the state as a dynamic historical phenomenon, developed and developing in the European context, is reflected in the writings of Rokkan (1999) and Bartolini (2005). They also document the precarious and shifting role of the political centre and of public authority and resources, of the variety of state–society relations, and the many different mixes of majoritarian and non-majoritarian institutions that have historically existed in Europe.

Identifying the 'old' mode of governance solely with formal political institutions, hierarchy, and coercion requires a weak disciplinary memory. Among students of politics, the belief in the importance (and explanatory power) of politics and government for the flow of history has varied over time. Liberalists and Marxists have usually given primacy to economic structures, forces and actors, viewing political actors as administrators of the great necessities or the instruments of the ruling, capitalist class. The behavioral revolution in political science was a reaction to a one-sided focus upon formal-legal institutions and actors. In the heydays of the welfare state, a growing agenda emerged together with participation of non-state actors that could provide information, other resources and legitimacy, involving corporate pluralism (Rokkan 1966), integrated organisational participation in government (Olsen 1981) and 'private government' (Streeck and Schmitter 1985). Generally, the limits of governing solely through coercion are well-known and the command theory of control has never been wholly valid (Goodin, Rein and Moran 2006: 12, 15). In modern democracies, including European states, consensus and support have been political achievements, not givens, and compliance has usually been based upon a mix of consent, incentives and sanctions.

An implication is that using 'the state', as portrayed in some state theories, as the backdrop for studying and assessing transformations of EU governance may lead to false interpretations of which transformations actually have taken place. It may be more promising to compare the Union with state practices and their many different modes of governance and political organisation. Analyses of the functioning, development, and effects of the EU's system of governance, then, have to take into consideration that what is called 'states' in everyday language involves a variety of actors, institutional structures, agendas, and public–private boundaries. States use complex repertoires of socio-political processes and structures, such as anticipation and autonomous mutual adjustment, voluntary exchange within the frameworks of markets and price systems, persuasion, bargaining and negotiations, majority voting based on political competition and accountability to citizens, and command and hierarchies (Dahl and Lindblom 1953). Bureaucratic organisation and processes are still an important part of these repertoires. Yet, like all other organisational forms and modes of governance, bureaucracy has had its ups and downs over time (Olsen 2008a). In this perspective, the EU may look less like a unique phenomenon if the Union is not compared to the ghost of 'the state'. It may also be argued that EU governance has become too complex to be captured by simple dichotomies.

Beyond the tyranny of dichotomies

The claim that there is a novel mode of governance in the EU is based upon a series of dichotomies. Examples are 'governance' versus 'government', 'new' versus 'old' modes, bottom-up governance versus top-down government, soft-law and legally binding law, self-governing and renewing networks versus hierarchies and bureaucracies, enlightenment-inspired informed debate, reason-giving, and voluntary acceptance versus formal authority, command and coercion, private versus public actors, power-sharing and Pareto improvements (creating no losers) versus redistribution based upon majority decisions, flexibility, learning and adaptation versus institutional rigidity with little room for variation and experimentation.

There have been periods and settings where a single form of governance has come close to being dominant, for example absolute monarchies in Europe from the 16th to the 18th century. Yet, mixed political orders, that is, orders blending different forms of governance and organisation are also well-known. European history involves mixed and shifting modes of governance and institutional arrangements, and contemporary systems of governance normally function through a mix of co-existing, partly inconsistent organisational and normative principles, patterns of participation, behavioral logics, standard operating procedures, and legitimate resources (Orren and Skowronek 2004, Olsen 2007). Both in the EU and in nation states, political order is created by a set of institutions that fit more or less into a coherent system.

In the EU different modes of governance and institutional arrangements are interdependent and interacting. Bargaining and deliberation over 'soft' laws take place in the 'shadow' of hierarchies, majority institutions and law-making. The Convention worked in the shadow of the forthcoming Intergovernmental Conference. Hierarchies function within a context of strong consensus norms. Competitive markets are embedded in complex frameworks of laws and regimes, for example, related to property rights and private contracts. Different modes then compete with, and complement each other and they operate in different and shifting mixes, variations that are unlikely to be captured by simple dichotomies seen as providing exclusive alternatives. When it is argued that it would be foolish to claim that the new governance has simply replaced old governance, or that the transition from one dominant mode to the other might be smooth and without obstacles, it is also necessary to discuss how the 'old' and the 'new' fit together (Eberlein and Kerwer 2004, Dehousse and Boussaguet 2008).[2] Can, then, a return to the general literature on democratic governance, and stronger links to the more enduring and recurring issues and theoretical ideas, around which the study of politics and governance has been organised historically, help to transcend the impediments and improve the understanding of EU governance? Can such a return, at least, contribute to getting the core questions right?

BACK TO THE BASICS: UNDERSTANDING DEMOCRATIC GOVERNANCE

The 'new' governance literature has been a reminder that governing in contemporary democracies involves more than formally organised political institutions and office-holders. The term has been central in a theoretical approach that has challenged intergovernmentalist conceptions of national executives as the powerful actors who drive European integration (Hooghe and Marks 2001), and it has been linked to the debate surrounding how far the EU is unique. While non-uniqueness facilitates comparison with other systems of governance (Börzel 2008), it has been claimed that the advocates of the 'new governance' agenda tend to conceptualize the EU as a *sui generis* phenomenon (Hix 1998).

The basic ideas behind the 'new' governance, however, are not really new. It is more a question of reactivating and re-emphasising ideas that are deeply rooted in Europe and the West, including anarchism's emphasis on individual liberty and the doctrine that human beings can live together in a civilised manner without any overarching centre of coercive power, and neo-liberal and conservative doctrines of economic laissez-faire and non-interference in the economy except for protecting private property, private enterprise and contracts. Historically, competing ideologies have expressed (excessive) faith in the benevolence or have stressed the problems of government, as well as of competitive markets and civil society. There have been struggles over the government's role in society, for example, what and how much governments should be responsible for, how it should be organised and work, how much authority and power should be endowed in public actors and institutions, how individual and public rights should be balanced, how much power should follow from numbers and numerical superiority, to what degree government should be neutral among life-projects and societal visions, and how citizens can and should control their rulers.

Now, such issues are activated again in Europe, and efforts to theorise EU governance can possibly benefit from taking into account the history of competing ideas and agendas of governance and the history of successive forms of government, pathways and performances (Finer 1997). Therefore, in order to clarify the particular features of the EU system of governance, this chapter holds that the Union could fruitfully be compared with the practices of other systems of governance, instead of comparing it with the theoretical ghost of 'the state'. Rather than relying on dichotomies, there is a need to attend to the variations within both 'new' and 'old' modes governance, including their different histories, formats, procedures and rationales (Citi and Rhodes 2007). Then the claims made by the advocates of competing modes of governance can be related to some well-known questions. Who governs? Within which institutional settings? With what agendas and with what impacts?

Who governs?

Since Aristotle, systems of governance have been classified in terms of the number (a single person, few or many) and the types of individuals (the wise, virtuous, rich, mediocre, and so on) who are involved in governance. Yet among students of the EU, there are different opinions about who the key actors are.

Analyses and doctrines of new forms of governance, characterised by private participation, public–private partnerships and informal networks have often been based on assumptions about the limited capacity of contemporary governments to steer societies. Governments are facing increasingly complex problems and they have become more and more dependent on resources held by societal groups, that is, expertise, information, technologies, and legitimacy. 'Participatory governance' is seen as a challenge to the authority of office-holders, and efforts to open up public policy-making and administration to society have been interpreted as a 'reconquest of political authority by societal actors' (Andersen and Burns 1996: 228). As societal groups are regaining control, the distinction between government and society becomes blurred.

Such issues have also been raised in the EU, often linked to an assumed democratic deficit and the hope that civil society and participatory governance will provide a remedy and contribute to 'good governance' (Kohler-Koch 2008b, 2008c). Nevertheless, while there may be frustration with political rulers and institutions, there has hardly been a revolt of the masses. The EU, furthermore, is not an example of 'governance without government'. Government actors are still the most central participants in EU governance, often filling 'double-hatted' roles in the interface between the European and the national level of government (Egeberg 2006), generating hybrid models and making it more difficult to separate levels of governance. There are a variety of public actors (elected representatives, bureaucrats, experts, judges, diplomats, military personnel), as well as private actors representing private enterprises and civil society organisations. While civil society participation has contributed to the debate and to some improvement of the democratic quality of the EU, the Union's system of governance does not live up to democratic normative standards (Kohler-Koch 2008b, 2008c). In sum, the complex patterns of participation in the EU can hardly be captured by the public–private dichotomy. Nevertheless, while there are strikingly different patterns of participation, for example across policy areas, some combinations of participants are more common than others, as documented in Gornitzka and Sverdrup's (2008) study of the EU Commission's expert groups.

Future studies have to consider who has formal access to different arenas of governance in the EU, who is actually mobilised, in what ways and compositions, and with what results. 'Who governs' has to be related to competing perspectives on human action, including assumptions about the motivations of those who govern, what they are capable of doing, and what behavioral logics they follow. What is the basis for the claim that human actors seek truth, justice, power, or material benefits; that they act on the basis of calculation of self-interest, the interests of some group or the public interest; or that they follow rules of appropriate behavior as defined for a specific identity or role by a specific culture or sub-culture? Future studies also have to ask what is the relevance of formally organised institutions of governance compared to informal networks for 'who governs'?

Institutional settings

Governance in contemporary democracies is (to some degree) determined by rules and norms; and according to Dahl and Lindblom, the first problem of politics is how citizens can provide rulers with the discretion and resources needed to fulfil their tasks and at the same time prevent them from becoming tyrants (Dahl and Lindblom 1953: 272–3). Historically, 'government by men' has often been seen as arbitrary rule, in contrast to government by laws, institutions, and constitutions. Yet, systems of governance institutionalise action and interaction to different degrees and on the basis of different normative and organisational principles and behavioural logics.

In everyday language, 'institution' may refer to a physical entity as well as an abstract idea. Here, institution refers to an organised system of behavioral rules, meaning, and resources (March and Olsen 1989). Institutionalisation is both a process and a property of organisational arrangements. As a process, institutionalisation implies increasing clarity, agreement and formalisation of (a) behavioural rules, including allocation of formal authority; (b) how behavioural rules are to be described, explained and justified; and (c) what are legitimate resources in different settings and who has access to, or control over, common resources. Consequently, *de-institutionalisation* implies that existing rules and practices; descriptions, explanations and justifications; and resources and powers are becoming more contested and possibly discontinued. There is increasing uncertainty, disorientation, and conflict. New actors are mobilised. Outcomes are more uncertain, and it is necessary to use more incentives or coercion to ensure that people comply with the rules and to punish deviance. *Re-institutionalisation* implies either retrogression or a transformation from one order into another, constituted on different normative and organisational principles (Olsen 2008b).

How, then, is governance organised in the EU? To what degree are there publicly recognised institutional arrangements that make it democratically legitimate to make and enforce decisions on behalf of citizens? According to what normative and organisational principles, behavioural logics, and forms of coordination are systems of governance organised and how are actors differently enabled or constrained? How are decisions made, implemented and enforced – what procedural mechanisms, processes and instruments are used? What resources, authority and power do EU systems of governance command? These are elementary questions to be raised in order to test claims about the importance of civil society involvement and informal networks, and the assumed reduced importance of public office holders and hierarchical political institutions. The significance of multi-level and polycentric structures, non-hierarchical informal networks, 'soft' instruments such as the OMC, public-private partnerships, independent non-majoritarian agencies, civil society participation and power-sharing, have to be held up against the significance of formally organised European-level and national institutions for legislating, executing, adjudicating and enforcing policies, the increased use of qualified majority voting in the Union, the strong tradition of constitutional and public law at the European continent, and the emergence of an autonomous and hierarchical European legal system. However, this chapter argues that focus should be upon how the different modes of governance are mixed, interact and supplement each other, and how the mix of modes of governance change over time, rather than seeing the different modes as dichotomies and alternatives excluding each other.

Generally, institutions of governance have been described as instruments of command, coercion and dominance, as tools for collective problem-solving helping societies to reach shared purposes and goals, as arrangements for regulating and facilitating exchange and helping citizens to fulfil their private desires, and as vehicles for constructing meaning and defining appropriate behaviour, helping society to construct individual and collective identities and accounts. In the EU all of these are present, and again it may be argued that simple dichotomies are unlikely to capture the complexity of the EU institutions, where hierarchies, networks and markets are supplementing each other in different combinations. The task of institutional approaches to governance is to somewhat improve our understanding of how the various aspects can be fitted together in democratic contexts (March and Olsen 1995: 245–6). Therefore, a challenge for the competing institutional approaches to EU governance is to figure out the relative autonomy and explanatory power of different EU institutions. That is, what is the explanatory power of properties of institutions, compared to properties of individual actors; broad global and European socio-economic and cultural forces; and chance events and garbage can processes where the explanatory logic is temporal coincidence and not human intentions or environmental determinism (Cohen, March and Olsen 2007). As a prelude to such analyses it is also necessary to ask what policy-makers aspire to achieve through different modes of governance and what are their agendas.

Agendas of governance

The 'new governance' debate within and outside the EU has fed on shifts in normative climate, ideologies and doctrines about how authority, power and control should be distributed in society. The renewed emphasis upon private enterprise and civil society participation in informal networks came together with an 'ideological shift from politics towards the market' (Pierre and Peters 2000: 55). Reform agendas included attempts to push back the state and make it leaner and less costly, using market and quasi-market mechanisms in the public sector, and introducing the principles of New Public Management. However, reforms also involved attempts to find a 'third way' between hierarchies and markets, giving primacy to civil society involvement in public policy-making.

The reform agendas have been contested within the EU as well as within nation states, reflecting opposing understandings of 'governance' and the office of government. Such contestations can be related to four stylised agendas of governance (March and Olsen 1995: 242–5), ideas that historically have been carried by individuals and groups and that have been embedded in different institutional arrangements. A *minimalist* agenda takes human beings as they are, with preferences and resources determined exogenously, and aspires to regulate their interactions and exchanges through a set of rules. Governance is a specific and limited activity, with the aim of administering the rules of common affairs and enforcing general rules of procedure. Power concentration is to be avoided and so is any large-scale vision and design of society. The regulating rules and principles are a result of spontaneous historical processes, evolving conventions and traditions, and not of imposed majority decisions.

Three other agendas encompass more ambitious roles for governance. A *redistributive* agenda emphasises substantive outcomes and the need to secure a more equal distribution of people's opportunities in society. Governance involves taking responsibility for the welfare of all citizens through reallocating resources and capabilities, an ambition that requires considerable taxation capabilities. A *developmental* agenda involves not only changing the environment of actors or their resources, but changing the actors themselves, their identities and sense of belonging. Governance includes improving citizens intellectually and morally by means of political participation and education. Citizens are supposed to collectively develop common purposes and projects and to create and sustain a shared culture, including shared concepts of good governance and the good society. A *structuralist* agenda gives primacy to governance through deliberate institution-building and reform, where societal impacts are achieved through designing, maintaining and developing institutions and organizational capacities for debate, analysis, and action.

While rhetorical battles usually give primacy to the purified stylised types, political practice involves finding acceptable balances among the four agendas, that is, how much and what type of regulation, redistribution, education and socialisation, and institution-building to pursue and in what constellations. In the EU literature the term 'governance' has been linked to the (re)emergence of 'the regulatory state' (Majone 1996, Armstrong and Bulmer 1998). It has been commonplace to argue that the Union does not have the resources required by the redistributive agenda or the control over education and socialisation required by the developmental agenda. The Union's record when it comes to governing through institution-building is more diverse. Nevertheless, all four aspirations are present in the EU, even if their significance in policy-making and their societal impacts are different. Modes of governance that have flourished in some policy areas have been seen as 'unthinkable' in other policy areas (Scharpf 2002) and a challenge is to understand the variations and their impacts on different policy areas as well as over time.

Performance

Advocates of the 'new' governance have made several claims concerning the superiority of this mode compared to other and presumably older modes. 'Improvements' and 'good governance' have been linked to policy effectiveness, democratic quality, and adaptive capacity through experimentation and learning. Yet, these claims have often been programmatic statements, supported only by modest documented evidence and, thus, creating a need for comparative studies of the actual performance of different modes of governance in different contexts (Citi and Rhodes 2007).

Policy effectiveness: Governance as policy making involves effective problem-solving and the ability to avoid sub-optimal solutions. It also involves conflict resolution capacities and distributional issues. Who gets what, when and how? Which and whose interests and values are accommodated and how are public and private interests balanced? A standard claim has been that civil society involvement and soft methods such as the OMC involve expertise and truth-seeking through deliberation, with appeals to reason and consent. Such methods are thought to create policy convergence in the EU by spreading 'best practice' through decentralised, informal networks. Yet, in practice, end results depend on to what degrees and in what ways agreed-upon standards and benchmarks are implemented at the national level (Börzel and Risse 2006).

Effective cooperation between public and private actors may, for example, demand both strong public authorities and strong civil society organisations, reliable partners with the ability to deliver what has been promised and to take responsibility. Such arrangements seem to work best in systems that combine some autonomy for both public authorities and civil society associations with a tradition of cooperation rather than state authoritarianism. This has been the case in the EU (Kohler-Koch 2000, Börzel 2008), as well as in the expanding welfare state (Olsen 1981). A growing agenda came together with increased participation from 'affected parties' (now: 'stakeholders'), a development that raised concern about possible co-optation of civil society organisations and capture of public agencies. The integration of resourceful societal organisations in public policy making in the EU, like elsewhere, has also raised concerns about the real influence of different kinds of interest groups and their possible impacts on substantive policy outcomes (Dür and De Bièvre 2007), as well as the impact on democratic accountability, the principle of one-person-one-vote, and the distribution of power in society (Benz, Harlow and Papadopoulos 2007).

Democratic legitimacy: What then are the moral doctrines and standards against which modes of governance are assessed and legitimated in the EU, so that citizens may become convinced that it is normatively acceptable that some have authority to make decisions about common affairs and others have an obligation to obey? In democratic polities, legitimacy depends on properties of both substantive outcomes and properties of the procedures used to make decisions. That is, legitimacy depends not only on showing that actions accomplish appropriate objectives, but also that actors behave in accordance with appropriate procedures ingrained in a culture; and in complex societies there is no guarantee for a perfect positive correlation between political effectiveness and normative validity (Merton 1938).

Because democratic governance involves the development, maintenance and change of normative standards legitimating institutions, behaviour, identities, meanings and resources, there is a special need to explore empirically how different modes of governance may impact definitions and interpretations of 'democracy' and 'democratic deficit'. In polities with democratic aspirations, such as the EU, there is also a need to understand how different modes of governance may help or hinder a transformation of individuals into law-abiding, consensus- and compromise-seeking citizens. Likewise, there is a need to explore how modes of governance affect the way in which elected representatives, bureaucrats, diplomats, military officers and judges may be turned into office-holders with an ethos of self-discipline, impartiality and integrity; and how different modes of governance may generate different balances between the requirements of public offices and individual calculated interests.

Adaptive capacity: Why are systems of governance what they are? How do they emerge, how are they maintained and changed, and why do processes of institutionalisation, de-institutionalisation, and re-institutionalisation take place? It has been claimed that historically, 'Europe has been much, much more protean, changeful, and innovative than any other part of the globe' (Finer 1997: 14), and in the EU the ability to engineer institutions to match shifting circumstances and policy demands has often been assumed in spite of well documented reform difficulties (Olsen 2007). The Union has, on the one hand, been more successful in developing supranational institutions than any other region in the world, and this development has to some degree been a result of deliberate decisions. For example, the Open Method of Coordination was launched by the Lisbon European Council in March 2000 and the OMC and other 'soft' methods were seen to increase the EU's ability to experiment, learn and reform itself. On the other hand, the a-political language of improvement through diffusion of 'best practice' stands in contrast with the fact that EU actors are usually wary of upsetting the balance of power between levels of governance and between institutions at each level of governance, a fact often turning major reform efforts into rather tortuous processes.

In practice, the EU's ability to learn and adapt has been far from perfect and new modes of governance and institutional forms often have been supplementing, rather than replacing old ones; generating composite systems of governance and accountability with layers of co-existing, interdependent and interacting institutions (Héritier 2003, Benz, Harlow and Papadopoulos 2007, Olsen 2007, Dehousse and Boussaguet 2008). For example, the Community method, with its legally binding and enforceable decisions is still important in the Union (Dehousse 2008) and bold statements about the withering of the nation state can be heard less frequently than some years ago.

Like other polities, the EU faces a balancing act between continuity and change, *Rechtsstaat* values and majority government, and between exploitation and exploration (March 1991, Olsen 2008b, Sabel and Zeitlin 2008). Exploitation involves using rules, routines and knowledge that are known to work. Exploration involves willingness and ability to experiment with rules, routines and knowledge that might, but often do not, provide improvements. Purification of exploitation will make a system of governance obsolete in a dynamic world that requires continuous adaptation to shifting circumstances and priorities. Continuous experimentation will prevent the organisation from realising the potential gains of new discoveries. What is less obvious is how to balance the two (March 1991).

The dilemma is observed in the EU, for example in regard to the struggles over treaty revisions. Intergovernmental Conferences (IGC) have often created 'leftovers' to be dealt with by future IGCs, in particular when it comes to institutional reorganisations, reflecting that member states hold conflicting views of what Europe should look like in the future. Those who are in favour of deepening European integration and developing efficient institutions in an increasing number of policy areas usually claim that current amendment procedures are 'excessively rigid' and they want to simplify revision procedures. Those who defend the status quo and member state sovereignty are more inclined to look for adequate protection and guarantees against undesired revisions of the treaties that involve a transfer of authority and power to 'Brussels'. They give priority to intergovernmental bargains that require unanimous consent and protect the member states' veto in treaty revisions, and they struggle to avoid change through (re)interpretations and every day practices in the Court of Justice and other EU institutions.

A possible implication is that students of the EU should hold models of change that assume easy equilibria through adaptation or competitive selection up against models that assume 'historical inefficiency'. That is, adaptation to deliberate reform efforts and environmental change is slower and less precise than assumed by equilibrium models (March and Olsen 1989). Another implication is that students of EU dynamics may fruitfully ask not only why policy-makers choose one specific mode, but rather to what degree and under what conditions forms of governance (practices, not blueprints) are the result of deliberate and informed choices. How important is governance as institution-building compared to other standard processes of change? To what extent are shifting modes of governance artifacts of attempts to cope with shifting problems, priorities and circumstances through a series of loosely coupled political compromises? If there is an increased use of civil society involvement in informal networks, is this due to their perceived superior performance, or is it due to member states defending their sovereignty and refusing to delegate authority and power to European-level institutions and actors? Is the OMC likely to be a transitory phenomenon that will disappear in policy areas when member states are able to agree on the Community Method, or is its use likely to increase in importance because the level of conflict increases in an expanding Union?

THE NEED FOR SYNTHESIS

The argument of this chapter is simple. The 'governance turn' in EU studies has called attention to some important political phenomena, changes in 'the real world' that require observation, analysis and interpretation. Nevertheless, there is disagreement among policy-makers, citizens and scholars on how the EU system of governance works and how it has changed over time. It is also questionable how useful dichotomies such as 'government' versus 'governance' and 'old' versus 'new' modes of governance, as exclusive alternatives, are for capturing these phenomena. The EU is certainly not a case of 'governance without government', and the old–new dichotomy is too crude (there is too much variation within each of the two categories) to provide precise insight into the degree and direction of change in the Union. This is the case, in particular, when the ghost of 'the state' is used as a comparative tool for understanding ongoing transformations. Then, where do we go from here? Arguably, the 'new' governance may be interpreted as an approach supplementing, rather than replacing older approaches. Adding new modes, therefore, can be understood as a contribution to an increasingly complex, multi-layered and multi-centered European system of governance, rather than to one institutionalised system of governance replacing an older system.

As a start, there is a need to get the core questions right. It has been argued that rather than seeing the EU as a unique entity, the study of EU governance can benefit from attending to standard questions about democratic governance. Who governs? To what degree and according to which normative and organisational principles are modes of governance institutionalised? What do the rulers aspire to achieve and what do they do when they govern? What are the effects of different modes of governance upon policy efficiency, democratic legitimacy, and change in systems of governance? Rather than seeing change towards the 'new' mode of governance as a general improvement and a development towards 'good governance', it has been suggested that it is necessary to take into account that historically the organisation of systems of governance has been contested, involving confrontations, power-struggles and efforts to find a democratically acceptable balance between competing conceptions and agendas.

Contemporary polities have repertoires of modes of governance and all the basic modes known from studies of democratic governance elsewhere are, more or less, present in the Union. The EU is to a large extent based upon legal integration. It is an experiment in building markets and formally organised political institutions, as well as informal networks with participation from civil society and private enterprises. There are complex and shifting patterns of co-existing actors, structures, behavioural logics, processes, agendas and resources, within a larger and shifting international environment. The coherence of the EU system of governance has varied over time through a variety of processes, rather than a single, dominant process of change. Yet the shifting mixes of processes and their outcomes are not well understood.

Efforts to explore to what degree and under what circumstances the EU systems of governance are likely to have independent and enduring impacts, and on which political phenomena they have such impact, cannot feed on an existing set of shared theoretical ideas. Unsurprisingly, different approaches give explanatory primacy to different factors (agency, institutions, chance events, macro functional and normative environments), and much work is needed in order to specify the scope of the conditions for different modes of governance, the factors that drive shifts in these modes, and the utility of competing analytical frames. The grand theoretical challenge, however, is to work towards possible syntheses between the competing approaches. That is, to figure out whether and how different modes of governance - including their possible institutionalisation, de-institutionalisation and re-institutionalisation – may be comprehended within a single theoretical framework. Beyond all question, this is a tall order to which this epilogue is a prelude.

NOTES

1. Thanks to Beate Kohler-Koch, Fabrice Larat, and James G. March for constructive suggestions and help.
2. Weiler makes a similar observation when it comes to international governance and law-making: 'the contention is not that international governance – and community – has replaced the older paradigm, but that they provide a new layer in a multilayered international system' (Weiler 2008: 2).

REFERENCES

Andersen, Svein A. and Tom R. Burns (1996), 'The European Union and the erosion of parliamentary democracy: A study of post-parliamentary governance' *Contemporary*

Developmental Analysis **1** (2): 33–66. Reprinted 1996 in Svein A. Andersen and Kjell A. Eliassen (eds.), *The European Union: How Democratic Is It?*, London: Sage Publications Ltd, 227–251.

Armstrong, Kenneth and Simon Bulmer (1998), *The Governance of the Single European Market*, Manchester: Manchester University Press.

Bartolini, Stefano (2005), *Re-Structuring Europe. Centre Formation, System Building and Political Structuring Between the Nation State and the European Union.* Oxford: Oxford University Press.

Bendix, Reinhard (1968), 'Introduction' In: Reinhard Bendix (ed.), *State and Society*, Boston: Little, Brown and Company, pp. 1–13.

Benz, Arthur, Carol Harlow and Yannis Papadopoulos (2007), *European Law Journal*, Special issue, **13** (4).

Bevir, Mark (2006), *Encyclopedia of Governance*, Thousand Oaks: Sage.

Börzel, Tanja (2008), *European governance – negotiation and competition in the shadow of hierarchy*, Berlin: Freie Universität Berlin (manuscript).

Börzel, Tanja and Thomas Risse (2006), 'Europeanization: The domestic impact of European Union politics', in Knud Erik Jørgensen, Mark Pollack and Ben Rosamond (eds.), *Handbook of European Politics*, London: Sage Publications Ltd, 483–504.

Boyle, Alan and Christine Chinkin (2007), *The Making of International Law*, Oxford: Oxford University Press.

Citi, Manuele and Martin Rhodes (2007), 'New modes of governance in the European Union: A critical survey and analysis', in Knud Erik Jørgensen, Mark Pollack and Ben Rosamond (eds.), *Handbook of European Politics*, London: Sage Publications Ltd, 463–482.

Cohen, Michael D., James G. March and Johan P. Olsen (2007), 'The Garbage Can Model', in Stewart Clegg and James R. Bailey (eds.), *International Encyclopedia of Organization Studies,* London: Sage Publications Ltd, 534–537.

Dahl, Robert A. and Charles E. Lindblom (1953), *Politics, Economics, and Welfare*, New York: Harper.

Dehousse, Renau (2008), 'The Community Method: Chronicle of a death too early foretold' in Renaud Dehousse and Laurie Boussaguet (eds), *The Transformation of EU Policies? EU Governance at Work*, Mannheim: Connex Report Series No. 8, 7–36.

Dehousse, Renaud and Laurie Boussaguet (eds) (2008), *The Transformation of EU Policies? EU Governance at Work*, Mannheim: Connex Report Series No. 8.

Dunleavy, Patrick and Christopher Hood (1994), 'From Old Public Administration to New Public Management', *Public Money & Management* **14**, 9–16.

Dür, Andreas and Dirk De Bièvre (eds.) (2007), 'Interest group influence on policy making in Europe and the United States', *Journal of Public Policy* **27** (1), 79–101.

Eberlein, Burkard and Dieter Kerwer (2004), 'New governance in the European Union: A theoretical perspective', *Journal of Common Market Studies* **42** (1), 121–142.

Egeberg, Morten (ed.) (2006), *Multi-level Union Administration. The Transformation of Executive Politics in Europe*, Houndsmill: Palgrave MacMillan.

Finer, Samuel E. (1997), *The History of Government* (3 volumes), Oxford: Oxford University Press.

Goodin, Robert E., Martin Rein and Michael Moran (2006), 'The public and its policies', in Michael Moran, Martin Rein and Robert E. Goodin (eds.): *The Oxford Handbook of Public Policy*, Oxford: Oxford University Press, pp. 3–35.

Gornitzka, Åse and Ulf Sverdrup (2008), *Who are the experts? The informational basis of EU decision making*, Oslo: Arena, University of Oslo (manuscript).

Héritier, Adrienne (2003), 'New modes of governance in Europe: increasing political capacity and political effectiveness?', in Tanja Börzel and Rachel Chichowski (eds.), *The State of the European Union. Law, Politics, and Society*, Vol. 6, 105–26.

Hix, Simon (1998), 'The study of the European Union II: The "New Governance" agenda and its rivals' *Journal of European Public Policy* **5** (1), 38–65.

Hooghe, Liesbet and Gary Marks (2001), *Multi-level Governance and European Integration*, Lanham, MD: Rowman and Littlefield.

Kohler-Koch, Beate (2000), 'Framing. The bottleneck of constructing legitimate institutions', *Journal of European Public Policy* **7** (4), 513–531.

Kohler-Koch, Beate (2008a), 'New modes and new promises of European governance' in Ulf Sverdrup and Jarle Trondal (eds.), *The Organizational Dimension of Politics*, Bergen: Fagbokforlaget, 104–122.

Kohler-Koch, B. (2008b), 'Civil society contribution to democratic governance: A critical assessment', in Beate Kohler-Koch, Dirk Bièvre and William Maloney (eds), *Opening EU Governance to Civil Society – Gains and Challenges*, Mannheim: Connex Report Series, No. 5, 9–18.

Kohler-Koch, B. (2008c), 'Does participatory governance hold its promises?', in Beate Kohler-Koch and Fabrice Larat (eds): *Efficient and Democratic Governance in Multi-Level Europe*, Mannheim: Connex Report Series, No. 9 (forthcoming).

Kohler-Koch, B. and R. Eising (eds) (1999), *The Transformation of Governance in the European Union*, London: Routledge.

Kohler-Koch, Beate and Berthold Rittberger (2006), Review article: 'The "governance turn" in EU studies', *Journal of Common Market Studies* **44**, 27–49.

Majone, Giandomenico (1996), *Regulating Europe*, London: Routledge.

March, James G. (1991), 'Exploration and exploitation in organizational learning', *Organization Science* **2**, 71–87.

March, James G. and Johan P. Olsen (1989), *Rediscovering Institutions*, New York: Free Press.

March, James G. and Johan P. Olsen (1995), *Democratic Governance*, New York: Free Press.

Merton, Robert K. (1938), 'Social structure and anomie', *American Sociological Review* **3**, 672–682.

Olsen, Johan P. (1981), 'Integrated organizational participation in government', in Paul C. Nystrom and William H. Starbuck (eds), *Handbook of Organizational Design*, Vol. 2, Oxford: Oxford University Press, 493–516.

Olsen, Johan P. (2007), *Europe in Search for Political Order. An Institutional Perspective on Unity/Diversity, Citizens/their Helpers, Democratic Design/Historical Drift, and the Co-existence of Orders*, Oxford: Oxford University Press.

Olsen, Johan P. (2008a), 'The ups and downs of bureaucratic organization', to appear in Margaret Levi (ed.), *Annual Review of Political Science*, Vol. 11, Palo Alto, CA: Annual Reviews.

Olsen, Johan P. (2008b), 'Change and continuity. An institutional approach to institutions of government', *European Political Science Review* **1** (1).

Orren, Karen and Stephen Skowronek (2004), *The Search for American Political Development*, Cambridge: Cambridge University Press.

Pierre, Jon and B. Guy Peters (2000), *Governance, Politics and the State*, Basingstoke: Macmillan.

Rhodes, Rod A.W. (1996), 'The new governance: governing without government', *Political Studies* **44**, 652–667.

Rhodes, Rod A.W. (1997), *Understanding Governance: Policy Networks, Governance, Reflexivity and Accountability*, Buckingham: Open University Press.

Rhodes, Rod A.W. (2003), 'What is new about governance and why does it matter?', in Jack Hayward and Anand Menon (eds), *Governing Europe*, Oxford: Oxford University Press, 61–74.

Rokkan, Stein (1966), 'Norway: Numerical democracy and corporate pluralism', in Robert A. Dahl (ed.), *Political Oppositions in Western Democracies*, New Haven: Yale University Press, 70–115.

Rokkan, Stein (1999), *State Formation, Nation-Building and Mass Politics in Europe. The Theory of Stein Rokkan*, edited by Peter Flora with Stein Kuhnle and Derek W. Urwin, Oxford: Oxford University Press.

Rosenau, James N. and Ernst-Otto Czempiel (1992), *Governance Without Government: Order and Change in World Politics*, Cambridge: Cambridge University Press.

Sabel, Charles F. and Jonathan Zeitlin (2008), 'Learning from difference: The new architecture of experimentalist governance in the European Union', *European Law Journal* **14** (3), 271–327.

Scharpf, Fritz W. (2002), 'The European social model: coping with the challenges of diversity', *Journal of Common Market Studies* **40** (4), 645–70.

Schmitter, Philippe C. (1996), 'If the nation-state were to wither away in Europe, what might replace it?', in Sverker Gustavsson and Leif Lewin (eds), *The Future of the Nation-State*, London: Routledge, 211–244.

Streeck, Wolfgang and Philippe C. Schmitter (eds) (1985), *Private Interest Government. Beyond Market and State*, London: Sage Publications Ltd.

Weber, Max (1970), 'Politics as a vocation', in Hans H. Gerth and C. Wright Mills (eds.), *From Max Weber. Essays in Sociology*, London: Routledge, 77–128.

Weiler, Joseph H.H. (2008), *The turn to governance: The exercise of power in the international Public Space*, New York: New York University, The Straus Institute for the Advanced Study of Law and Justice (Orientation paper).

Annex

LIST OF NATIONAL REPORTS

The reports are available online at:
http://www.connex-network.org/govdata/national-reports/

Austria: Falkner Gerda, Michalowitz Irina, Tajalli Eric. 2006. Research on EU multilevel governance in Austria: A state of research.

Belgium: Kerremans Bart, Drieskens Edith, Van den Brande Karoline and Delreux Tom. 2006. Research on EU multilevel governance in Belgium: A state of research.

Bosnia and Herzegovina/Croatia/Serbia: Adam Frane. 2006. Research on EU multilevel governance in Bosnia and Herzegovina, Croatia and Serbia: A state of research.

Bulgaria: Salkin Svetoslav, Sedelmeier Ulrich. 2006. Research on EU multilevel governance in Bulgaria: A state of research.

Czech Republic/Slovak Republic: Šlosarčík Ivo. 2006. Research on EU multilevel governance in the Czech Republic and the Slovak Republic: A state of research.

Denmark: Bogason Peter, Thomsen Jannie. 2006. Research on EU multilevel governance in Denmark: A state of research.

Estonia: Augustinaitis, Spurga, Maciukaite-Zviniene, Grigaliunaite, Stracinskiene. 2006. Research on EU multilevel governance in Estonia: A state of research.

Finland: Kemilä Sampo. 2006. Research on EU multilevel governance in Finland: A state of research.

France: See Fabrice Larat's chapter 'Europe's South: Similarities and Differences in Governance Research' in this volume.

Germany: Beate Kohler-Koch, 2007, Regieren in der Europäischen Union, Abschlussbericht [http://www.connex-network.org/govdata/reports/Kohler-Koch_2007_DFG.pdf] See also the chapter 'German Governance Research: Advanced but Mono-Disciplinary' in this volume.

Greece: Pagoulatos George. 2006. Research on EU multilevel governance in Greece: A state of research.

Hungary: Horvath Anna, Sedelmeier Ulrich. 2006. Research on EU multilevel governance in Hungary: A state of research.

Ireland: Auer Stefan, Shaw Colin. 2006. Research on EU multilevel governance in Ireland: A state of research.

Italy: Cassese Sabino. 2006. Research on EU multilevel governance in Italy: A state of research.

Latvia: Reich Norbert. 2006. Research on EU multilevel governance in Latvia: A state of research.

Lithuania: Augustinaitis, Spurga, Maciukaite-Zviniene, Grigaliunaite, Stracinskiene. 2006. Research on EU multilevel governance in Lithuania: A state of research.

Netherlands: Thomassen Jacques, Rosema Martin. 2006. Research on EU multilevel governance in the Netherlands: A state of research.

Norway: Lie Ragnar, Egeberg Morten. 2006. Research on EU multilevel governance in Norway: A state of research.

Poland: Iszkowski Krzysztof. 2006. Research on EU multilevel governance in Poland: A state of research.

Portugal: Mateo Gonzalez Gemma. 2006. Research on EU multilevel governance in Portugal: A state of research.

Romania: Potec Lia, Sedelmeier Ulrich. 2006. Research on EU multilevel governance in Romania: A state of research.

Russia: Strezneva Marina, Voitolovsky Fiodor. 2006. Research on EU multilevel governance in Russia: A state of research.

Slovenia: Bahovec Igor. 2006. Research on EU multilevel governance in Slovenia: A state of research.

Spain: Mateo Gonzalez Gemma. 2006. Research on EU multilevel governance in Spain: A state of research.

Sweden: Gustavsson Sverker. 2006. Research on EU multilevel governance in Sweden: A state of research.

Switzerland: Braun Dieter. 2006. Research on EU multilevel governance in Switzerland: A state of research.

United Kingdom: See Simon Bulmer's chapter 'United Kingdom and Ireland: Leading in Governance Research' in this volume.

European University Institute: Eckert Sandra. 2006. Research on EU multilevel governance at the European University Institute in Florence: A state of research.

Name Index

Country Index